The Renaissance of American Indian Higher Education

Capturing the Dream

Sociocultural, Political, and Historical Studies in Education
Joel Spring, Editor

The Renaissance of American Indian Higher Education

Capturing the Dream

Edited by

Maenette Kape'ahiokalani Padeken Ah Nee-Benham
Michigan State University

Wayne J. Stein
Montana State University

LAWRENCE ERLBAUM ASSOCIATES, PUBLISHERS

2003   Mahwah, New Jersey   London

Lawrence Erlbaum Associates, Inc., Publishers
10 Industrial Avenue
Mahwah, NJ 07430

Cover design by Sean Falcon Chandler

Library of Congress Cataloging-in-Publication Data

The renaissance of American Indian higher education : capturing the
dream / edited by Maenette K. P. AhNee-Benham, Wayne J. Stein.

p. cm. — (Sociocultural, political, and historical studies in education)

Includes bibliographical references and index.

ISBN 0-8058-4320-5 (cloth : alk. paper)
ISBN 0-8058-4321-3 (pbk. : alk. paper)
1. Indians of North America—Education (Higher)—United States.
2. Indian universities and colleges—United States.   I. Ah Nee-
Benham, Maenette K. P. (Maenette Kape'ahiokalani Padeken),
1956–   . II. Stein, Wayne J., 1950–   .   III. Series.
E97.55 .R46   2002
378.1'982997 —dc21

20020024354
CIP

Books published by Lawrence Erlbaum Associates are printed
on acid-free paper, and their bindings are chosen for strength
and durability.

Printed in the United States of America
10 9 8 7 6 5 4 3 2

*We dedicate this work to the love and teasing, humor and laughter,
dancing and pushing, reflections and song, passion and compassion,
and commitment and honesty shared with all of us.
Thank you, Doris and Fred Leader Charge, Jack Barden,
and Henrietta Mann.*

*The editors acknowledge the support of the following people:
Valorie Johnson, Betty J. Overton-Adkins, and Sue Flint.
The commitment of our family at the W. K. Kellogg Foundation
and all our transcribers: Sue, Diana, and Karen; our copyeditors:
Sue, and the staff at Lawrence Erlbaum; and support staff
at Michigan State University: Linda, Cathy, and Betty*

Contents

Part III: Nurturing and Advocating Spirit and Voice

Part IV: Extending the Reach of Tribal Colleges and Universities

About the Cover: Indigenous Model of Education

Sean Chandler

The initial drawing of this piece was actually inspired by Maenette Benham's book about Indigenous models of education. It was also only done in pencil to show that ideas about and methods of education can be changed (or erased) to adapt to new challenges that each particular indigenous community may face over time. Within this drawing, I specifically erased and redrew a mark or line to show that change. The wavy "imperfect" lines demonstrate the molding that an educational system has gone through to fit a certain community; it may look imperfect to a quick judging outsider but to an individual inside this system, it symbolizes the community's ongoing existence in the universe. This line also could define the searching or wandering of our place in life.

Within this round form are symbols representative of my culture, Aaninin. These symbols represent certain animals, such as horses, buffalo, and deer. They may not necessarily represent the actual animal but instead their teachings or our elders' teachings. The stars could represent people, goals, ancestors, the universe, or the environment. Toward the center is a star, which could represent education itself, or a goal that could be reached through educational achievement.

On or in the outer edges of this form are a total 12 sets of 2 circles that could represent 12 new and full moons of the year. They also stand for people—some of these circles are within the form and some are outside—interestingly, one is about to start this educational road or trail.

The buffalo represents everything that my ancestors needed to survive. My father, Al Chandler-Good Strike, tells me of a story of the buffalo coming back to us, and that it has come back in the form of education.

Sean Falcon Chandler (A Ani nin, Gros Ventre) is a young artist gaining recognition throughout the art world for his contemporary perspective and insightful view of the lives of native and indigenous peoples. His artwork has been shown at The Heard Museum in Phoenix, Arizona, The Eiteljorg Museum in Indianapolis, Indiana, The Suitcase Museum, Paris Gibson Square Museum of Art in Great Falls, Montana, The Holter Museum of Art in Helena, Montana, The Oscar Howe Art Center in Mitchell, South Dakota, The Minneapolis Institute of Art in Minneapolis, Minnesota, and the Museum of Natural History, in Paris, France. He is currently at Fort Belknap College developing a curriculum for their Native American Studies Degree.

Foreword

Gerald E. Gipp
Executive Director,
American Indian Higher Education Consortium

The concept of providing higher education programs for native students through an American Indian university was first proposed at the turn of the 20th century. The catalyst for the tribal college movement was in large part due to mainstream higher education's lack of attention to and failure to address the unique needs of American Indian and Alaskan Native students nationwide. However, it was not until the 1960s, during President Johnson's Great Society and war on poverty, which promoted community action programs on Indian reservations, that the social and political environment became conducive to the radical notion of tribal governments chartering and operating institutions of higher education for their own people. The movement was initially championed by a dedicated handful of educators, native and nonnative, who committed their professional careers to the success of educating Native American youth. Despite numerous challenges, tribal colleges and universities (TCUs) have proliferated since that time through their tenacity and unwillingness to fail.

In 1973, the leaders of the six original colleges (Diné College, D-Q University, Oglala Lakota College, Sinte Gleska University, Sitting Bull College, and Turtle Mountain Community College) created a parent organization, the American Indian Higher Education Consortium (AIHEC), to serve and represent them in that nationwide movement. In turn, AIHEC created the American Indian College Fund (AICF) in 1989, and later, was instrumental in establishing the AIHEC Student Congress in 1990, and the Alliance for Equity in Higher Education in 1999, all of which have contributed to the development and success of TCUs and the students they serve.

Through the organizing mechanism of AIHEC, a small nucleus of individuals worked tirelessly in the halls of Congress, advocating for support of the tribal college movement. Finally, a level of stability was reached when federal legislation was enacted in 1978 through the Tribally Controlled Community College Assistant Act (renamed in 1998, The Tribally Controlled College or University Assistance Act) to provide funding for the core operations of the colleges.

Since the 1970s, the success of the original schools has led to the growth and accreditation of 33 tribal colleges and universities throughout the United States, with the promise of many more to follow. New colleges are now being organized in Arizona, Michigan, and Wyoming with others being developed in Alaska, New York, and Oklahoma; and, Native Hawaiians have expressed interest in joining the higher education movement among native people.

Many accomplishments have been realized since the Navajo Nation created the first tribal college, Navajo Community College, in 1968. Since that time, the number of colleges has multiplied, the number of programs and the quality of offerings have increased, colleges have expanded into 4-year and graduate programs, the number of students entering TCUs directly from high school is on the upswing, and, tribal colleges are playing a more significant role in their respective communities and tribal governments as well as in regional and national arenas.

Despite the success of the TCU movement within the tribal communities, TCUs continue to be the most underfunded institutions of higher education in the United States, which has hindered their ability to gain financial parity with their mainstream sister institutions. Continual financial stress threatens the caliber of the programs they offer and their ability to attract qualified faculty and staff. In partial response to this financial stress, AIHEC and the TCU presidents promoted major policy initiatives in the early 1990s to improve funding from federal agencies. Two of the most important successes of these initiatives include (a) in 1994, legislation that was written and passed by congressional supporters of the TCUs, which bestowed land grant status to 29 TCUs, and (b) on October 19, 1996, President Clinton created an important partnership between the TCUs and federal agencies by signing the White House Initiative on Tribal Colleges and Universities. The Executive Order mandated that all federal agencies develop strategic plans to increase services and resources to tribal colleges. Most recently, President Bush (2001) reaffirmed the TCU Initiative by extending the Executive Order for the White House Initiative on Tribal Colleges and Universities and appointing a new executive director.

Over the past 6 years, as a result of the Executive Order, the TCUs have realized a dramatic increase in federal funding through a variety of government programs. However, as important as this infusion of resources has been to the TCUs, these funds are often competitive, supplemental, short-term, and they tend to come with restrictions and limitations that can stifle innovation and creativity. Consequently, the initiative-driven programs might not benefit all colleges equally, nor do they always have the necessary flexibility to address the colleges' basic needs. An additional concern with this type of funding is that it may detract from one of the colleges' primary missions, that is, to provide quality culturally relevant education.

The success of the TCUs also depends on their individual and collective ability to create partnerships outside the federal sector. Among the most significant of these partnerships has been with the W. K. Kellogg Foundation. During the early discussions between tribal college presidents, Kellogg staff and board members, it was recognized that TCUs needed flexibility in planning and developing their institutional operations and course offerings. It was in this spirit of cooperation that the W. K. Kellogg Foundation and the TCUs began the Native American Higher Education Initiative (NAHEI). The primary focus of the initiative was to strengthen the governing structures and fiscal capabilities of individual TCUs and their national organization, AIHEC. The funding made available to each NAHEI-participating college through AIHEC's technical assistance programs and directly from the W. K. Kellogg Foundation has demonstrated how private philanthropic organizations can make an important contribution to ensuring quality and sustainable programs within the TCUs.

The following chapters, written by a number of senior and emerging TCU scholars and Indian education experts, and edited by Dr. Maenette K. P. Benham and Dr. Wayne J. Stein, tell the story of NAHEI and the vision of the tribal college movement. The authors have captured the essence of NAHEI's accomplishments that have taken TCUs, as well as AIHEC, to a new and higher level of productivity and program development. TCU and AIHEC must capture and institutionalize the lessons learned from this experience to ensure the sustainability of the good work produced through NAHEI-sponsored activities, and to use this new knowledge and wisdom to widen the circle of partnerships with other philanthropic groups.

As the TCUs enter a new era of greater accountability and increased expectations, there are new challenges to be met. TCUs must maintain a delicate balance as they move forward in developing quality education that reflects the culture and traditions of their tribal communities. TCUs represent bright lights of hope in the skies over Indian Country as they bring a new dawn to a vision that benefits the seventh generation.

Prologue
Elder Reflections

Henrietta Mann
Montana State University-Bozeman

Long ago at the time of creation, Great Mysterious Spirit established some teachings that all the children of this extraordinary "Turtle Island" had to learn and live by. Such teachings were encyclopedic, impeccable, linguistically appropriate, and culturally specific to each indigenous tribal nation. They constituted diverse bodies of traditional knowledge and thinking that each individual had to study and master in order to become a skillful and educated tribal member. Thus, indigenous tribal/Indian education has its roots in creation, and indigenous educational systems are ancient systems of knowledge, as old as creation itself.

Thousands upon thousands of years before 1492, indigenous people had evolved their unique educational systems. The period following 1492 brought unimaginable changes to indigenous education and ways of life. The Anglo-European immigrants instituted their own culturally different educational systems that were blatantly oriented toward assimilation, which for the initial 300 years of contact were under the control of the church. Richard Henry Pratt, of Indian off-reservation boarding school fame, succinctly articulated the assimilationist intention of early Anglo-American education in his maxim, "Kill the Indian, save the man" (Adams, 1995, p. 52). This was the avowed goal of schools that educated Indian students, regardless of whether they were located on or off reservations, operated by religious denominations, or eventually handled by the various state governments. Historically and culturally, it was a difficult time to be Indian and to retain one's Indian self-identity.

A lack of tribal participation, inferior quality of education, assimilation, and deliberate destruction of indigenous tribal languages unfortunately characterized the indigenous tribal education journey from the late 16th century to the mid-20th century. This was confirmed by the findings of a 1969 investigation of the educational status of American Indians, which were cogently described by the title of the report, *Indian Education: A National Tragedy—A National Challenge* (1969). This special senate subcommittee on Indian education made numerous recommendations for improving the quality of Indian education. One of its key recommendations was to increase the involvement of American Indians in the education of their children. The report resulted in federal legislation that ushered in the era of Indian self-determination in education and the genesis of the tribally controlled community college movement.

Navajo Community College, now Diné College, became the first of 33 such tribally controlled institutions of Native American higher education. Individuals such as Dillon Platero, Robert Roessel, and the late Ned Hataali were Indian education visionaries at the forefront of this movement. As one tribally controlled community college after another was established, other individuals assumed leadership roles in laying the cultural and academic foundations necessary for maintaining the continuity of these unique tribally controlled institutions. Many of their names appear in this publication, and they truly are the heroes and heroines whose visions of change and commitment make them all worthy of inclusion in the Hall of Fame of American Indian Education.

The tribal colleges and universities (TCUs) leaders have struggled to create over the past three decades are miracles of persistence and an answer to the prayers of many generations of our ancestors. Because of their experiences and observations, grandfathers and grandmothers from the four sacred directions of this "Turtle Island" have prayed for the recurrence of culturally based education that nurtures traditional knowledge and develops strong Indian identities. TCUs are those places of hope. They also symbolize the enduring spirit of the first peoples/nations of this sacred homeland. They are places that honor and celebrate the dignity and cultural integrity of first nations, which are balanced with contemporary and innovative academic programs of educational excellence rooted in the archetypal teachings of Great Mysterious Spirit.

Cognizant of their respective cultural imperatives, Indian educators worked with advocates of Indian education to reassert their rights and responsibilities to educate their own. Through federal legislation, the United States Congress affirmed the existence of TCUs, but congressional authorizing legislation has resulted in a considerable disparity in actual appropriations. Historically, TCUs have been underfunded and have had to build their institutional foundations dollar-by-dollar, grant-by-grant, program-by-program, and literally brick by brick. Tribal college presidents and other administrators have been equal to the challenge, have learned through experience, and have developed community models of educational excellence.

In 1992, at a critical time in the development of TCUs, the W. K. Kellogg Foundation (WKKF) established a task force for the purpose of planning a new educational initiative. One of its previous significant initiatives was a multimillion dollar undertaking with historically Black colleges and universities, and WKKF was interested in the possibility of a similar initiative with Native Americans. Subsequently, Dr. Valorie Johnson, Dr. Betty J. Overton-Adkins, and other key WKKF employees invited tribal college presidents and several other Indian educators to a meeting at their corporate headquarters in Battle Creek, Michigan. After discussion of initial funding and to avoid any possibility of competitive funding situations, Dr. Lionel Bordeaux, President of Sinte Gleska University, articulated the basic ground rule for the W. K. Kellogg Foundation initiative by stating, "It is all of us, or none of us." This position was culturally congruent with the concept of inclusiveness that has characterized the TCU movement.

In 1994, the WKKF entered into a 7-year initiative with TCUs, initially to provide these indigenous higher education institutions with an opportunity to reflect on, think about, and share their knowledge about tribal colleges. The WKKF called this partnership the Native American Higher Education Initiative (NAHEI). In describing the initiative, Dr. Valorie Johnson stated that it is "more than a grant" of $30 million; it is "a work of art in progress."

NAHEI targeted three different categories of participants. The primary group comprised all of the TCUs and three federal entities; Haskell Indian Nations University, Southwestern Indian Polytechnic Institute, and the Institute of American Indian Arts. A second category was composed of four national Indian organizations; the American Indian Higher Education Consortium (AIHEC), the American Indian College Fund (AICF), the National Institute for Native Leadership in Higher Education (NINLHE), and the AIHEC Student Congress. The third category included mainstream institutions of higher education that had programs focused on meeting the needs of Native American students.

In its NAHEI program description entitled "The Challenge," the WKKF (1994) envisioned its initiative of "Capturing the Dream" as follows:

> The WKKF initiative will help Native American colleges to articulate their vision of higher education, to strengthen their planning process, and to iden- tify major initiatives that will facilitate strategic development. Assistance to mainstream institutions will help to strengthen and disseminate results-ori- ented programs and information. WKKF will also support activities to help institutions in creating greater access to higher education, strengthen edu- cation programs for Indian students, and help increase graduation rates. A major focus will be educating Indian people who know and identify with their own culture and yet are prepared to live in and contribute to a multicul- tural, global society. (1994, pp. 3–4)

NAHEI was designed as a multiyear initiative that was divided into two phases. Grantees shared their progress and thinking in networking confer- ences held in different geographic locations—the Flathead Reservation of Montana; Oneida, Wisconsin; Albuquerque, New Mexico; Phoenix, Ari- zona; and Santa Fe, New Mexico.

The conferences were held in Indian country, which reaffirmed the im- portance of indigenous tribal cultures, one of the unique aspects of NAHEI. Consequently, cultural ways of seeing and knowing, referred to as "elder re- flections," were incorporated into the agenda at each gathering through the voices of three native elders; Doris and Fred Leader Charge and Dr. Henrietta Mann. The three elders were to observe the processes and reflect on the proceedings at the end of each day. They also shared the honor of greeting each new day with thanksgiving and prayers for spiritual guidance, which sometimes were accompanied by the burning of sacred incense. Dr. Mann commented as follows: "The smell of sage and sweetgrass is as an- cient as the land and the stone mountains. These grandmother's perfumes connect us to our sacred past and to all our ancestors. Tomorrow, our grand- children too will be reminded of our collective past when they use them to bring blessings to their lives" (2001). In consistently recognizing youth and elders, the NAHEI family also remained cognizant of its cultural past and its cultural future. TCU personnel have provided and continue to provide the critical bridge between yesterday's, today, and tomorrow's generations.

NAHEI was an incredible, respectful 7-year journey, filled with thinking, sharing, learning, and visioning. The initiative was a time of high-level think- ing and impeccable use of language when the group developed its shared vi- sion for "Capturing the Dream." The product is an insightful and powerful collective statement: "Native Americans will shape their own futures and that of their communities through higher education that perpetuates tribal culture and honors the people, the land, the air, the water, and the animals that are essential for a healthy America and for world survival." Essentially, this is a succinct futuristic statement of individual and community empowerment and cultural continuity that can be attained through native higher education, which also honors everything that exists within the sacred circle of life and is necessary for a healthy nation and planetary survival. Native educators are global visionaries who are just as concerned about the future of the world as they are about their respective communities.

The NAHEI odyssey is a continuing adventure of epic proportions. It is the story of a diverse group of people whose history includes being this country's first teachers and first students, who established the first educational systems on this land, and whose university was the entire natural world. NAHEI is a story about the faith and commitment of two women, Valorie Johnson and Betty J. Overton-Adkins. Both have walked on an ever-expanding journey that reaches from "Turtle Island" to Hawai'i and *Aotearoa* (New Zealand). The story of NAHEI captures the dreams of TCU presidents and staff, night after night—year after year, dreams that they dreamed into existence and that have taken indigenous cultural ways and indigenous knowledge and wisdom to another dimension of time and space.

NAHEI in book form bears the vision of the WKKF initiative, *Capturing the Dream: Native American Higher Education Initiative*. Under the capable editorship of Dr. Maenette Kape'ahiokalani Padeken AhNee-Benham and Dr. Wayne J. Stein, the authors have told the stories of the issues, challenges, and lessons learned over the 7-year duration of NAHEI. The book is dedicated to four individuals, two of whom have walked up the Milky Way back to the stars.

The first is Doris Leader Charge, Fred's beloved wife of 38 years. She was a good Lakota woman and a powerful role model. She was a mother, grandmother, sister, aunt, friend, and an elder for both NAHEI and NINLHE's Summer Institutes. She pursued her college degree as a nontraditional student and was a cultural studies instructor at Sinte Gleska University. She also was an actress and a Lakota dialogue coach in the movie *Dances With Wolves*. Valorie Johnson remembers the time when Doris sent Kevin Costner to Wal-Mart to purchase a new pair of Wranglers so he would not have to wear his designer jeans with holes to her class. Kevin Costner may have made *Dances With Wolves*, but we know he was doing Doris' dance. As a NAHEI elder, Doris presented insightful reflections that were guided by her generous heart. She was wisdom, joy, respect, humility, peace, light, and love. Albert White Hat described her as being fiercely loyal to Sinte Gleska University, and she had that same loyalty to all TCUs.

The other individual who walked to that place of eternal peace and beauty during the course of NAHEI is Dr. Jack Barden. Like Doris, Jack was strongly committed to TCUs, and he was a cofounder of Sitting Bull College, formerly Standing Rock Community College. In the conclusion of his chapter in this book, he notes that "tribal colleges, by virtue of the fact that they are local and are attuned to the contemporary and traditional cultures of their reservations, are positioned to make significant contributions to the social and economic development of their communities. The Northern Plains Bison Education Project, the Learning Lodge Institute, and the Sicangu Policy Institute are instances in which TCUs have brought their knowledge of these cultures to bear on improving their reservations." TCUs were the love of Jack's life, and his literary contribution to *Capturing the Dream* is a sound piece of scholarship.

Another aspect of the initiative is that it has had other stellar individuals besides Dr. Jack Barden and Doris Leader Charge walking the NAHEI journey. Dave Warren, historian and Santa Clara Pueblo, was one such person. He participated, as a local elder, in the NAHEI Cluster Writing Session in Santa Fe. He reminded the scholars that their discussion and writing had to be grounded in certain knowledge areas, which he catalogued as (a) culture matters, (b) sovereignty matters, (c) community-building matters, and (d) empowerment matters. All of these are embedded in NAHEI. Empowerment is a strong element of the initiative, and education is playing a significant role by improving and forging interrelationships that enhance native communities.

This publication documents the story of NAHEI; it is intended to be a practical chronicle that tells a story of success and how to maintain that success with a genuine sense of hope. The chapters in this book address four themes and represent issues that have a significant bearing on the continuing evolution and viability of TCUs. They are (a) language and culture, (b) social and economic (community) development, (c) student access and success, and (d) institutional capacity building. All are important in the ongoing refinement and development of TCU programs. It is noteworthy that WKKF incorporated culture into its initiative, sending out a strong message to its grantees that culture is important and that it does matter. This alone is significant in that such a strong proculture position represents a drastic departure from the norm for Native Americans.

Dr. Maenette Benham and Dr. Henrietta Mann address the language and culture issue in chapter 9, "Culture and Language Matters: Defining, Implementing, and Evaluating." They note that the issue of language and culture runs throughout all of the chapters in this book. Despite the historical assault on indigenous languages in the past, the "miracle" stories told in each chapter speak to the enduring spirit of the first languages of this land. Native America is fortunate to have the number of language/cultural programs that exist in the TCU academic world at this time.

The matter of maintaining living languages is of grave contemporary concern to indigenous people, inasmuch as some of their languages are facing extinction unless drastic and immediate measures are taken to reverse the trend. When a language is at risk, so is a culture. In indigenous thinking, language is the lifeblood of culture. In one Plains Indian cultural ceremony, sinew represents the lifeline of the people. Both the symbols of the ceremony as well as the native language are life. What the reader must be mindful of, while reading this book, is that the themes of language and culture are like a strong length of sinew that runs throughout the chapters, with the dual purpose of holding the NAHEI story together and simultaneously securing the story to the mission of TCUs.

Language and culture are interrelated and interdependent, and so is the rest of life. The interdependent nature of all life that exists within the inclusive and sacred circle of earth creates sacred relationships like the connection between language and culture. Four projects that illustrate connections are Little Big Horn College's Learning Lodge Institute; United Tribes Technical College's Northern Plains Bison Education Network; Brigham Young University—Hawai'i's Center for Hawaiian Language and Cultural Studies; and the University of California-Los Angeles' American Indian Studies Center and Sinte Gleska University's Project HOOP. Grantees are aware at the most elemental level that sacred relationships exist between humans and all that makes up the environment, primarily water, air (the sacred breath of life), earth, and fire (the light of life). Also embedded in these projects is the knowledge that kinship exists between the two-legged native people and the four-legged bison, between the land and the sea, between native theatre and the community, between cultural scholars and curriculum, and between teachers and learners.

Benham and Mann take the position that indigenous languages must be taught from prekindergarten through postsecondary education. They ask whether culture can be taught without mother-tongue instruction. Among their conclusions, they state that "because language embraces the spiritual, intellectual, historical and cultural competencies and capacities of the people who use it, the syntax, the lexicon, and the cultural treasures embodied in languages must be taught in safe places." TCUs are among the safest of places to teach indigenous languages and culture.

Culturally based education is important in TCUs, but it is even more important in teacher preparation programs at TCUs and mainstream institutions. This issue is comprehensively explored in chapter 10, "A Gift to All Children: Native Teacher Preparation" by Dr. D. Michael Pavel, Dr. Colleen Larimore, and Matthew VanAlstine. They discuss the need to increase the number of both native and nonnative teachers who are appropriately trained to teach Indian children in culturally respectful ways. The authors note that "knowledge of native languages and culture can positively influence school, students, and communities." They further state that all constituencies of the educational community must feel a connection to the school, and each must do everything possible to make the educational experience of this land's first children positive, which is an incomparable gift.

The gift of a positive educational learning experience based on indigenous languages and culture can only be enhanced with positive leadership. Native leadership is another facet of this first thematic area, which Dr. Valorie Johnson, Dr. Maenette Benham and Matthew VanAlstine explore in chapter 8, "Native Leadership: Advocacy for Transformation, Culture, Community, and Sovereignty." This topic is important in view of the fact that, over the past three decades, TCU presidents have demonstrated persistent, knowledgeable, consistent, and competent leadership in the field of indigenous tribal education. Individually and collectively, they have maintained the momentum of the on-going evolution of TCUs. They are individuals, both male and female, who are passionate about education, who are committed to serving the people in their respective communities, who have a strong sense of identity and culture, and who are concerned about the next generation of leaders being trained in their institutions. As the authors point out, these individuals cross sometimes-invisible community barriers, tribal boundaries, cultural/racial lines, and geographic/international borders as "cultural brokers" who promote understanding. Thus, TCU leadership is a critical concern in that a generational change is approaching, and younger native leaders will have to assume the responsibilities heretofore carried by TCU presidents.

TCUs are complex, multifaceted, community conscious, and student centers of higher learning. Their curricular offerings and special programs address the diverse natures of their communities as well as current trends in higher education and across the country. They are keenly aware of the need for social and economic (community) development, the second of the four themes that run throughout the initiative. As an example, they are concentrating on native teacher preparation, strengthening of the family, issue-oriented curriculum development, youth entrepreneurship, and economic "recovery," a term that a few individuals prefer to substitute for development.

Five projects that demonstrate such efforts are Northwest Indian College's OKSALE Native Teacher Preparation Program, Diné College's Teacher Education Program, Fort Peck Community College's Family Education Service Model, Sinte Gleska University's Sicangu Policy Institute, and Turtle Mountain Community College's Center for New Growth and Economic Development. To say that these NAHEI projects are impressive is a virtual understatement. The key aspect of their success is that they encompass the requisite knowledge of and familiarity with their respective communities that has long been missing from other initiatives. TCUs with native leaders, educators, planners, and staff know the needs of their respective communities, and they know how to formulate appropriate solutions that will benefit them. Drawing on their experience in previous social change movements, TCUs are on the journey of creating healthy institutions and communities through social and economic (community) development.

In addition to the general overall development of communities/reservations, the third thematic strand of NAHEI is student access and success. As part of their primary mission, TCUs are oriented to community education, and they recognize the need for knowledgeable, trained, skilled, and educated people to make up the workforce. As articulated in chapter 11 by Dr. Anna M. Ortiz and Iris Heavy Runner, it is a given that TCUs offer their students increased access and opportunities to transfer to mainstream postsecondary institutions. It has been demonstrated that native students who have attended a TCU have a greater degree of success at postsecondary institutions. TCUs are increasingly concerned with gender-balanced recruitment, retention, and graduation of native students.

Through NAHEI, Fort Peck Community College has developed an excellent Family Education Service Model that involves the entire family in the matriculation and educational success of the native student, and that also considers the student's responsibility to the community. NAHEI also has supported greater student access to education through online distance education. The Eagle Project at Salish Kootenai College is only one example of a distance-education project that offers a world health course to students in Australia, Canada, and the United States (Focus Group Discussion, March 2001). Crownpoint Institute of Technology's Kellogg Initiative also provides educational opportunities in training, employment, small business management, and alternative livestock and animal health/range management to the students and communities in its geographic area.

Another factor that influences students' access to and success in higher education is faculty. In chapter 12, "Native Faculty: Scholarship and Development," Dr. John Tippeconnic, III and Dr. Smokey McKinney examine faculty development at TCUs and compare it with development of native faculty at mainstream institutions. They discuss differing faculty roles, the ongoing necessity for supporting faculty development, and the need for TCUs to recruit native faculty. The authors also point out the value of mentoring between junior and senior faculty or as is the case at Leech Lake Tribal College, establishing a mentoring relationship between each faculty member and a tribal elder. The overall goal of faculty development is to have the best prepared and culturally knowledgeable faculty in order to make the education of native students a positive and successful experience.

The fourth and final thematic area of NAHEI is institutional capacity building, the focus of NAHEI. The authors of the chapters devoted to this topic are eminently qualified to write on this subject. They include two current presidents, Dr. James "Jim" Shanley and Dr. Gerald "Carty" Monette; a former president, Dr. Wayne Stein; a former TCU administrator, the late Dr. Jack Barden; Paul Boyer, who has written the definitive study for the Carnegie Foundation on American Indian Colleges; Richard Nichols, a consultant of national stature; and Timothy Sanchez, an emerging scholar who is pursuing his doctorate degree at Teacher College, Columbia University. These native educators are the American Indian intelligentsia of this period of the TCU movement, as are the others whom Dr. Stein mentions in his chapter 2.

In chapter 2, "Developmental Action for Implementing an Indigenous College," Dr. Stein presents an historical framework for contemporary TCUs, along with several TCU mission statements covering 25 years, beginning with that of Diné College. He notes that each mission statement is the "crucial element that makes a tribally controlled college unique in the world of higher education." In the second part of his chapter, Stein lays out in detail the pragmatic steps to be taken in establishing a TCU; these range from adopting a philosophy and mission statement to formulating a realistic developmental action plan.

The first section of chapter 4, "The Effect of the Native American Higher Education Initiative on Strengthening Tribal Colleges and Universities," which Dr. Stein wrote in collaboration with Dr. Jim Shanley and Tim Sanchez, examines the general governance and financing of TCUs and their differences from and commonalties with other institutions of higher education. The second section covers the interrelationships between TCUs and the national organizations that support them—AIHEC, The American

Indian College Fund, the AIHEC Student Congress, NINLHE, and the Alliance for Equity. In the third section, the authors assess the impact of NAHEI on TCUs and discuss how the initiative has strengthened the governance and finance of AIHEC, the central organization of the TCUs. The authors conclude that WKKF made a substantial contribution to strengthening TCUs and the national organizations and that its initiative is a model that can or should be emulated by other philanthropic organizations nationwide. Although this initiative was successful and made a substantial, positive difference, TCUs still face challenges; the primary one is the continual quest for adequate and stable funding.

In chapter 3, "Limitations and Alternatives to Developing a Tribally Controlled College," Dr. Jim Shanley cogently explores issues and provides answers to questions about the future development of new tribal colleges that must meet the varied needs of particular communities. He discusses the issues of resource availability, accreditation, critical mass of students, and alternative models. His final thought is that any group that is serious about initiating a tribal college should ask the tough questions, give truthful answers, and if an answer is "no," seek alternatives to developing a college.

In chapter 5, "Tribal Colleges and Universities Building Community: Education, Social, Cultural, and Economic Development," by the late Dr. Jack Barden, corroborates Dr. Stein's and Dr. Shanley's assertion that TCUs, indeed, "are creatures of their communities," which results in a focus on community building. Described in this chapter are a number of NAHEI projects; the discussion ranges from providing access and opportunity for all children and youth at the precollege level to developing intra and intertribal partnerships that enhance social and economic (community) development. In the words of experience, wisdom, and love contained in this article, Jack Barden has left a valuable legacy for the future development of TCUs.

In chapter 6, "Linking Tribal Colleges and Mainstream Institutions," Dr. Carty Monette and Richard Nichols discuss the effectiveness of or obstacles to partnerships between TCUs and mainstream institutions of higher education. They intersperse their narrative with several examples of positive partnerships and include ideas about the importance of interpersonal relationships and the need for clearly delineated and written articulation agreements between TCUs and mainstream institutions.

The last chapter on the theme institutional capacity building is "Building Tribal Communities: Defining the Mission and Measuring the Outcomes of Tribal Colleges" by Paul Boyer. Boyer discusses accountability and assessment, using Fort Peck Community College and Turtle Mountain Community College as examples. At Fort Peck, accountability begins at the individual level and spirals outward to the community, to accreditation agencies, and ultimately to the entire natural world as an inclusive model that is also accountable to past and future generations. The author states that "when individuals and communities become accountable for themselves and each other, they strengthen both culture and sovereignty." At Turtle Mountain Community College, cultural outcomes are important and faculty are integrating "the Seven Teachings of the Ojibwe—wisdom, love, respect, bravery, honesty, humility, and truth—into the curriculum." At Turtle Mountain, as at Fort Peck, accountability also expands outward to the community and beyond with the message that "culture matters." Paul Boyer concludes that TCUs must develop their own internal assessment tools and share alternative assessment techniques with each other.

The closing chapter, "Information Technology and Tribal Colleges and Universities: Moving Into the 21st Century," was written by Dr. Michael O'Donnell and five of his associates at Salish Kootenai College. They note that, whereas the United States benefits from information technology, "Indian tribes lack the physical and human resources to use information technology to improve the lives of Indian people," primarily because of a lack of infrastructure and Indian computer professionals. They also discuss NAHEI and its support of Indian college students, explore the issues surrounding information technology in Indian country, and assert that TCUs must determine a strategic direction concerning appropriate technology use. The authors contend that technology provides an opportunity for empowerment and conclude that partnerships offer the best hope for indigenous people to share in the information age.

The 1969 Indian Education report, made public at about the time tribally controlled colleges were in their infancy, documented the effect of economics on the education of American Indians and the fact that Indians consistently lag behind all others in terms of available material resources. It appears that TCUs are once again lagging behind in the field of information technology, and the gap might have been even wider were it not for NAHEI support to some TCUs in this area. This is but another challenge facing TCUs.

TCUs represent an exercise in tribal self-determination and sovereignty. They continue to exist despite seemingly overwhelming obstacles, which have failed to impair their growth and development. The W. K. Kellogg Foundation's NAHEI gave TCUs the necessary time and financial support to reflect on, evaluate, plan, dream, and map the renewed journey into this new millennium. As articulated by Dr. Richard Little Bear, President of Chief Dull Knife College, it was a time to break the cycle of being resigned.

It was a time to build on the strong native ways of knowing and to reaffirm institutional commitment to language and culture.

NAHEI was a sacred 7-year journey of renewed hope characterized by mutual learning and respect. As Buffy St. Marie of the Nihewan Foundation sang in her NAHEI song, "Learning is a sacred thing." Everyone played a critical role in creating and nurturing a strong and positive NAHEI community and voice. This book contains a wonderful story, written by native educators and native-hearted educators, about how education has improved and can continue to improve indigenous communities. It is a story about climbing the next mountain range and reaching out across the ocean to Aotearoa and sharing the best practices of tribal college development with Maori relatives. It is a priceless gift from TCUs to the four related children of the world and to their ancestors. It is a beautifully painted and hopeful academic winter count that symbolizes the outstanding achievements of indigenous institutions of higher education, institutions that maintain indigenous traditions in a dynamic contemporary context.

For this I thank you, Maenette and Wayne, for your passion, commitment, understanding, and great intellects. I will never forget you, Valorie and B. J., for your 7-year gift of this landmark study that documents a partnership of spirit and the heart between the W. K. Kellogg Foundation and TCUs. Speaking for your elders, we thank you, all our relations, for your great work and add our prayers to all the others that your journey on earth will be long and rewarding.

It is finished in love and peace.

REFERENCES

Adams, D. W. (1995). *Education for extinction: American Indian's and the boarding school experience, 1875–1928.* Lawrence, KS: University Press of Kansas.

W. K. Kellogg Foundation. (1994) *The Challenge* [Brochure]. Battle Creek, MI: Author.

Kennedy Report. Senate Subcommittee on Indian education. *Indian Education: A national tragedy—A national challenge.* 91st Cong., 1st Sess. (1969) S. Rept. 501 (Serial 12836):25.

I
INTRODUCTION

1

The Journey of the Native American Higher Education Initiative and Tribal Colleges and Universities

Maenette K. P. Benham
Michigan State University

In the 1960s, social disadvantage due to social class and compounded by ethnicity, which brought with it a history of assimilation and cultural legitimization issues, found native/indigenous people of North America in a position where they had little capacity to take advantage of the fruits of equity or choice. One might argue that the market-liberal utilitarian procedural policies of the times, which sought to achieve the greatest good for the greatest number, defined education as a commodity delivered through a uniform pedagogy. The social outcome, therefore, was that those who had the advantage (class, race/ethnicity, gender, and language) acquired the benefits and the choice, and those who had less social capital did not. In the end, disproportionate acquisition of resources brought about by educational polices grounded in choice and efficiency dismissed the principles of social justice and equity (for more on this topic, see Benham & Heck, 1998).

Early leaders of the tribal college movement understood that possession of mainstream (American) literacy was essential to their participation in this imperfect market-advantaged society. They further understood that whatever they created had to be the antithesis of the ethical dimensions of market-liberal utilitarianism that drove current procedural educational policy. What was required to guide this new tribal college movement were culturally substantive policies, concerned with the legitimacy of native ways and wisdom. This movement toward sovereignty and self-determination illuminated the principles of social justice that spoke of success not as the accomplishment of the advantaged, but instead, as the growth and accomplishment of the disadvantaged. This investment would require the allocation of resources to pockets of the community that had grown invisible.

The tribal college movement, as a strategy of resistance, would challenge the notion of legitimate control of education by mainstream institutions of higher education as well as press federal governing agencies to address deeper issues of equity and legitimacy. The autonomy of tribal colleges would enable an indigenous people to achieve educational sovereignty—that is to say, to affirm a collective vision grounded in their particular cultural knowledge and wisdom, to create policies and practices that place native communities in control of their community's life, and to create a wave of political power that makes a place for native/indigenous people in an environment that has been historically hostile.

How tribal colleges were able to build this enterprise over the last 40 years, attaining tribal-, state-, and national-level supportive legislation, is a story best told in a number of texts and talking circles (see Stein, 1992; see also *The Tribal College Journal of American Indian Higher Education*[1]). Some of this history and how it interplays with the W. K. Kellogg Foundation's visionary Native American Higher Education Initiative (NAHEI) are recorded here.

THE TRIBAL COLLEGE MOVEMENT
AND THE NATIVE AMERICAN HIGHER
EDUCATION INITIATIVE

It is important to build individual institutional capacity, but as a movement we must be comprehensive and inclusive.   (Gonzales, 2000)

Tribal colleges and Native American/indigenous-serving higher education institutions are unique as a whole and as individual institutions of postsecondary education. Among their unique features are their deep connections with (as articulated in mission statements and programs) and

---

[1]*The Tribal College Journal of American Indian Higher Education* is a rich resource for students and scholars of native/indigenous postsecondary education. Several issues that provide historical information about TCUs include; Summer Special Edition, 1989, Vol. 1; Summer, 1990, Vol. 2; Summer, 1995, Vol. 7; Summer 1996, Vol. 8; and Fall, 1996, Vol. 8.

involvement in the historical, cultural and social, political/policy and governance, economic/business, and educational institutions of their communities. Because tribal colleges are seen as integral and contributing partners (in some situations, leading ones) in the cultural and economic growth of a community, these linkages are vital. Given their importance to the communities they serve, it is essential that native thinkers and leaders as well as philanthropic agencies focus their attention on the fiscal health of individual tribal colleges and Native American-serving higher education institutions, as well as the Native American higher education movement as a whole. In light of this need, NAHEI has provided both an opportunity to examine the past and present evolution of Native American higher education and a call to plan for a healthy future. Additionally, NAHEI offers many lessons regarding planning, developing, initiating, and evaluating comprehensive educative and community-based programs in native and tribal settings.

In an annual report by the W. K. Kellogg Foundation (2000) entitled, "Profiles in Programming: Native American Higher Education Initiative, Educating the Mind and the Spirit," what has been learned about effective partnerships and the fundamental goals of the initiative are illuminated:

> The Native American Higher Education Initiative (NAHEI) took a departure from these approaches (top down, assimilating, and exclusive programming) by supporting the Native American educational leaders' efforts to articulate their vision of higher education, strengthen their planning process, and identify major initiatives that facilitate strategic development. The Native American Higher Education Initiative began in 1995 with a goal of catalyzing significant, positive changes in higher education in the United States. The goal was to increase the access and success of greater numbers of Native American students who will provide leadership in their communities, the nation, and the world by strengthening Native American communities and the higher education institutions that serve them. (p. 2)

To better understand the importance of NAHEI's goals and the meaningful partnership that it has created between the W. K. Kellogg Foundation and tribal colleges (including Native American-serving institutions), we must view the initiative within a broader, historical context. At a project advisory meeting in June, 2000, Ms. Veronica Gonzales, Executive Director of the American Indian Higher Education Consortium, and Dr. Betty Overton-Adkins, Program Director of the W. K. Kellogg Foundation, presented a glimpse of NAHEI's place in the history of tribal colleges and the role it has played in the much larger movement (see Fig.1.1[2]).

What we learn from their presentation is that (a) within the larger higher education picture, tribal colleges are still young, developing institutions; (b) NAHEI came at a time in the tribal colleges' history when funding and focus were needed to increase their effectiveness and reach as sources of learning, leadership, and economic development; and (c) tribal colleges will make much more "history" with support from a number of sources. This historical accounting represents only a small part of the story.

A Current Assessment of Tribal Colleges and Universities

In his report, "Capturing the Dream: Creating Systemic Change, The Evaluation of the Second Year Implementation of the W. K. Kellogg Foundation's Native American Higher Education Initiative," Nichols (2000) suggested seven topics that warrant deeper examination; (a) policy development and change, (b) partnership and collaboration, (c) technology, (d) improved institutional viability, (e) engagement, (f) improved access, and (g) national leadership. At the level of policy development and change, the report encouraged tribal college leaders to conduct ongoing examinations of the shifts of tribal, state, federal, and corporate world policy and practice. Current exemplary policy initiatives include the efforts of Turtle Mountain Community College's Center for New Growth and Economic Development, Sinte Gleska University's Sicangu Policy Institute on the Rosebud Sioux Reservation, and the work of the American Indian Higher Education Consortium (AIHEC) on behalf of tribal colleges and native-serving institutions. In essence, the function of policy analysis is to understand the relevant policy networks in which tribal colleges and native-serving institutions, both individually and collectively, are situated and that, in the end, determine strategies and outcomes that serve to benefit native people and communities.

Regarding partnerships and collaborations, Nichols stated that 30 of 33 tribal colleges and universities (TCUs) have viable partnerships. Of those 30, 22 are tribal college and mainstream partnerships in academic programs and/or facility-sharing projects. According to the report, "Fourteen

---

[2]Further development of this mapping could include (a) following the journey of individual Native American and indigenous-serving higher education institutions, (b) surveying social and political movements both locally and nationally that have affected native communities and education specifically, (c) highlighting critical moments in mainstream higher education history that have impacted native higher education, and (d) placing "faces" on the map with stories of people and communities.

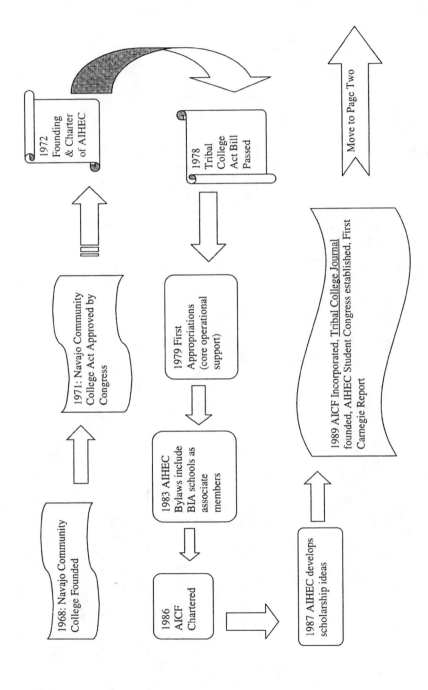

FIG.1.1. Overview of tribal college movement and NAHEI (Veronica Gonzales & Betty Overton-Adkins).

1972
Founding
& Charter
of AIHEC

1978
Tribal
College
Act Bill
Passed

Move to Page Two

1971: Navajo Community College Act Approved by Congress

1979 First Appropriations (core operational support)

1968: Navajo Community College Founded

1983 AIHEC Bylaws include BIA schools as associate members

1986 AICF Chartered

1987 AIHEC develops scholarship ideas

1989 AICF Incorporated, Tribal College Journal founded, AIHEC Student Congress established, First Carnegie Report

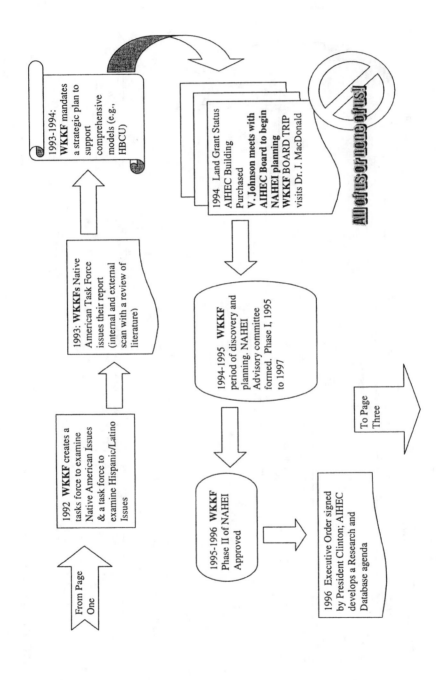

1993-1994: **WKKF** mandates a strategic plan to support comprehensive models (e.g., HBCU)

1993: **WKKFs** Native American Task Force issues their report (internal and external scan with a review of literature)

1992 **WKKF** creates a tasks force to examine Native American Issues & a task force to examine Hispanic/Latino Issues

1994 Land Grant Status AIHEC Building Purchased **V. Johnson meets with AIHEC Board to begin NAHEI planning WKKF BOARD TRIP** visits Dr. J. MacDonald

All of us or none of us!

1994-1995 **WKKF** period of discovery and planning. NAHEI Advisory committee formed. Phase I, 1995 to 1997

1995-1996 **WKKF** Phase II of NAHEI Approved

1996 Executive Order signed by President Clinton; AIHEC develops a Research and Database agenda

From Page One

To Page Three

FIG.1.1. *continued*

8

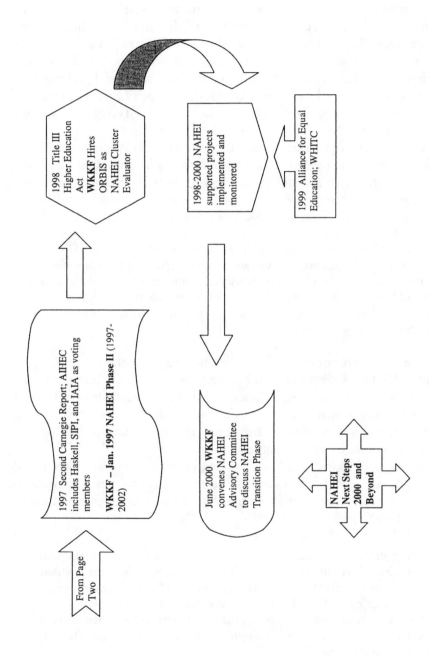

FIG.1.1. *continued*

9

of these projects (or 64%) involve collaborations among TCUs and a mainstream university. Four of the partnerships solely involve Native IHEs (Institutions of Higher Education), while two others reflect Native community-TCU partnerships, one reflects a mainstream IHE and Native community collaboration, and one reflects a Native IHE collaboration with national Indian organizations" (p. 16). Two successful projects that were briefly discussed were Little Big Horn College's Learning Lodge Institute and the United Tribes Technical College's (UTTC) Northern Plain Bison Education Network.

The report placed special emphasis on the issue of closing the digital divide. As electronic technology begins to saturate (as a result of decreased prices and increased availability) many educational institutions and communities, tribal colleges and native-serving institutions face unique issues of infrastructure, skill, and access. The report (Nichols, 2000) stated:

> Unfortunately, this prerequisite does not always exist in Indian Country, where most NAHEI projects operate. Among often cited examples of infrastructure problems are: (a) too few telephone lines at tribal schools/colleges, (b) old wiring incapable of supporting high-speed video transmissions necessary for distance learning, and (c) lack of personnel with requisite knowledge of how to use new technologies. (p. 45)

The report encouraged TCU researchers to study the successful programs at Sinte Gleska and Salish Kootenai, as well as the intertribal initiative of the North Dakota Association of Tribal Colleges, for lessons learned about building partnerships that decrease the digital divide and making computer technology relevant. In essence, using electronic technology is a means to ensure equity through empowerment.

With regard to improved institutional viability, the report highlighted the strides that tribal colleges and native-serving institutions are making to build internal infrastructures to support their work. As stated in the report (Nichols, 2000):

> Earlier, in another document, the author of the Carnegie report also noted that most Native IHEs would probably evolve to become "a unique combination of community college and research university." That these trends are, in fact, occurring, and that Native IHEs are indeed moving toward becoming the unique institutions described in the 1997 report is borne out in this evaluation when one examines the extent to which these institutions have improved their viability. (p. 47)

The report highlighted four areas that are supporting and shaping tribal colleges and native-serving institutions' viability into the future; (a) improving internal administrative processes, (b) building fund-raising capacity, (c) developing new degree programs, and (d) strengthening scholarship programs.

The report recognized the importance of tribal colleges' and native-serving institutions' efforts to engage in the communities they serve. It included several examples of these engagement activities that have resulted in strengthening economic empowerment, rebuilding cultural traditions, and healing communities (health and social welfare) through a variety of initiatives. Indeed, the report stated that tribal colleges and native-serving institutions "by their very nature and missions—exemplify the characteristics of engagement that other institutions of higher education are currently striving to actualize" (p. 50).

The report continued, "Increased student access to TCU-level higher education is evidenced in the increased enrollments at Native IHEs. Although data are limited thus far, it is clear that there has been a continued growth in TCU enrollments" (p. 53). Nichols reported that access, retention, and graduation are increasing in several tribal colleges and native-serving institutions. For example, Leech Lake Tribal College reported cutting its junior-year dropout rate by 50% at Oglala Lakota College, there were 30 graduate students pursuing master's degrees; and at Haskell Indian Nations University, there were more then 80 graduates in four teacher education programs. Melanie Two Eagle shared a recent AIHEC Student Congress report indicated that 27,000 students were enrolled in TCUs, an increase of 7,000 since the 1997 Carnegie Report (Boyer, 1997). Although numbers are increasing, Nichols cautioned the advisory committee that increased attention to the pipeline model (a metaphor for bridging and retention) is needed across all tribal college communities and native-serving institutions.

Finally, Nichols affirmed the need for continued support of national leadership activities, especially in the areas of (a) human and financial resources, (b) advocacy and outreach to relevant higher education institutions and organizations, (c) institutional data collection and policy-related research, (d) technical assistance and professional development, and (e) organizational development and strategic positioning. All five areas, Nichols stressed, are important to the sustained excellence and growth of the Native American higher education movement. Furthermore, the role of supporting agencies, which include AIHEC, the AIHEC Student Congress, the National Institute for Native Leadership in Higher Education (NINLHE), and the American Indian College Fund (AICF), is essential in championing collective efforts that support leadership development, policy analysis, and strategic positioning.

Summary

We need to learn about our own capacities, we need to learn how to use new technologies that will help us to build capacity [e.g., information systems]. We [also] need to know that these projects have grown [current and future] Native American leaders. And, we need to know which barriers are real or not ... We learned [that] how we define our goals are different, we need to define our ideas and the words we use.

(Dr. Janine Pease Pretty on Top, June, 2000)

Although the lessons learned from this journey are essential wisdom, persistent questions on two topics remain. The first topic relates to how TCUs have met the educational needs of the communities they serve. To address this topic, Dr. Pease Pretty on Top advocated for a collection of rich, textual stories that reveal the "echo" effect of community-based and educative programs. She explained that often a program gives birth to other programs that engage students, families, and their communities in unexpected, yet fulfilling ways. It is the impact—the So what difference does it make?—of these clusters of programs that is important to the mission and work of tribal colleges. The chapters that follow provide extensive discussion on this topic in the hope that continued examination of processes and outcomes will enable us to learn more about how we might organize and structure the work of other native/tribal institutions.

The second topic concerns what it means for tribal colleges to address the issues of social justice and the dilemmas of legitimacy that spring from a postcolonial history. Although thoughts about this issue are alluded to throughout the book, an in-depth discussion of this topic is not within the scope or purpose of the book. Suffice it to say that the authors define the advocacy of social justice and legitimacy as a political process that attends to the rights of each individual within the community to be heard and to reap the rewards of citizenship. In essence, educational policy and praxis, from a social justice perspective, is grounded in the belief that whatever is done must benefit the least among us. Therefore, policy and practice denotes the local community's (in this case, tribes) legitimate right to define, in a concrete sense, the educational experiences offered by the formal school institution. Substantive policies, then, must be established to create learning communities that empower the individual and the community, and result in language and culture competency, and individuals who are highly skilled in the vocations and the academic disciplines.

THE 21ST CENTURY WINTER COUNT: ANTICIPATING A NEW PLACE OF PROMISE

Let's go back to the founding principles. We must remember these principles as a guide to our actions. We have an incredible opportunity, but character and integrity must go with us to foundations or it will destroy us.
(Dr. Janine Pease Pretty on Top, June, 2000)

We need to write a story about NAHEI. It is a movement of engaged institutions that have done several things very well.
(Dr. George Cornell, June, 2000)

This is a movement within, of, and among engaged institutions.
(Dr. Gwen Shunatona, June, 2000)

In our current capital structure, there is a belief that money follows value. If this is true, then the value that tribal colleges have to society (providing the best possible educational experience) must be further illuminated. In this book, the stories sharing the work of tribal colleges and Native American-serving institutions to engage their communities in teaching and learning their mother tongue, in building stable economies, and in supporting the health and well-being of their community members reveal the powerful reach of these institutions. Although these stories speak to the accomplishments of TCUs, the value of the work is that it also explicates troublesome issues and makes recommendations that are useful to both native and mainstream institutions.

In short, because they are unique institutions of learning in that their missions are linked to people, land, air, water, and animals, TCUs must launch their future efforts on a journey toward a place of promise. To do so, the writers of this book, in partnership with native scholars and tribal college presidents, have defined eight elements of planning, which are explicated in the following pages.

Element I: Communication Systems

Communication systems have multiple purposes and links, including (a) communication within an institution, across institutions, and with TCU-supporting organizations (AIHEC, AICF, AIHEC Student Congress, NINLHE); (b) communication with stakeholders; and (c) external communication (e.g., to broader native and nonnative communities, philanthropic foundations, and state and national agencies). With regard to communication within and across institutions, there is consensus that dynamic discourse is extremely important to growth in both institutional practices and learning. However, time and attention are scarce resources, especially among tribal college leaders; hence, communication often declines. Because a myriad of responsibilities and increasing concerns constantly compete for the attention of many individuals involved in the work of TCUs, effective means of communication and quick dissemination of information should be established. Scholars and practitioners of this work have suggested that an electronic network that maintains comprehensive and ongoing communications, keeping everyone involved and informed, is an important option.

Communication with stakeholders (e.g., tribal governments, special-interest groups within the community, and community elders) is vital. Strategic plans must be communicated in a compelling and comprehensive narrative that incorporates statistics, stories, trends, and implications. Persuading, in language and actions that are appropriate and respectful, can help tribal colleges and native-serving institutions more seek support for their diverse endeavors. Dr. Janine Pease Pretty on Top made evident this point when she said, "The least of our relatives need to come along as well." Keeping in mind that the success of strategic plans strongly depends on the ecology of attention (who participates, when, and how), any task force must consider how individuals across the tribal community might participate at appropriate times during the planning and implementation processes.

Communication strategies are important to the vitality of tribal colleges' and native-serving institutions' connections, not only with one another and the communities they serve, but also with potential funding and supportive agencies. Indeed, communicating the statistics and stories of success is important to families, to community leaders, and to funders (the notion of "return on investment"). However, as both Richard Williams and Dr. Janine Pease Pretty on Top confirmed, many tribal colleges are high-risk developing institutions located in communities that are poor and disenfranchised. Given this, many tribal colleges and communities have driven off potential funders and supporters. The question then becomes: How might next-step strategies provide essential learning for potential funders regarding how they might effectively work with native communities? Also, how do we work with the least of our relatives to teach them how to work with funding agencies?

To enhance understanding among, across, and between diverse communities is the overarching goal of disseminating new knowledge and lessons learned in a variety of forms to a broad audience. This knowledge should be shared with current and future leaders of tribal colleges, as well as with mainstream university and college faculties. In addition, information should be used in teaching funders about the issues and possibilities of supporting innovative engaged institutions. Information should also be shared with policymakers and decision makers at all levels of governance (e.g., tribal to federal to international).

Element II: Leadership Development

Into the 21st century, tribal colleges and native-serving institutions will need leadership at all levels; college administrators, faculty and staff, and student leaders. A unique aspect of native/indigenous leaders is that they often do not take a position of autocratic power. In most cases, a tribal college president, a student leader, and a community leader are individuals who possess spiritual qualities that guide them to facilitate and promote cultural values and vision through interactive and participatory activities (see Johnson, Benham, & VanAlstine, chap. 8). Although native leadership has been romanticized in the public media and mainstream scholarship, the work is difficult and often exhausting.

Tribal College Presidents.   Presidents of tribal colleges and native-serving institutions serve as leaders of the Native American higher education movement, which has created professional communities of shared cultural values and symbols. They are the administrators of small to large, often complex institutions that must meet the demands of different stakeholders, for example, students, tribal governments, and communities, as well as state and federal expectations and global pressures. And, in many cases, they must teach, counsel students and their families, promote and raise funds, develop information systems and record-keeping strategies, and serve their communities in ceremonial assignments. As administrators, they perform all the functions of a leader of an organization, for example, supervising, allocating resources, designing systems of accountability, and establishing priorities (including what they cannot do) and assessment strategies that measure outcomes in relation to the institution's impact on and contribution to the community. College presidents are also politicians. They must be ever vigilant as to the needs of constituents (e.g., faculty, students, and alumni) and form coalitions that work together to build effective learning environments. College presidents are team players who often work side by side with construction workers as well as teachers and, in some cases, are paid no more than the school janitor or bus driver. Further, college presidents are entrepreneurs, working to garner resources to maintain their current programs, as well as to fund future, long-term innovative initiatives.

Although fundraising is an essential component of a college presidents' role, communication and public relations consume much of their effort. The pace and intensity of this position require further attention. Questions that need further examination include: What are the factors that best characterize the role and functions of the college presidency? For example, what are the unique organizational and cultural features of tribal and native-serving colleges that define the presidency? What strategies of organizational leadership do college presidents identify as being effective and not effective (e.g., administrative strategies and cultural strategies)? How do college presidents sustain their own spirit (e.g., time for contemplation) in light of the challenges of their jobs (e.g., isolation and multiple expectations)?

Faculty Leadership.   Leadership, as conceived and practiced by many native-controlled institutions, is regarded first and foremost as subjective. That is, the act of leadership is interactive and inclusive, and has at its focus the health and welfare of people, the good of the community, and the celebration of life. Given this, the role of faculty and staff as leaders within the college community is not taken lightly. Each member of the college community has insight, knowledge, and skills that enhance the collective efforts of the whole. Ongoing professional development should focus on content knowledge and increased electronic-technology skills, as well as leadership development.

Questions that require further discussion include: How do we best involve faculty and staff in the policymaking functions of the college, thereby providing opportunities for the enhancement of professional and personal journeys? How do we create a time and place for our faculty to discuss, problem solve, and learn about the issues confronting our colleges (other than staff meetings)? How do we provide opportunities for our faculty to have meaningful experiences with other tribal college and native-serving institutions' faculty as well as mainstream university and college faculty?

Youth Leadership.   Designing programs to build leadership among native youth requires ongoing dialogue and planning with an increasingly diverse population of young people. To assume that our youth are homogeneous would be a serious mistake. Indeed, our youth come from unique tribes, have varying levels of academic needs, bring with them different interests and ways of thinking, and deal with isolation, culture, and self-identity in diverse ways. Given all this, we must continue to engage our youth in activities that contribute to the quality of life and success of our native communities. To provide a supportive environment, TCUs, in partnership with AIHEC, AICF, and the AIHEC Student Congress, might reflect on several resources that must be brought to bear on youth leadership development activities. These include (a) bringing together youth from tribally controlled and mainstream colleges and universities to learn about and become active in important movements; (b) having seasoned individuals mentor emerging scholars and leaders during their college years and through their early careers; (c) funding attendance and participation in leadership development activities across institutions (business, research, teaching, economic development, and government); and (d) providing opportunities for youth leaders to collaborate on innovative and important community-based initiatives.

Element III: Land Grant Opportunities

The Land-Grant Act of 1862 and the Second Morrill Act in 1890 did two things; (a) established a law that required colleges to provide an array of disciplinary subjects (including agriculture, industry, and mechanical arts) that might otherwise be found in only elite, private institutions; and (b) provided direct annual federal funding to TCUs. For tribal college presidents and leaders, important questions might be: What does it mean to tribal colleges to have land-grant status? What might be the benefits of land-grant status, and at what cost (if any)? Given that the benefits are substantial, what procedures must be followed to attain the benefits of land-grant status? What are needed now, as TCUs enter the 21st century, are strategies to assist tribal college presidents, native-serving institutions, and AIHEC to think more deeply about land-grant opportunities and to encourage TCUs to implement projects that make full use of the privileges currently available.

Element IV: Accreditation

The idea and practice of accreditation have been of concern to tribal colleges since the movement's beginnings. Although accountability may be meritorious, the questions of "accountable to whom" and "accountability by what standards and criteria" have been contested terrain. In particular, accreditation is bounded by a rational model that values individual competition and merit, which in many cases diverges from the basic values of tribally controlled institutions (e.g., interdependence, generosity, and the importance of linking all living things with mother earth). The debates surrounding accreditation over the past decade have been complicated by increased involvement and oversight by both state and federal agencies. Concerns that must be addressed include the creation of an accreditation model that is respectful of unique cultural systems and values; the potential of aligning with other accrediting agencies without sacrificing institutional autonomy; and policy development and articulation statements that support the values of quality, equity, and excellence.

In addition, TCUs might want to think more carefully about designing collaborative arrangements with K–12 schools, other tribal and native-serving colleges, 2-year and 4-year mainstream institutions, and business or community organizations (under the aegis of AIHEC, for example). Through these collaborative undertakings, participants could honestly discuss accreditation issues and problems; thoughtfully and actively begin to address barriers that stifle forward-looking, authentic accreditation models; create principles and design a model of accreditation that promotes student success; and commit to creating policies and procedures that ensure the establishment of new models of accreditation.

Element V: Financing and Facilities

With large portions of tribal college and native-serving institutional resources coming from a combination of corporate and private sources, federal and state pockets, tribal resources, and student fees, funding has been (and will continue to be) a highly competitive enterprise. Fiscal constraints often present college presidents and their boards with painful decisions that might lead to a reduction or elimination of academic programs; loss of faculty and staff; delay of new educative initiatives; decrease in construction, maintenance, and repair of facilities; and (most unfortunate) cutbacks in resources students need to complete their degrees. Increased enrollments in tribal colleges due to the need for higher education for skilled positions, advanced certification and , and the perpetuation and enhancement of native knowledge have brought with them the need to consider innovative ways of thinking about and designing funding and financing strategies.

In the broader context of higher education, the well educated and well off predictably persist and succeed. Tribal colleges, on the other hand, have worked and continue to work to reverse this inequity. However, in light of increased competition for decreasing pools of monies, resistance to acknowledgment of native/multicultural values by a conservative elite (i.e., the assault on affirmative action that has redirected state and federal taxpayer revenues), and ambiguity regarding how much an efficient and productive enterprise should cost (e.g., how much a particular degree, scholarship, or academic program should cost), candor and thoroughness about finances are vital to the success of tribal colleges. To begin to address these concerns, attention should be given to the following questions: What have been successful funding formulas for tribal colleges, native-serving institutions, and other alternative as well as mainstream higher education institutions? What can we learn that might help college presidents and their boards develop and implement future funding formulas and policies to sustain these practices to build the viability of their colleges?

Attention to facilities is an important component of future work that requires focused attention. At the forefront of this objective is the need to think about how to build and sustain new campus utilities that support information technology. In light of this, tribal colleges and native-serving institutions must be able to: (a) define how electronic technology will affect their teaching and learning (define multimedia and distance learning options); (b) locate ways to help the college organizational structure shift and grow to embrace transformed facilities and the use of electronic technology (policies and procedures); (c) support people, champions who will direct the implementation and evaluation of electronic technology (create and support the network infrastructure), and (d) finance and train through policy support.

Regarding the topics of funding and financing, the growing effectiveness and success of the AICF has enhanced the efforts of tribal colleges and native-serving institutions. In partnership with this organization (and others), tribal colleges can design and support fundraising models that align with their needs (e.g., budgeting, planning, evaluation, and academic process). These models should attract the best emissaries (native and nonnative) who can build strong networks of support. The outcome of these models should support students, construct and maintain facilities, build the infrastructure needed to introduce and employ computer technology systems, and support and sustain innovative academic programs. In essence, the advisory planning task force could develop a model to assist college presidents to think about financing plans for facilities and program development as a sophisticated, long-range institutional process that builds sustained constituent and donor commitment.

Element VI: Relationship Building With Philanthropic Foundations

Philanthropic support has primarily funded mainstream university research and development agendas. Indeed, a large portion of private foundation funds has been granted to higher education (e.g., Ford, Kellogg, Johnson, Lilly, Carnegie, MacArthur, Hewlett, and Murdock). The past successes of the Native American higher education movement, however, cannot be solely attributed to the voluntary contributions of philanthropic foundations, but also to the innovativeness, creativity, and persistence of individual and cluster members of the tribal college community. Because tribal colleges and native-serving institutions have had to build their facilities, organizational structures, and faculties with little financial support, they have maintained their autonomy, sovereignty, and academic freedom, but at what cost? Lacking the mechanisms (i.e., entrée) to establish or compete for viable funding arrangements with private, philanthropic institutions has made their work to nurture excellence, to attract and retain native students in the pipeline, and to support the efforts of talented faculty a difficult, uphill challenge. Although it is true that funding must come from a number of sources, increased support from philanthropic foundations cannot only enhance the good works of native-controlled higher education institutions, but can also address the uneven, skewed funding history of many of them.

Element VII: Technology

Leaders in native/tribal institutions have recognized the growing possibilities of teaching, learning, and disseminating new knowledge/research through electronic/computer technology. How information technology is reshaping the way we learn, the content of what is learned, and the nature of who we are as native/indigenous people is still being discussed and contested. Is technology a "cure-all"? How can technology enhance, but not jeopardize or destroy, unique lineages and oral languages, symbolic histories, and the rhythms that define native integrity? Whatever the question(s), technology has become omnipresent in our daily lives and in the educational process. Given these contemporary advancements, college leaders must consider a number of factors as they think about and employ computer technology. Specifically, they need to understand the implications of computer technology on the nature of knowledge, to understand the influence of computer technology on the ways in which we learn and teach, and to define policy that ensures efficiency, access, quality, and equity.

Element VIII: Collaboration and Linkages

Partnerships, real partnerships, honor the strengths, needs, and shared values of all partners. Authentic partnerships are important to tribal communities because they demonstrate a concern for the welfare of all community members, the environment, and the language and culture of the people. Tribal colleges and native-serving institutions are important to creating meaningful partnerships due to their regular interaction with constituents within and outside the tribal community. Through NAHEI, we have learned that partnerships comprise organizations and individuals who grow to trust one another and understand that it is not the "other" who needs to change, but that all participants must work to move toward another promised and hopeful place. In addition, we have learned that partnerships involve multiple players within organizations, for example, teachers, faculty, staff, parents, students, and administrators. These partnerships often lead to strong professional networks among college presidents, financial/budget officers, counselors, teachers, and students. The power of partnerships is that they have the potential to create comprehensive, integrated systems that support student learning and that can integrate other factors, such as health and wellness, volunteerism, and community leadership, into the learning journey.

The Fit Between K–12 Schools and Tribal/Native-Serving Colleges. Ongoing concerns regarding the journey between K–12 and postsecondary education have led many teachers, school leaders, and scholars to recognize the interdependence of the two. That is to say, K–12 schools and tribal colleges should share in the responsibility for educating and providing every opportunity for students to succeed in their transition as well as academically. Several questions might begin some thinking about K–12 partnerships: What can tribal colleges learn from current K–12 school reforms in curriculum (e.g., native-language based, interdisciplinary frameworks), teaching and learning (e.g., interdisciplinary, activity based, collaborative), and assessment (e.g., portfolio based, performance based)? How can tribal colleges work with their secondary schools (K–12 school system, both private and public) to ensure appropriate and successful articulation between high school and college? What role should the tribal college play in K–12 school reform (e.g., native-based learning, teacher preparation, assessment standards)?

Tribal/Native-Serving College and Business/Industry Linkages. The value of such linkages is that they can provide the tribal college with resources and support for student learning. Indeed, the 1980s and 1990s saw increased funding in the fields of technology, biotechnology, and engineering. Although funding is available from business and industry, the questions that we might want to pose to help us think more deeply about this particular linkage include: How can native and/or tribal integrity be maintained in the face of these collaborations? How can native knowledge and intellectual/cultural rights be preserved?

Tribal College/Native-Serving and Mainstream Institutions.   Consortia arrangements range from simple (single area/discipline and one-directional) to complex (multiple, reciprocal, or bidirectional) services. Collaborations between institutions can consist of sharing library resources and computer services, linking enrollment and admissions (cross-registration), joint purchasing, sharing faculty and staff resources/services, and sharing responsibility for community economic development. Concerns regarding this form of collaboration include sustained leadership and participation, institutional autonomy, and reciprocity or multidirectional support and learning.

Collaboration and linkages give rise to several challenges. First, any new partnership or collaboration must be given time to grow. Participants must learn to trust one another and have time to adjust their structures and processes before they can be expected to commit to a new initiative. This time of growth and trust building can be extraordinarily rocky as several barriers, for example, different cultures, priorities, values, and languages, must be overcome. In short, it is wise for TCU leaders to think more deeply and to plan more strategically for rich, creative, productive, and mutually beneficial partnerships.

CONCLUDING THOUGHTS

The past history of our journey, coupled with the present diligence and energy of our work, has clearly affirmed the continued growth and success of our tribal and indigenous postsecondary institutions. Indeed, the legitimacy of our people's defining the epistemological terrain of our educational institutions has been a long-fought struggle, but it has become both our right and our responsibility in the 21st century. Because it is within our hands and our hearts to create a way to educate in a context that is true to our unique cultural integrity, we must continue to study and conduct critical dialogues to ensure that we never become stagnant and complacent. The value of this book is that the dialogue it presents and engenders is both descriptive and instructive and it leads us to important places. We must look closely at what we are doing to ensure that even the least among us is being served. It is, after all, how we hold ourselves accountable in this process that will be the key to our legitimate sovereignty and sense of community.

REFERENCES

Benham, M., & Heck, R. (1998). *Culture and educational policy in Hawai'i: The silencing of native voices.* Mahwah, NJ: Lawrence Erlbaum Associates.

Boyer, P. (1997). *Native American colleges: Progress and prospects.* Princeton, NJ: The Carnegie Foundation for the Advancement of Teaching.

Cornell, G. (2000, June). *NAHEI Project Advisory Council Meeting*, Battle Creek, MI.

Gonzales, V. (2000, June). *NAHEI Project Advisory Council Meeting*, Battle Creek, MI.

W. F. Kellogg Foundation. (2000). *W. K. Kellogg Foundation profiles in programming: Native American Higher Education Initiative, Educating the mind and the spirit.* Battle Creek, MI: Author.

Nichols, R. (2000). *Capturing the dream: Creating systemic change, The evaluation of the second year implementation of the W. K. Kellogg Foundation's Native American Higher Education Initiative* (Report from ORBIS to the W. K. Kellogg Foundation). Battle Creek, MI: Author.

Pease Pretty on Top, J. (2000, June). *NAHEI Project Advisory Council Meeting*, Battle Creek, MI.

Shunatona, G. (2000, June). *NAHEI Project Advisory Council Meeting*, Battle Creek, MI.

Stein, W. (1992). *Tribally controlled colleges: Making good medicine.* New York: Peter Lang.

2

Developmental Action for Implementing an Indigenous College: Philosophical Foundations and Pragmatic Steps

Wayne J. Stein
Montana State University

PART I—PHILOSOPHICAL FOUNDATIONS OF TRIBAL COLLEGES AND UNIVERSITIES

A Philosophy

To build something worthwhile that is lasting, whether as an individual or a community, one must have a working philosophy that also allows one to dream and envision a better future. For American Indian people and indigenous people around the world who have suffered the ravages of colonization, this becomes especially true as they set out to build educational institutions to serve their communities. A strong core of ethics, a clear set of professional education principles, and a worldview of their own can and should be their guiding force as they build their dream educational institution.

The Struggle to Be

The effort to assimilate indigenous tribal nations and individuals by the governments of the colonizers who have usurped their lands has, in fact, worked in thousands, maybe millions, of separate cases. Yet, at the core of those indigenous tribes and nations that have survived into the 20th century, there are several million people who have managed to protect and nurture some or all of their cultures, religions, and languages. Equally important are those indigenous individuals who have learned to walk in both worlds, for they in many ways are the first line of defense in protecting what is left of their people's folkways and lands.

Those indigenous people who have chosen not to be assimilated require and ask only one thing; the right to be members of their communities on their own terms, not the oppressive and foreign terms dictated by their colonizers. James Zion, attorney for the Navajo nation, said it this way in a paper delivered at a fair housing conference in 1989:

> However many Indian nations and individuals are not interested in assimilation, they desire the "right to be Indian." It's not that they want more from the American way—it's that they are struggling to hang on to what they have left after 500 years of war, disease, and forced acculturation by non-Indians who have subjugated them and conquered their lands or taken most of their lands. (pp. 4–5)

Why an Indigenous People's Philosophy

However clear it remains that American Indian tribal nations are working hard to hang on to their folkways, as are most indigenous people around the world, it is also clear that the Western cultural ways that have flooded the world through colonization, and now commerce, have made substantial and at times overwhelming inroads into all American Indian and indigenous cultures. The free-enterprise system of economics, based on capitalistic principles, gluttonous consumerism, high technology, and faster and better systems of communication and transportation, has shrunk the world and erased most barriers protecting any culture, not just the indigenous ones. It seems ironic that the very people who started this movement of worldwide mass consumerism, high-tech mass transportation, and mass communication now complain that their children no longer listen to them or value the culture ways of their own people but would rather embrace this new world culture movement that exploded on the world scene at the end of the 20th century.

The earth is in crisis as it relates to the people of the world, their folkways and cultures, the fauna and flora kingdoms, and the world's water systems, both freshwater and oceans. The world population of human beings and their careless use of nature's resources have so stressed the natural world that many knowledgeable individuals now despair over what the future holds for humankind and our relatives on this planet. It is not just diverse cultures that are in danger of disappearing from the face of this earth in the near future, but life as we know it today.

John Collier (as cited in Forbes, 1972), Commissioner of Indian Affairs of the United States in the 1930s and 1940s, showed remarkable foresight when he discussed American Indian societies:

> They had what the world has lost. They have it now. What the world has lost, the world must have again lest it die. Not many years are left to have or have not, to recapture the lost ingredient ... What, in our human world, is this power to live? It is the ancient, lost reverence and passion for the earth and its web of life.
>
> This indivisible reverence and passion is what the American Indian almost universally had and representative groups of them have it still.
>
> If our modern world should be able to recapture this power, the earth's resources and web of life would not be irrevocably wasted within the twentieth century, which is the prospect now.
>
> True democracy, founded in the neighborhoods and reaching over the world, would become the realized heaven on earth. And living peace—not just an interlude between wars—would be born and would last through ages. (pp. 11–12)

Environmental conservationists and world leaders who truly understand and care about the crisis facing humankind and their use of the world's resources are now turning to the American Indian and other indigenous people of the world for philosophical insights into how to live in this world without destroying the very things that support all life. Even as the concerned segments of the world's dominant cultures and nations turn to the American Indian and other indigenous people for guidance concerning the preservation of the environment, other more powerful segments of those same nations continue to ravage the earth for material and political gain. And if indigenous people happen to live where coveted resources are located, they are immediately attacked through the colonizers' legal and political systems.

While those nefarious activities are under way, adventurers, outlaws, missionaries, businesspeople, and homesteaders illegally flood the homelands of the indigenous people, bringing with them disease, alcohol, rape, and murder. In such cases, there is little or no help to be had from the international community, little or no help from the national legal and political systems because they are often part of the problem, and fellow nonindigenous citizens look away in the names of national interest and monetary gain. So once again the cycle begins for another indigenous people and their homeland. Lest one think that the cycle of destruction is a part of the past for indigenous people now that the world begins the 21st century, one has only to look to South America, Southern Asia, and much of Africa to see that the cycle of destruction is going on as it did in the 15th century. Indigenous people located on today's coveted lands are on the front line, facing the very destruction that may be causing the end of humankind on this earth.

All the cultures and people of the world were at one time tribal people who understood that, to live in harmony with nature, one must respect all other life that makes up the natural world. It is only in the last several centuries that industrialized people have sought to completely harness nature as nation-states have grown and prospered through the rise of the industrial age and now the information age. In themselves, these developments have brought good to humankind in the form of medicines, foodstuffs, and the general spread of democracy around the world. It is the simultaneous loss of community that large cities engender, the steamrolling of any smaller indigenous people that might be in the way of perceived progress, the lust for wealth, and the disconnection from nature that industrialization has caused that are the real problems for all human beings.

The philosophical answers to the environmental and communal welfare problems of the world that are being sought from American Indian and indigenous tribal communities are at once simple and intricate. Most American Indian and indigenous people have within their cultures (or had before industrializing and commercializing influences) a version of three guiding philosophical principles. First, humankind must live in balance and harmony with the rest of the Creator's world. All things of this earth, and the earth itself, must be given respect and allowed to operate the way the Creator intended. Second, we who are living today have not inherited this earth to do as we please with it, but rather have only borrowed it from our children and grandchildren. We must take good care of it for their sakes and leave it in at least as good or better condition as when we received it. And third, every decision, whether about the use of the earth and its bounty or how communities are to function from now into the future, must be made with the utmost consideration of how that decision will affect, positively or negatively, the seventh generation to follow.

To state that the philosophical principles presented above have been under continuous threat of eradication by the powerful nation-states created by the colonizers of the indigenous people of the world would be an understatement. The founders of the American Indian tribally controlled college movement stepped into this philosophical, cultural, economic, and educational storm in the mid-1960s. They had to develop a philosophy that at once protected and enhanced their own cultures, and at the same time, embraced much of the philosophy and tools of their oppressors' educational system of higher education. The tribal college pioneers recognized that they could not just prepare tribal students to be proficient in their own cultures, but must also prepare them to be proficient and strong in a world now controlled by a colonizing foreign culture. The founders knew that most, if not all, of their people must be able to understand and compete successfully in two worlds. It had to be that way if their people were to survive, to retain some semblance of their true identity, and to protect what they had retained of their homelands and sovereign rights into the 21st century.

Tribal College Philosophy

Although seriously eroded by disease, economic collapse, war, and forced acculturation, one of the important segments of most American Indian communities still in existence by the mid-1960s and making something of a comeback was the American Indian intelligentsia. In fact, there were at least three distinct groups of American Indians that could be considered an intelligentsia thinking and acting on behalf of the American Indian people of the 1960s, sometimes in direct contradiction to each other. The first group was those tribal members (often referred to as elders) who still struggled to practice and teach the traditional values, language, and cultural ways of their people. Often they were also the poorest of their tribal nation and pushed furthest away from the mainstream of American life. The second group included those American Indian persons who had accepted nearly total acculturation and were working with the federal government and other assimilationist agencies to totally transform all American Indians into "real Americans." The third group was a small but emerging cadre of mostly younger American Indians who were educated in the Euro-American fashion but desired to preserve and enhance their own tribal values, languages, and traditions, although many of this group had been denied knowledge of their own cultures and languages by often intimidated or indoctrinated parents and the acculturation-minded school systems they had attended as children.

As it turned out, each of these groups were needed by the tribal college movement, as the movement's founders started the journey to create the tribally controlled colleges of the American Indian. Any movement that would resist or change a major segment of a society and one of its most powerful institutions must have an intelligentsia. Without a cadre of individuals devoted to the development of a philosophy, to rational short- and long-range planning, and to the education of others within their group, a movement will ultimately fail. Providing these elements of unifying philosophical principles, systematic planning, and internal and external education is what its intelligentsia can do for a movement (Forbes, 1972; Lutz, 1980).

Since the beginning of the 20th century, there have been Americans who believed that American Indians could and should manage their own higher education institutions. In 1911, an American Indian with the Euro-American name of August Breuninger proposed the creation of an American Indian university that would focus on American Indian cultures and be connected to an Indian museum. He believed that such a university would create opportunity for Indian people as well as demonstrate the vitality of American Indian cultures (Boyer, 1997). There were others of like mind, but their ideas could not overcome the assimilationists who had powerful allies in the United States Congress, the business world, and the philanthropic community.

A second serious proposal to start an American Indian-controlled college was made by the Rosebud Sioux (Sicangu Lakota) community of South Dakota in the mid-1950s, during the administration of Tribal Chairman Robert Burnette. The idea and project was a precursor of what was to come in the area of tribally controlled education, although the idea didn't come to fruition because of lack of funds (Sinte Gleska Community College, 1973).

Dr. Jack Forbes made another proposal for an American Indian university in the early 1960s, which was well thought out and had the support of many well-known American Indian leaders and intellectuals. Forbes and the small group working with him advocated and lobbied with passion and persistence the administrations of Presidents Kennedy and Johnson for such an institution. Although their efforts did not bear immediate fruit in the form of an American Indian university, they did lay the philosophical base and groundwork for tribally controlled institutions that were established later, in particular D-Q University. Forbes's proposed American Indian university would have developed pride in American Indian heritage, promoted use of native languages, developed a written version of each native language, trained American Indian teachers for tribally controlled K–12 schools, educated and trained American Indian students in the arts and professions, created precollege courses to bring insufficiently educated students up to college level, and carried out many equally good ideas that would have enhanced all American Indian communities (Forbes, 1985).

The guiding principle of Forbes and his group was that American Indian people must control the university. This principle, although not popular with government officials and mainstream educators of the time, also became the guiding principle for the tribally controlled college movement. This principle is very much at the center of all successful movements of indigenous, poor, or minority people. It was the visionary educator and poor people's advocate, Myles Horton, founder of the Highlander Folk School, who said that no outsider must be given the right or privilege of defining or qualifying the primary group. Outsiders tend to set false presuppositions and goals for primary group members to work toward, such as telling them to clean up and then they will all be "okay," then telling them to get an education and they will be "okay," then offering them low-salary jobs and if they take them, they will be "okay." Instead, the people must set their own goals, independent of outside input, and pride in self is the key (Adams, 1975).

The Navajo intelligentsia of the mid-1960s was first able to put together the necessary internal and external politics, people, and resources to found a true tribally controlled college in 1968. Navajo Community College (now known as Diné Community College), located in the arid Southwest of the United States, was founded with the clear intention that the local community would control the institution in order to enhance the understanding of their heritage, language, history, and culture. The college would selectively transmit these values for the survival of the Navajo as individuals and as a nation (Navajo Community College, 1976). To ensure that the proposed college would achieve the ideals envisioned by the founders, they developed a detailed mission and purpose statement. They understood that, in its infancy, Diné Community College must have a clear, detailed, and powerful mission if it was to weather the many questions and critics that would greet its founding. The founders also understood that these questions and critics would not come just from outside, but would also arise from many of their own people and from other American Indians who had come to believe the words of the colonizers—that American Indians are just not capable of managing and successfully overseeing an institution of higher education, even one dedicated only to the education of their own people.

The founders of Diné Community College, the Navajo community and the Navajo tribal government, to give themselves guidance and a touchstone when developing their college, adopted the following philosophy, mission, and purpose statements.

Philosophy of Diné Community College

1.   For any community or society to grow and prosper, it must have its own means for educating its citizens. And it is essential that these educational systems be directed and controlled by the society they are intended to serve.

2.   If a community or society is to continue to grow and prosper, each member of that society must be provided with an opportunity to acquire a positive self-image and a clear sense of identity. This can be achieved only when each individual's capacities are developed and used to the fullest possible extent. It is absolutely necessary for every individual to respect and understand his culture and his heritage; he must have faith in the future of his society.

3.   Members of different cultures must develop their abilities to operate effectively, not only in their own immediate societies, but also in the complex of varied cultures that makes up the larger society of man.

4.   In light of the difficulties experienced by traditional educational programs in meeting the needs of individuals and societies, it is important that Navajo Community College make every possible effort to search out and test new approaches to dealing with old problems. It is also important to build the capacity of the College so that it can respond effectively to problems arising out of rapidly changing conditions.

5.   To assure maximum development and success of individual students, Navajo Community College accepts the responsibility of providing individualized programs and of assisting students with their academic and social adjustment.

Purpose and Objectives

In order to carry out its purpose, Navajo Community College has defined its objectives as follows:

1. To provide academic foundations for students who plan to transfer to a senior college or university.
2. To provide vocational-technical training programs for students.
3. To provide adult education courses for individuals who desire to further their education.
4. To provide a program of community service and community development.

5. To provide assistance and consultation upon request to public, church, and Bureau of Indian Affairs schools and other organizations or institutions in the area which the College serves.
6. To foster in its Indian students the development and preservation of a healthy pride in their heritage.
7. To serve as a center for development of Indian cultures, with special emphasis on the Navajo. (Navajo Community College, 1976, pp.5–7).

The American Indian and native tribal nations in the United States and Canada that have followed the example of the Navajo nation and Diné Community College by founding their own tribally controlled colleges have developed philosophical statements with many of the same guiding principles. They have agreed that it must be clear that, although their intention is to educate their tribal people so they have the tools to compete in the larger world, they must also ensure that they do so on their own terms. Any mission statement must incorporate their tribal cultures, languages, and histories, and place these elements at the center of the colleges' purposes. Given below are examples of the philosophical and mission statements of Oglala Lakota College of South Dakota chartered in 1971, Little Big Horn College of the Crow (Apsaalooke) nation of Montana chartered in 1980, Fond du Lac Tribal and Community College of the Ojibway of Minnesota chartered in 1987, and the College of the Menominee of Wisconsin chartered in 1993.

Mission and Purpose of the Oglala Lakota College

To establish and to operate post-secondary institutions on the reservation granting certificates and degrees. This mission includes a diverse range of education from community service offerings to graduate courses. The College will coordinate and regulate all higher education on the Pine Ridge Reservation. The ultimate goal is the establishment of a Lakota university.

In carrying out its mission, the Oglala Lakota Board of Trustees stresses Lakota culture and Tribal self-determination. The College prepares students to understand the larger society as well as the customs and beliefs of the Lakota people. Working towards these ends, the College has defined its purposes:

-Tribal-

❖ To provide the Oglala Sioux Tribe as a sovereign people, with educated and trained human resources and personnel.
❖ To assist people in being active, productive members of their families, communities, and of the Oglala Sioux Tribe.

❖ To provide the Oglala Sioux Tribe with expertise and information needed for its development.

❖ To actively seek to place graduates.

-Cultural-

❖ To present the Lakota cultural perspective in teaching within the academic, occupational and community programs.

❖ To promote study of the Lakota culture as an area of study in itself.

❖ To research, study and disseminate the Lakota language, culture and philosophy.

-Academic-

❖ To maintain high academic standards for staff and students.

❖ To maintain open enrollments.

❖ To be accessible to potential students.

❖ To teach students necessary skills and human values which will assist them in fulfilling themselves and making a productive living.

❖ To work with other institutions and agencies in furthering the interests of the college.

-Community-

❖ To assist with the determination of development needs of the reservation districts and communities.

❖ To assist the reservation districts and communities in achieving their goals.

❖ To provide continuing and community education.

(Oglala Lakota College, 1998–1999, p. 4)

Philosophy/Mission of Little Big Horn College

Purposes and Powers:

Purposes include establishing, maintaining and operating educational institutions at the post-secondary level on the Crow Reservation, with educational, vocational and technical programs and curricula leading to degrees and certificates that may be granted by the college.

Little Big Horn College is the Crow education and cultural center that provides Associate of Arts degrees and certificates in areas that reflect the developing economic opportunities of the Crow Indian Reservation community. The college is dedicated to the professional, vocational and personal development of individual students for their advancement in the workplace or in higher education. The college is committed to the preservation, perpetuation and protection of Crow culture and language. Little Big Horn College respects the distinct bilingual and bi-cultural aspects of the Crow Indian Reservation community, aspects that are foundations of strength for the Crow and American Indian community. Little Big Horn College is committed to the advancement of the Crow Indian family through understanding and knowledge of pertinent issues and participation in community building. Little Big Horn College vitalizes Crow and American Indian Scholarship, thus strengthening the unique, self-governing Crow Tribe of Indians. (Little Big Horn College, 1997–1999, p. 8)

Mission of Fond du Lac Tribal and Community College

MISSION: The mission of Fond du Lac Tribal and Community College is to acknowledge the right of each individual to achieve a sense of self-actualization and to provide for the building of educational and civic relationships through the medium of education and life-long learning.

Fond du Lac Tribal and Community College will enhance the academic, economic, and cultural growth of the community through programs of educational excellence and a commitment to celebrate the diverse cultures of our community.

To achieve the principles of its mission, Fond du Lac Tribal and Community College shall:

✧ Promote scholarship and academic excellence through transfer and career education.
✧ Provide educational opportunities to community residents of all ages to foster a commitment to lifelong learning.
✧ Provide access to higher education by offering developmental education.
✧ Provide educational access to historically under served populations, particularly Anishnaabe communities.
✧ Promote the language, culture, and history of the Anishnaabe.
✧ Promote teaching excellence.
✧ Provide opportunities for applied research.
✧ Provide programs that will celebrate the cultural diversity of our community and promote global understanding.
    (Fond du Lac Tribal and Community College, 1995–1997, p. 7)

Mission Statement of the College of the Menominee

The College of the Menominee Nation (CMN) is founded from the highest ideals of the Menominee Indian Tribe and the Menominee people. Its first emphasis is upon its students: to provide a quality environmental and educational experience which will allow those choosing to pursue their individual goals to achieve a significant position in the world's economy and social structure. This overall goal will be pursued out of the history, traditions, values and aspirations of the Menominee Indian Tribe, thus strengthening and preserving the Tribe's history, traditions, values, and aspirations.

In pursuit of these ideals the College dedicates itself to pursuing research and development goals which promise to better the educational and economic lives of the Menominee people, other tribal people, and the world at large, thus, allowing the Menominee, in this way, to contribute to a strengthening of tribal peoples within American society.

The College, as an institution of higher education, also dedicates itself to developing educational strategies built around concrete projects that enable students to learn by doing. Educational concepts will be embodied in tasks, which have the potential to provide significant benefits to the student, the student's family, the Menominee Tribe, Indian people, or to the world at large. These strategies will pay special attention to the barriers, which prevent student success and will provide resources, which will allow students to reach their full academic potential.

The College functions as a tribally controlled institution of higher education on the Menominee Indian Reservation focusing on general studies, specialized degrees, or certificates of completion, which meet the professional or paraprofessional needs of the Menominee Reservation communities or other reservation or regional non-reservation communities, and vocational education programs. It serves Indian students from the Menominee Reservation and any other Indian students needing its educational programs as well as students from communities in North-Central Wisconsin.

It is through these missions, the provisions of a quality educational environment which is centered in Menominee culture, the development and pursuit of research and development projects designed to improve the educational and economic lives of the College's students, and implementation of a curriculum designed around the twin concepts of learn by doing and community service, that the College of the Menominee Nation is founded.

(College of the Menominee Nation, www.menominee.com, 1999)

The previously quoted mission statements were written over a 25-year period, and each still retains the crucial element that makes a tribally controlled college unique in the world of higher education. Each maintains the philosophy that the protection, enhancement, and teaching of its tribal culture and language are central to its college's mission, curriculum, and values. The founders of tribally controlled colleges and the chartering tribal governments have remained true to the ideal of tribal and community control of their colleges throughout the 30-year history of the tribally controlled college movement.

It should be noted that the philosophical and mission statements of the tribally controlled colleges have evolved and been refined as the tribal colleges in question have become more secure in their own identities, and well enough established to handle any concerns or challenges, internal or external, to their existence. An example is how Diné Community College's philosophical/mission statement was changed and refined from 1968 to 1999. The current mission statement is presented below.

Diné College Mission

- ❖ To strengthen Personal Foundations for Responsible Learning and Living consistent with Sa'ah Naagháí Bik'eh Hózóón.
- ❖ To Prepare Students for Careers and Further Studies.
- ❖ To Promote and Perpetuate Navajo Language and Culture.
- ❖ To Provide Community Services and Research.
    (Diné College, crystal.ncc.cc.nm.us/about/dcfacts.html, 1999)

These philosophical and mission statements are good examples any other American Indian or indigenous people should look at carefully if they are serious about developing their own community-controlled colleges. These statements contain most of what is needed to guide an indigenous community through the difficult task of founding a community-controlled college and the even more challenging task of developing and maintaining such an institution.

PART II—PRAGMATIC STEPS IN STARTING AN INDIGENOUSLY CONTROLLED COLLEGE

Community

The local indigenous community is the most important base and touchstone for any indigenous group that is planning the development and building of an indigenously controlled college. At the very least, there must be implicit consensus among the local indigenous community that it is desirable to add a locally controlled college to the community. With either the implied consent or the active participation of the community, the persons who will do the actual work, usually a small cadre of tribal activists and supportive educators, can begin the arduous task of planning, lobbying for, and building the community's locally controlled college.

A number of important questions must be asked in a community with regard to starting an indigenously controlled college, beginning with whether it is desirable or necessary to start such a college. These questions are best answered by using community meetings as a vehicle for bringing interested segments of the community together. The group in favor of a college must not dominate these meetings, but must work hard to get attending community members to speak their minds on a host of issues, for these early meetings will truly give a clear picture of whether the action committee should go ahead with their plan to build a college controlled by the indigenous community. The action committee must be willing to guide but also to sit quietly by while all in attendance have their say. They must not become offended and argumentative when people criticize their idea and dream. They must understand that those in attendance may, for the first time, be feeling free and safe enough to say what is really on their minds. Given time and discussion in an atmosphere where it is safe to air differences, even the most negative community members will usually come around to supporting the idea of an indigenously controlled college. If, deep down, they really did not support the idea of a community-controlled institution of higher education that takes into account the community's identity and culture, they probably would not have come to the meetings in the first place.

Once these community meetings have taken place and permission has been given to go ahead, fewer meetings are necessary. Another necessary outcome of the community meetings is the formation of an advisory board made up of community members who can meet periodically with the action committee to review and advise on strategies, local politics, and a host of issues that will arise as the indigenous college's developmental action committee moves forward.

Local Leadership/Tribal Council

Once the members of the community-at-large have had ample opportunity to express their thoughts and support, the advisory board and action committee must make an extensive effort to ensure that the local political system supports the idea and is willing to contribute to the development of an indigenous college. Although it is possible to start developing an indigenously controlled college without the support and consent of the local political machine and leadership, it will prove impossible to sustain the effort under such circumstances. The enabling charter for the college must come from the local tribal or indigenous government in order to legitimize the college in the eyes of the local community and the outside world. The local government often can provide some of the necessary resources needed by a fledgling indigenous college, such as meeting space for the college's early classes, funds to help defray the ever-present expenses of even the most modest effort, and land on which to build if and when that day comes. The local government also may need to offer support in dealing with various levels of state and national government and with their funding agencies, as well as help when the action committee solicits funds from private sources.

The advisory board and action committee must not become discouraged if local government leaders do not immediately become wildly enthusiastic supporters of the college's development. The action committee must remember a number of important facts. First, the committee is dealing with men and women who have seen many programs come and go that were supposed to help their people overcome years of oppression but failed to do so. Second, the governmental, political, and family clan leaders are probably the elite of the homeland and have grown used to making decisions for their people. These leaders will recognize that, at the very least, the new college will change the makeup of the homeland (reservation) in some manner that will upset the status quo. Third, there are already tribally or indigenously controlled colleges throughout the United States, Canada, New Zealand, and other nations that have shown a remarkable ability to improve the lives of their people by giving indigenous students the intellectual tools and cultural strength to change their homelands for the better, and these stories of change have not gone unnoticed by tribal and indigenous leaders around the world. Finally, if the local tribal or indigenous community has given clear support to the idea of a locally controlled college, in time, with gentle but constant pressure from the advisory board and action committee, this community support will bring the local government to a stronger position that sustains the indigenously controlled college and its continued development and growth.

Indigenous leaders usually recognize that a group of indigenous people must learn to protect themselves and what remains of their homelands from rapacious international business conglomerates and national governments that are under tremendous economic pressure to develop any and all natural resources or that have little respect and regard for indigenous cultures and claims to their homelands. There is strong evidence coming out of the indigenous communities of the world that it is often their leaders who are promoting the development of an indigenously or tribally controlled college in their community. At the World Indigenous People's Education Conference (WIPEC) held in Hilo, Hawai'i, during the summer of 1999, one of the central activities was the exchange of ideas and information presented to the conference participants by the American Indian Higher Education Consortium (AIHEC) concerning the question "What is a tribally controlled college?" Participants' interest in every aspect of what makes up a tribal college was intense, with questions posed on topics ranging from funding to culturally relevant curriculum.

Indigenous leaders are searching for answers to these seemingly overwhelming problems in a way that will prepare their people to compete in today's world, help restore much of what has been lost culturally, protect what remains, and allow them to remain true to their basic or central identity as individuals and as an indigenous people. What was shared at the WIPEC conference in Hawai'i about the tribal college movement and its success in the United States and Canada provides many of the answers that indigenous leaders and community activists are seeking.

In 1997, at the request of the Carnegie Foundation for the Advancement of Teaching, based on his research, Paul Boyer wrote a report entitled *Native American Colleges: Progress and Prospects*. He found a number of compelling motivating factors that might impel an indigenous community to consider founding a local tribally controlled college. Boyer discovered that, even as the American Indian tribal colleges must continuously struggle to fulfill their mission mandates because of the difficult financial situations in which they often find themselves, they are still crucial to their communities' economic, cultural, and spiritual survival.

Boyer recorded a number of important characteristics of tribally controlled colleges. First, tribal colleges provide a learning environment that supports students who have come to view failure as the norm for themselves in any nonindigenous educational system. American Indian students attending a tribal college often say that, for the first time in their lives, they actually feel welcome in a classroom when they begin their tribal college classes. The alienation of indigenous students as they attend mainstream schools and colleges is a well-documented fact, and this has led to horrendous dropout rates and added to a climate of failure in indigenous communities (see Ortiz and HeavyRunner, chap. 11). Tribally controlled colleges have changed that climate of expected failure to an atmosphere of expected success for American Indian students in those communities that have planned and built their own locally controlled colleges.

Second, tribal colleges celebrate and help sustain American Indian traditions. In established non-Indian institutions of higher education, the values and traditions of American Indian students are undermined and often ridiculed. In contrast, tribal colleges' mission statements declare

that one of their most important reasons for existence is to preserve, protect, and enhance their people's cultures, languages, and traditions by em-
bedding them into their curricula and into the ways in which they conduct
the colleges' business.

Third, tribal colleges provide essential services that enrich the surrounding communities. These colleges have become community institutions in
every respect by providing more than just traditional educational services.
They also offer social and economic programs, such as alcohol and substance abuse counseling for their students, daycare services for students,
transportation services for students and community members, economic
development workshops for tribal members, tribal culture and language institutes for the community, and much more.

Fourth, the colleges have become centers for research and scholarship.
Tribal colleges increasingly are undertaking research that is of direct benefit to their communities' and tribes' economic, legal, and environmental
interests. Tribal members trained as scientists, professionals, and paraprofessionals in a host of critical fields are having a positive influence on their
communities' abilities to protect and preserve what is important to them.
In many fields of research and scholarship, partnerships with non-Indian
colleges and universities substantially increase what can be accomplished
by the tribal colleges' students and administrators. These partnerships
benefit both parties because together they can compete for many national
education, science, and social programs and grants that neither party
would be eligible for on its own. Tribal college researchers and faculty
members have raised the awareness of many non-Indian education personnel by taking them into the American Indian world and sharing with
them a worldview that honors and respects all things of this world, not just
that which can be exploited and turned into a business opportunity. Tribal
college researchers have also added greatly to scholarship on the American Indian by offering an insider's scholarly interpretation of what happened historically in a given tribal community and what is happening yet
today in that same community. Tribal college scholars have, in an important sense, taken back from the non-Indian scholar their own tribal or indigenous people's story (Boyer, 1997).

How, then, do indigenous communities that desire to build an indigenously controlled college put themselves in a position to emulate the successes of the American Indian tribal college movement? They must start at
the very beginning and implement each part of their dream step-by-step.
The important components that must go into building an indigenous community's college are described in the following sections.

Charter

One of the most important tasks the advisory board and action committee must accomplish is shepherding of the enabling charter of the envisioned tribal or indigenous locally controlled college through the approval process of the tribal council or local indigenous government. This may be an easy task if the local governing council already fully supports the college, or it can be difficult if the local governing council must be convinced that the college is a good idea that it will benefit the whole community.

If the local governing council does need convincing, the advisory board and action committee must remember that their primary goal is to obtain an enabling charter so that they can begin building their college. They must not allow themselves to get into a political struggle with a reluctant governing council because their chances of winning a direct political confrontation against an entrenched governing council are almost nil. The first strategy to gain a positive vote for an enabling charter should be one of gentle political persuasion from the advisory board and supportive community members, with the action committee providing research about the benefits a locally controlled indigenous college will bring to their homeland (reservation).

If that strategy does not work, the next approach should be to use the local equivalent of a public referendum spearheaded by the advisory board and action committee. Again, the advisory board, the action committee, and their community supporters should not directly attack the governing council. Not only will that tactic be unproductive in the present, but it may create long-term ill will that can only hurt the college in the future. The community referendum will allow the entire community electorate to show their direct support for the establishment of a local indigenously controlled college with a positive vote. That accomplishes two things. First, it obtains the charter to create the indigenous college without directly confronting reluctant local leaders and thus avoids making long-lasting powerful enemies at home. Second, it sends a strong message to all concerned, both within and outside the community, that the local indigenous community strongly desires an indigenously controlled college.

Board of Trustees and Advisory Board

The charter should include articles of incorporation or a similar set of guidelines that describe how the college will operate as a legal entity of the tribe or indigenous community. Once the charter has been secured, a governing board of trustees for the college must be selected. The board of trustees will have numerous responsibilities in ensuring the success of their locally controlled college. Thus, the way they are selected and their relationship with the local governing body are crucial and should be spelled out in the college's charter.

A key factor in the success of an American Indian tribally controlled college is that its board of trustees must act as a buffer between the college and the local governing body (the tribal council) and clearly set policy for the college's administrative practices. By acting as a buffer between the college and its local governing body, the board of trustees ensures that good educational practices will be maintained, rather than policies phasing in and out because of the colleges becoming involved in the local political scene. An indigenously controlled college must be an intimate part of its local community, yet remain politically and administratively separate from the local governing body, in order to be a true institution of higher learning. Becoming too close to the daily business of the tribal government or local governing body is a sure formula for the college's failure.

The board of trustees can be selected in a number of ways, any of which will work if the process is clearly stated and followed faithfully by the local governing body and community. How the board of trustees is selected must be spelled out in the college's enabling charter and articles, with provision for changes in the selection process if the community so desires. Three examples of selection processes that have been used by American Indian tribally controlled colleges follow.

In one system, the communities of the reservation (homeland) are divided up into districts, and the members of each local community district elect a representative to the college's governing board of trustees for a set term. In addition, the tribal council (the local governing body) has the right to select and appoint a set number, usually one to three, of the board members, also for set terms.

In another approach, the tribal council (the local governing body) is authorized to appoint all members of the board of trustees, but with staggered terms, to ensure continuity of policy for the college. The Turtle Mountain Chippewa Tribe of Belcourt, North Dakota, has created an innovative process for selecting and appointing their tribal college board of trustees. In 1971, the action committee founding community college assembled the components to develop a tribal community college and accepted the advice of Gerald One Feather, chairman of the Oglala Sioux Tribe and a founder of Oglala Lakota College. He advised the Turtle Mountain Community College founders that avoiding tribal politics was essential. The method he suggested was to set up a two-tiered board of trustees system to govern their college.

The action committee took his advice and, upon receiving the charter for Turtle Mountain Community College, instituted a two-tiered system of governance, which is still unique among tribal colleges (C. Davis, personal communication, March 3, 1987). Legal control of Turtle Mountain Community College rests with its 9-member board of trustees and a nonvoting chairman who is appointed by the tribal council for life (or until the chairperson chooses to resign). The board consists of two tribal council members, two representatives-at-large from the community, two representatives from local educational agencies, two students, and two representatives of operating tribal programs. The board of trustees, in turn, elects a 5-member board of directors, who guides the college administration through monthly meetings and acts as a business review board. The board of directors is, in turn, responsible for overseeing operating policies and fiscal aspects of the college. The board of directors also has final say over all staff hired and supervises the president of the college. The board of trustees meets quarterly to review the actions of the board of directors and when necessary, to handle major policy needs. The board of trustees was established to ensure that the college carries out its mission and to serve as a buffer and liaison between the board of directors and the tribal council (Stein, 1992).

Administrators

The American Indian tribally controlled colleges were founded by small cadres of dedicated activists made up of grass-roots tribal members, often referred to as troublemakers by federal and tribal government officials. Sometimes the cadres also included concerned nontribal activists, young and educated tribal activists, and elected tribal officials who wanted change for their people (Stein, 1992). Often, it was within these groups that the new boards of trustees found administrators to establish their newly chartered tribal colleges and get their operations under way. That was not the case in every tribal college's start-up, however. A number of tribally controlled colleges sought experienced college administrators from already established institutions; some were American Indian and several were Euro-American. However the boards of trustees selected them, the leaders of the new colleges had key characteristics in common. They were leaders, risk takers, and educators, and they possessed strong character and the desire to see tribal (indigenous) people regain control of their institutions and lives.

Any new indigenous college must select its founding president with great care, for the tone and character of the new institution will reflect the president's personality. If the new president has the above-described characteristics, the college will be well on its way to success. If, however, the board of trustees makes an unwise choice of a founding president, the college will suffer as long as that individual is at the helm. A poor selection, one made for the wrong reasons, could set an indigenous college back several years, whether early or late in the college's life, and could inhibit the natural growth the college should experience as it expands its service to the community.

To select the right president, the board of trustees must take their time and allow only considerations having to do with the management of the college to influence their judgment. Although the founding board of trustees will not have had experience at filling such a position, they can do the necessary research to ascertain whether the person or persons being considered have leadership skills, have demonstrated loyalty to indigenous people and their goals for self-determination, have a history of acting with good character, have a background in education or a related field, and are willing to take calculated risks in carrying out the necessary tasks to get the college operational as an educational institution. If possible, the board of trustees should call on board members or administrators from established indigenously controlled colleges to assist them in their initial search for a founding president, as every bit of advice and experience in making this important decision will help in making the right choice.

In turn, the president must seek out and retain the best possible team of support administrators he or she can find to carry out the tasks of creating each part of the fledgling college. The board of trustees will assist in this important task. They may know of fellow tribal members or other qualified indigenous persons who can be recruited to serve as administrators of the college. The board and the president must take a firm stance in the community and with the local governing body, stating that the college's administrative, professional, faculty, and support staff positions are to be filled by well-qualified individuals. The college will not serve as an employment agency, but rather the board of trustees and the president are committed to building, for the community, the very best college possible from its founding date.

The board of trustees, the president, and the administrative team will develop a management style tailored to their specific institution, as they go about building their college. However, they must remember that, although there are good educational, administrative, and management practices to which they must adhere, each tribal or indigenous community has a unique culture and set of family based values that must also be taken into consideration as the college's management style evolves and strengthens. Schuyler ("Sky") Houser, with 20 years of experience as an administrator and developer of tribally controlled colleges, stated in a 1991 article in the *Tribal Col-*

lege Journal of American Indian Higher Education entitled "Building Institutions Across Cultural Boundaries" that management is not a Euro-American invention. Rather, tribal and indigenous communities have always had ways of accomplishing important community tasks that require well-timed, well-organized collective activity. He went on to say that, in many tribal and indigenous communities, traditional ways of organizing and managing important events such as spiritual and cultural activities persist into the present, although an outsider might not easily discern them.

The fact that today many tribal and indigenous communities have become hybrid societies adds to the challenge of developing the right management style for a new locally controlled college. Indigenous communities now reflect in part that which has always been their culture and values, but they also reflect pieces of the Western majority's culture that has been forced upon them, as well as welfare cultural values resulting from the destruction of their indigenous economic systems. New indigenous colleges and their administrators will confront all of the above value systems as they somehow address the expectation that they develop an educational institution with the easily recognizable patterns of a traditional European-style college, yet one that is also truly a part of the indigenous community and its cultural management style. Houser (1991) went on to say that American Indian colleges have faced difficult management concerns that lie at the center of current indigenous community and economic development. Each successful American Indian college has had leaders who correctly identified how their tribal community got business done and what its management methods were. The college leaders have then incorporated the best of those methods into their management styles. By incorporating the best management practices of the local tribal community, administrators are clearly demonstrating to their community that the college and its administrators value the tribal culture and its value system.

American Indian tribal colleges have experienced an interesting trend over their 30-year history in relation to the percentage of native and nonnative administrators of their colleges. In the early years of the tribal college movement, the ratio was about 50:50 between the two, but as the years passed, the proportion gradually changed to today's ratio of about 90% natives to 10% nonnatives serving as tribal college administrators. Another interesting fact about the makeup of American Indian tribal college administrators is the number of women who serve in leadership roles in their colleges. At any one time, at least one third of the presidents of American Indian tribal colleges are women, and 50% of all other administrators are also women.

Both of the preceding items illustrate several important benefits of having a locally controlled college in an indigenous community. First, the college will draw home a number of well-educated persons who were originally from the community, but who left to secure an education and found positions elsewhere after completing their educational programs. Second, indigenous women have always been leaders in their societies in education and in cultural preservation and transmission, which has allowed them to move into leadership roles in the tribal college movement. Third, just having a locally controlled college in a community has changed those communities in many tangible and intangible ways, which has led to the education of community members so they might go on for 4-year and graduate degrees, and return home to assume leadership roles in the tribal college and the community-at-large. AIHEC, the American Indian tribal colleges' national organization, has also sponsored several short-term leadership training institutes specifically aimed at increasing the pool of trained tribal college administrators.[1]

Faculty

The board of trustees, president, and academic dean or academic vice-president of a new indigenously controlled college will find that another difficult challenge is the recruitment and selection of faculty. They must keep open minds and be flexible because there will be numerous ways in which they can meet their students and the college's need for classroom instructors. Early on in the life of the college, the administrators themselves may also serve as instructors, when they are qualified and in their own fields of study. In their formative years, American Indian tribally controlled colleges often had their administrators teaching in addition to performing their administrative duties. Although today in the more established tribally controlled colleges that need is not as intense, administrators in many of the smaller or more recently founded American Indian tribally controlled colleges still teach as a necessary part of maintaining the college's course offerings.

A newly founded indigenously controlled college has an important resource in their community that they must not overlook; professionals (such as program administrators, lawyers, and doctors) and traditional persons (elders and culture keepers) who live and work in the community. These professional and traditional persons can become the part-time instructors

---

[1]New indigenously controlled colleges from around the world would be wise to contact AIHEC and ask to be informed and included when such leadership institutes are going to be offered. The leadership institutes would give the new indigenously controlled college administrative personnel a head start on the professional development and network building they will need throughout their careers.

who will supplement the ranks of the instructor pool for any new or small indigenous college. Once a college has successfully recruited a cadre of part-time instructors from its community's professional and traditional ranks, the college should make an organized effort to help these new part-time instructors develop their course materials and syllabi. It is unlikely that many, if any, of these part-time instructors will have had formal training or experience as teachers. They, and the students they will be teaching, deserve all the help the college can give them so that students have a positive learning experience in the classroom. It is also important that the part-time instructors want to continue teaching for the college after their initial semester or quarter of teaching, as it is likely that the college will need them for some time in the future.

Administrators of a new indigenous college will plan for fewer and fewer part-time instructors as their college matures and its financial resources grow, but they should plan to continue to search out and recruit part-time instructors from the ranks of community professional persons. Part-time instructors will be needed when the college is unable to find a full-time instructor for every course its students need.

The traditional persons, those individuals best suited to teach the tribe's or indigenous group's culture and language, who agree to become part-time instructors, will need special attention from the college for three important reasons. First, they often come from that part of the community that has chosen to keep the greatest distance between themselves and formalized Western educational institutions, and, being respected elders of the community, they are often, although not always, elderly. This can mean that they have little formal Westernized education, and they could initially be uncomfortable in a formal college classroom. It would be wise to team them up with experienced teachers who can help them prepare for the first few semesters or quarters they teach for the college.

Second, the college will want to retain the traditional instructors who find that they enjoy teaching in a tribal or indigenous college and who are good at it. They will become the backbone of the college's native studies department as the college grows and matures. The native studies department is that part of the indigenous college that makes it a unique institution of higher education. No other institution of higher education can or will teach the local culture and language with the love and accuracy that the locally controlled indigenous college's native studies instructors will offer, over time.

Third, a strong native studies department that has respected traditional persons teaching within it, who come directly from the community, should gain important support for the college from the traditional segment of the community. The support of the community's traditional members can and will bring special rewards to the college and its students in a variety of ways.

The full-time faculty and their quality as instructors will be, over time, the true measure of how well the new indigenously controlled college is serving its students. As its financial position is strengthened, the young college must do everything it can to find, recruit, and hire the best possible full-time instructors. The improvement and growth of its teaching corps should be made a top priority of the college each year when the annual plan and budget are generated. The college should also cast a wide net when advertising for new teachers, for it will find that there are dedicated teachers of all races, religions, and parts of the country or world who truly want to work and serve in an indigenous community. Their reasons for wanting to teach in the indigenous community will vary as much as the individuals will, but that should not detract from their abilities as teachers. In most cases, the college will find that, as a group, these individuals are in the profession of teaching for all the right reasons. There may be the rare time when the college's administration will have to remove a teacher from the college instructors' ranks for the benefit of the students and the teacher, but that will happen no more often than it does in any mainstream higher educational institution. (For more on faculty issues, see Tippeconnic and McKinney, chap. 12, this volume)

The administrators of an indigenous college, whether it is a new or an established one, should make every effort to locate and hire indigenous instructors. In addition to being good teachers, indigenous instructors can be excellent role models for the local indigenous students. They are living testimony that an indigenous person can succeed in the majority society and yet remain true to oneself as an indigenous person. And, if that person originally was from the local community, so much the better.

Support Staff

The support staff of an indigenous college should be a vital link to the indigenous community that is being served by the locally controlled college. The support staff positions (secretaries, paraprofessionals, custodial staff, technical staff, and other employees) are those most likely to be filled by local community members. For the new indigenous college, the persons selected to fill these behind-the-scenes but important positions will send a direct message to the community about the college's willingness to reach out to the community and be a part of it.

In hiring individuals to fill support staff positions, the new college must take special care to ensure that a fair and honest process is followed to employ the best qualified persons, regardless of family connections, political contacts, or personal friendships. In offering these positions for which local community members can compete, the new college can show that it is a fair and impartial community institution, endeavoring to find the best possible people to serve its students. Every person selected for a support staff position will become an unofficial ambassador for the college in all of its relationships with students, the community-at-large, and the local governing body. Thus (like new faculty, administrators, and board members), each of these individuals must be a person of good character and must have a talent for working with others. The old cliché that an institution and its administrators can work only as well as their support staff is true in this case, and the builders of the new indigenous college must understand this principle and ensure that the best support staff possible are in place at their college. An added benefit to being a locally controlled educational institution is that the college can begin educating and training its own support staff as the college matures, and can employ those graduated students as positions open up within the college.

Students (and Student Services)

Every action taken to start a new indigenous college and continue to develop an established indigenous college has the primary goal of serving the indigenous student to the best of everyone's ability—the board of trustees, administrators, faculty, and support staff. Established American Indian and other indigenous colleges have found that their students enroll at an indigenously controlled college for many of the same reasons that majority/nonindigenous students attend college. Newly founded indigenous colleges will most likely find that their students desire to better themselves intellectually, that they hope to improve their chances of securing satisfying and financially rewarding employment, that they seek the skills to manage their own futures, and that they want an opportunity to provide a better life for their families.

A newly founded indigenous college will probably see initial student demographics that reflect the experience of the American Indian tribally controlled colleges. Many students will be older (over 30); the majority will be single, female heads of households with extended family obligations. Some will have failed at nonindigenous higher education institutions and find college an unusually heavy burden, and virtually all will be the first in their families to attend college. Indigenous students attending a tribal or indigenous college present their instructors and counselors with many challenging cultural, linguistic, and personal characteristics and situations. For the past century, most indigenous people around the world have existed in abject poverty, and this will generally be true of the native students who attend indigenous colleges. It must be remembered that indigenous students will bring with them to college a value system that is a hybrid of native culture, mainstream culture, and welfare culture. Instructors and students often have to sort through this cultural mix in order to create for each student a productive and healthy plan to get through the college program. Staff members at all levels of a new indigenous college need to recognize that nearly 90% of the students attending their college are first-generation students. Programs especially tailored to increase the likelihood that these students will stay in school will need to be developed (Stein, 1992).

The mission statement of a new indigenous college should declare that it will help preserve, promote, and teach its tribal or indigenous culture and language. Students will be given an opportunity to learn more about their indigenous culture, which in turn will build in them a sense of identity and pride. These qualities are important to indigenous students as they struggle to overcome poverty, lack of self-esteem, and poor educational preparation in their quest for a higher education. Students will be encouraged to actively seek proficiency in their own languages and cultures because traditional spiritual ceremonies and arts remain an integral part of most indigenous students' communities. Indigenous colleges have generated great pride in their communities' indigenous heritages (Boyer, 1990).

As its resources grow, the newly founded indigenous college should develop special support programs for its students. College staff should constantly examine existing programs to ensure that they are the most beneficial in assisting students through the college experience. The special challenges facing students will reflect the demanding environment from which indigenous students come. Several examples of special programs developed by American Indian tribally controlled colleges are transportation programs, child-care programs, and student peer support groups, which have greatly enhanced students' success in completing their programs of study.

American Indian tribal colleges are often located (as most new indigenous colleges will be) in some of the most isolated rural parts of their respective nations. In addition, most American Indian reservations and indigenous homelands have poor road systems with few paved highways, as well as severe weather conditions and long distances between the small

communities of the reservation or homeland. Many students will have un-
reliable vehicles (if they have any vehicle at all), and thus may need to use
the college's transportation system, even in the best weather. An added
benefit of having a college bus system is that all community members can
use it and help defray the cost by paying a small fee to use it.

Child-care programs help those students who have children, grandchildren, or younger siblings imposing demands on their time and resources. Indigenous students reflect their culture at its best when they take on the
responsibility of child care. Unfortunately, this responsibility can lead to ab-
senteeism, insufficient finances to cover the needs of an extended family,
and a lack of time to study and prepare for class. Indigenous colleges that
have developed child-care programs for their students have gone a long way
toward helping students at a basic and necessary level.

An example of a successful student support program is the Blackfeet Community College's Women's Support Group. The group meets regularly after
classes to discuss and develop strategies to help members cope with burdens
of filling so many demanding roles at once; student, mother, wife or single
head of household, and often major economic provider. The Women's Support Group program became so visibly successful for the women participating
that several male students at Blackfeet Community College asked the college
to sponsor a similar program for them (C. Murray, personal communication,
January 8, 1991).

New indigenous colleges should also consider some of the more traditional student service programs because of their potential contribution to
the success of students at indigenous colleges. These programs illustrate
how important a wide variety of counseling and service programs is to these
students. For example, most established tribally controlled colleges place
importance on adult basic education (ABE) programs (also known as graduate equivalency degree or GED programs) because a substantial number of
their student recruits lack a high school or secondary school diploma. Tribal
colleges' ABE programs have become a significant part of reservation or
homeland educational scenes because of the alarmingly high percentage of
indigenous students who drop out of junior and senior high school. It should
be noted that, on American Indian reservations where tribally controlled
colleges have taken over the responsibility for ABE programs from the state
education systems, GED rates have increased by as much as 1,000% (Bordeaux, 1990).

Financial aid programs are also a necessity for more than 90% of indigenous students. The new indigenous college needs to establish a mechanism
by which its students can receive financial aid, whether that aid comes di-

rectly from the tribe or indigenous community's governing body; from the state, provincial, or national government's educational financial aid programs; from private foundations; or from a combination of these sources. Indigenous students will be hard-pressed to attend college even with this aid, and it will be almost impossible for them to do so without it, unless the college assesses no tuition or fees. (For more on students and student issues, see Ortiz and HeavyRunner, chap. 11.)

Facilities

Although bricks and mortar are important to a school, founders of a new indigenous college need to understand that they do not need to wait for substantial buildings to establish their institution. The most important ingredient for starting a community-controlled college are its people (especially its students and instructors), not its buildings. However, if the founders of the new college have the good fortune of owning or having access to adequate facilities, they will have a strong start on developing their college, and can turn their attention to other important matters affecting the college's future.

New indigenous colleges that do not have access to their own classrooms and office space should follow the example of the many American Indian tribally controlled colleges that also lacked facilities when they were founded, but made do with whatever space they could beg, scrounge, borrow, or share in their communities. Tribal college founders understood that learning could take place almost anywhere if the instructors and students were motivated to have classes, and were not concerned with where those classes were being held. It is the sincere effort of the participating teacher and students, not whether the classroom is attractive, that really creates a quality teaching and learning experience in the classroom.

American Indian tribally controlled colleges that had no facilities when they started used some of the following strategies. Some tribal colleges shared office space with other tribal programs, brought in used (often condemned) mobile homes for office space and classrooms, or borrowed classrooms from the local K–12 school system and held night classes. Others moved into condemned and abandoned federal and tribal buildings and renovated them into office space and classrooms, or they borrowed enough funds from their tribe to purchase old and empty privately owned buildings in the community and renovated them into offices, classrooms, and libraries. Some shared space in their local community library and added higher education materials to its collection (often donated materials from more prosperous, longer established institutions). Eventually, the tribal college would run the library for the community and add to it a tribal archive. Other colleges borrowed funds from their tribal government for materials and had their vocational technology and carpentry students and instructors build college office buildings and classrooms as a part of their curriculum. In one instance, college founders borrowed a jail cell from the local police department to hold a class in one of their outlying communities. These examples illustrate that many options are available in indigenous communities for creative indigenous college administrators to find or create office space and classrooms.

Because the board of trustees and administrators of a new college must improvise when it comes to finding office space and classrooms, they should develop for their college, as soon as possible, a long-range plan that includes provisions for and a designated committee focused on securing a permanent home for the college. This will mean developing a financial plan that outlines specific ways to raise the necessary funds for renovating an already existing facility, or for building a new facility that meets the college's needs for office space and classrooms. The administrators and board members of already well-established indigenous colleges can be of valuable assistance to newer colleges by sharing successful strategies they were able to use in carrying out their facility and college campus building plans. Facility planning committees for new indigenous colleges should develop good relationships with their local governing bodies, state or provincial legislators, and national legislators and committees that approve the funding of these types of community projects. They should also contact private philanthropic foundations for project funds and investigate borrowing the necessary funds from the tribal or local governing body, a local lending agency, or a bank to build or renovate, using as collateral the future revenues the college will bring in from its funding sources.

Finances

Securing finances for the establishment and continuation of a new indigenous college is a serious challenge that does not get any easier as time goes by and the institution matures. Most indigenous people live on the margins of the majority society, which means that poverty is a general community problem and that the indigenous community does not usually wield political power on the national scene. Hard work, creativity, and accountability must be the creed of the new college's fund-raisers as they go about the business of securing the funds necessary to establish their college and ensure its financial security.

The resources to start a college can come from any legitimate source, whether tribal funds, state or provincial funds, national funds, or private philanthropic funds. To secure start-up funds, the college founders need to be astute and tenacious politicians and grant-proposal writers. Each of the potential contributors to the college's creation must be approached with that contributor's special characteristics in mind. There are a number of tasks that college fund raisers need to carry out:

1. Do the necessary research on each potential contributor—whether public or private—and tailor the college's funding appeal to meet that contributor's specified areas of giving.
2. Understand that the burden of proof of need is with the college and not the potential contributor when making the case for funds or resources to be granted to the college.
3. Attend conferences and meetings that staff members of the funding source frequent so that college personnel can develop personal relationships with staff and decision makers of potential contributors.
4. Send at least two college representatives when meeting with potential contributors; this allows for mutual support and flexibility in presenting the funding request.
5. Develop the best possible written materials and visual aids the college can afford, to share with potential contributors; continually update these materials as the college matures.
6. Send materials to potential contributors whenever some interesting event takes place within the college or with its students. Materials telling the story of the tribe or indigenous group, as well as individual students' stories, are effective in reaching contributors.
7. Invite potential contributors' representatives to the college campus and community. This is especially effective during a pow wow or other community or college ceremony that is open to the public.
8. Make sure that the prospectus is well written when soliciting a grant or program funds.
9. Be courteous but proud of what the college is doing when sharing information about the college and its mission, while also making the contributor feel important, trusted, and needed (Oregon State University Development Office, 1993).
10. Finally, do not pursue contributors just to obtain general operating funds; have a specific goal in mind for those resources. Contributors that do not fit the college's needs can become a burden and can lead to financial and legal problems if the college tries to use them for purposes other than those for which they were granted.

Once funds to establish an indigenous college are secured, the founding administrators and board of trustees must immediately put together a long-range funding plan that includes a solid budgeting and fund-accounting process for the college. (For more on this topic, see Shanley's chapter.)

Instruction

A major challenge that the new indigenous college will face is building its instructional program to meet the many demands placed upon it. There will be pressure to focus on mainstream curriculum to prepare students for the majority's competitive society, similar pressure to develop curriculum that is focused on the indigenous/tribal group's culture, and requests from the indigenous governing body and administrators for the college to use its resources (personnel and funds) immediately for economic development of the community. The challenge will be to find the right balance when the fledgling college allocates its resources in fulfilling its stated institutional mission. Because most new indigenous colleges will declare in their mission statements a desire to carry out all of the above-mentioned tasks, the determining factor will be what resources and personnel in the community are available to teach the designated curriculum and to work on special projects for the community.

In its search for the right balance for the curriculum, the new college should probably first develop that part of the curriculum that is readily accessible in most indigenous communities; its indigenous cultural and language studies. By developing this area of the curriculum, the new college will accomplish several important tasks for its students, its community, and itself. First, studies have indicated that American Indian students attending established American Indian tribally controlled colleges benefit greatly from the opportunity to study the history, culture, and language of their own people as taught by their elders and truly knowledgeable teachers. By better understanding their identities as members of an American Indian tribe with its own distinct and ancient way of life and by understanding better the cultural values and way of life of their people, students' sense of pride is enhanced and their self-esteem is strengthened.

Second, by immediately stressing the fledgling college's commitment to the development and teaching of the indigenous community's culture and language, a strong tie to the community's traditional and elderly members is established. Indigenous studies will also help build the sense of pride in itself that is necessary to any community's well-being (Boyer, 1997). Third, by developing an indigenous-studies program, the college will bring into the institution traditional tribal members and tribal elders who can provide valuable advice to administrators about operating in the community.

Finally, developing an indigenous-studies program will strengthen the college on the local and national political fronts and will quickly provide a strong foundation for later curriculum development. The new college will also be developing an aspect that will make it unique among its country's higher education institutions, its own indigenous studies. Indigenous studies at established mainstream higher education institutions are at best skimpy, undervalued, and usually a neglected part of the curriculum. The new indigenous college can quickly make indigenous studies its area of strength and expertise, putting it ahead of even the strongest higher education institutions in the country. No other higher education institution will ever have the kind of access to indigenous cultural experts that the new indigenous college has the day it opens its doors to students from the community.

The development of mainstream curriculum will, at first, be dictated by a number of needs that all colleges have for a well-balanced curriculum for their students. All students will need to be able to read, write, and do mathematics at a basic level of proficiency upon completing their education at the college. Thus, the new college must dedicate the necessary resources to ensure that these basic classes are in place before any other curriculum is developed. If the college has the necessary resources, it should bring instructors on board full time to start building strong departments in these basic areas. If the requisite funds are not available, the college can start by looking to the community and local educators for part-time instructors for these important classes.

The new college may want to look to established institutions of higher education located nearby (both indigenous and nonindigenous colleges) to offer needed courses. This practice worked well for many of the American Indian tribally controlled colleges in their early stages of development. In fact, such arrangements should be easier to establish than in the past because of the distance-learning technology that is available today. Also, collaborations between established institutions and developing indigenous colleges may provide both partners new opportunities to qualify for funding support of jointly offered courses and programs from state, provincial, or national governments, or from private agencies.

While these basic needs are being met, the college can conduct a survey to identify additional educational needs that are unique to their community. The surveyed population should include all potential employers, educators in the K–12 system, local governing officials, members of the community-at-large, and the nearest private and public 4-year colleges and universities. This constituent base can identify for the college the areas of curriculum that they see as necessary and desirable for students to gain employment or to continue on to 4-year colleges and research universities. Identified curricular needs should then be prioritized by the board of trustees and college administrators with the help of a committee comprising students and community members. Appropriate courses can then be developed as the college secures the necessary resources for their inclusion in the college's course offerings.

As the new college gathers faculty and develops curriculum for its students, it will increasingly be seen by community organizations and the local governing body as an intellectual resource to be used for the community's benefit. The local governing body will ask college administrators and faculty to assist in writing grants for the community, to serve on community committees, and to provide other such assistance. The new college's administrators and faculty must carefully weigh each request and decide whether they have the time and energy to work on additional tasks and still perform their official college duties. At times they will have the time, energy, and expertise to be of real service to the community or local governing body; then they should serve when requested. When college personnel take time to serve on committees or help to write important community-service grants, the college will acquire strong and important community support. Strong support from the community and local governing body will translate into opportunities to pursue grants that require joint participation and will benefit each of the partners and their constituents.

FINAL THOUGHTS

To succeed in founding an indigenous or tribally controlled college, there must be a sound philosophical foundation and a realistic developmental action plan. The philosophy of the founding group of an indigenous college will be the guiding light for the mission of the institution, will tie the college to its community, and will dictate what will be taught at the college. The developmental action plan is the blueprint that must illustrate the step-by-step actions necessary for the founding of a new indigenous/tribally controlled college.

Implementing the philosophy, mission, and developmental plan is just the beginning. Much additional work must be done by the new college's board of trustees and administrators as they prepare to interact with the many outside agencies that will affect the new college within and outside the community as it matures. These agencies range from the private vendors with whom the college will do business to the agencies and branches of tribal, state, and national governments. These outside agencies are important to the success of the new college for a multitude of reasons. The college must be certain of its philosophy and developmental action plan and use both advantageously.

REFERENCES

Adams, F. (1975). *Unearthing seeds of fire: The idea of Highlander.* Winston-Salem, NC: John F. Blair.
Bordeaux, L. (1990, May). *Higher education from the Tribal College perspective.* [speech]. Montana Pipeline Conference, Montana State University, Bozeman, Montana.
Boyer, P. (1997). *Native American colleges: Progress and prospects.* Princeton, NJ: Carnegie Foundation for the Advancement of Teaching.
Boyer, P. (1990, May). *Tribal Colleges: Creating a new partnership in higher education.* [edited speech]. Opening the Montana Pipeline Conference. Montana State University, Bozeman, Montana. Conference proceedings. Sacramento, CA: Tribal College Press.
College of the Menominee Nation. (1999). Available: *www.menominee.com.*
Diné Community College. (2000). Available: Fond du Lac Tribal and Community College. (1995–1997). *Fond du Lac Tribal and Community College catalog.* Cloquet, MN: Author.
Forbes, J. D. (1985). *Native American higher education: The struggle for the creation of D-Q University, 1960–71.* Davis, CA: D-Q University Press.
Forbes, J. D. (1972). *Why Deganawidah-Quetzalcoatl University? An Indian-Chicano university in 5082 A.C.* Davis, CA: D-Q University Press.
Houser, S. (1991, Winter). Building institutions across cultural boundaries. *Tribal College: Journal of American Indian Higher Education, 2* (3), 11–17.
Little Big Horn College. (1997–1999). *Little Big Horn College catalog.* Crow Agency, MO: Author.
Lutz, H. (1980). *D-Q University: Native American self-determination in higher education.* Davis, CA: Department of Applied Behavioral Sciences, University of California, Davis.
Navajo Community College. (1976). *Institutional self-evaluation report.* STsaile, AZ: Author.
Oglala Lakota College. (1998–1999). *Oglala Lakota College catalog.* Kyle, SD: Author.
Oregon State University Development Office. (1993). *Fund raising.* Eugene, OR: Author.
Sinte Gleska Community College. (1973). *Sinte Gleska College's history.* Rosebud, SD: Author.
Stein, W. J. (1992). *Tribally controlled colleges.* New York, NY: Peter Lang.
Zion, J. W. (1989, Fall). *Human rights, law, and Indian culture: Five centuries of unfinished business.* Article prepared for the Fair Housing Conference. Bozeman, MT: Montana Human Rights Commission.

3

Limitations and Alternatives to Developing a Tribally Controlled College

James Shanley
Fort Peck Community College

INTRODUCTION

This chapter is intended to answer a number of critical questions about the future development of new tribal colleges. Is there a limit to the number of tribal colleges that can be developed in the United States? If so, what are the limitations? Given limitations, how many tribal colleges should or will be developed? What are the essential characteristics that will lead to successful tribal college development? Finally, are there alternatives to the tribal college model?

The answers to the preceding questions will vary widely from community to community. Every tribe lives in a unique environment, and the tribal colleges that have developed to date reflect the uniqueness of the chartering tribes. In addition, many factors that are intertwined with the development of mainstream higher education need to be considered, the major factors being resource availability, accreditation, and critical mass.

Resource Availability

In North America, tribal colleges arose out of the Indian education movement of the late 1960s and early 1970s, when there was a renaissance of hope, pride, and resolve aimed at strengthening tribes and improving life for

American Indians, particularly those living on reservations. A key concept in the development of the tribal college movement was the strengthening of sovereignty expected by tribes through the chartering of their own unique institutions. This exercise of legal authority was a key element in the overall effort that, at the time, was being called self-determination.

Many values and goals were embodied or sought in this exercise of sovereignty. There was recognition of the value and need to legitimize (from a mainstream point of view) cultural knowledge, language, and world perspectives. There was a need for job training at the tribal level, for community development, and for services and the technical assistance necessary to promote lasting community development. There was a need to provide higher education opportunities that had not been readily available from the Bureau of Indian Affairs (BIA) in the preceding decades. Finally, a tribal higher education institution was a potentially powerful source of pride and tribal esteem.

All of these goals or needs helped to form the parameters of what a tribal college model could be. Unfortunately, the model did not readily fit the template of existing higher education institutions in the United States. The closest model that contained many of the characteristics desired by tribal colleges was the community college model, which was a post-World War II innovation that, at the time, was 20 years old. However, there were some distinct differences between the standard community college model and tribal colleges.

Community colleges, for the most part, were an extension of the public education (K–12) system that developed in the United States over a 100-year period. The key characteristics of this public education model were local control and open access to schools. The foundation of local control came from the provision of local resources to build, staff, and maintain the local schools. Eventually, the financial responsibility shifted to state governments, with the local communities retaining the responsibility to provide basic resources and local control.

This financial structure is based on taxation of local and state citizens, and on the local level, is usually based on a property tax. At the state level, the money is generally raised from individual income taxes or other special tax levies. Although public school districts were overlaid on reservation trust property, Indian tribes did not control local public K–12 education systems. Tribes, because of their unique trust relationship with the federal government, could not develop a property taxation system. The tribes, although theoretically able to tax tribal citizens, have never been in a position philosophically or actually to tax their members. This lack of a tribal tax base is due largely to the impoverished nature of most Indian reservations and the reliance on Federal transfer payments, such as BIA or welfare funds, to provide minimum standards of living.

Therefore, in the case of tribal colleges, the key provision of local resources provided through taxation that serves as a fiscal basis for mainstream community colleges was not and is still not available to tribes. This has proved to be very problematic. Most tribes do not have sufficient income from other sources that can be used as a local fiscal base for a postsecondary institution. So, despite the pride- and confidence-building expression of tribal independence and sovereignty created by chartering colleges, the resources do not exist locally to provide for tribal colleges.

In their formative years, the tribal colleges were pieced together with different federal grants, such as Title III, Strengthening Developing Institutions. These funds, however, were very insecure and far from sufficient to develop an institution. The colleges, through the American Indian Higher Education Consortium (AIHEC), turned to the federal government, and, after a lengthy struggle, the Tribally Controlled College or University Assistance Act was passed in 1978 (formally named Tribally Controlled Community College Assistance Act). However, the amounts appropriated under the Act were inadequate to realistically develop and maintain an institution. The Act also created a continual struggle to maintain local autonomy and control with the purse strings being held by Congress and the BIA. One of the primary fears expressed by congressional opponents of Tribally Controlled College or University Assistance Act in the fight for the initial legislation was that the tribal college movement would proliferate and consume more and more federal resources. This opposition was offset somewhat by congressional skeptics who thought the movement would fail. The proliferation fear became a reality as tribal colleges have been successful and have multiplied.

To address the proliferation argument, certain requirements or limiting entrance characteristics were built into the Tribally Controlled College or University Assistance Act. When a tribe's request for a Tribally Controlled College or University Assistance Act designation was made to the BIA, the applicants were required to complete an eligibility study to determine whether their proposed college could participate. There are eight primary criteria that the BIA uses to define the minimum organizational capacity needed to be recognized as a tribal postsecondary institution.

First, organizational documents provide proof of an institution's meeting the following criteria:

1.   Does the college meet the definition of an "institution of higher education" as defined in Title 20, Sec. 1001 as incorporated in 25 U.S.C.A. §1801?

2.   Does the institution admit as regular students only persons having a certificate of graduation from a school providing secondary education or students holding the recognized equivalent of a high school diploma? Or does it admit as regular students persons who are beyond the compulsory school attendance age for the state in which the institution is located and who have the ability to benefit from the training offered by the institution?

3.   Does the institution provide not less than a 2-year program, which is accepted toward a bachelor's degree?

4.   Is the college a non-profit or public institution?

5.   Is the college accredited by a recognized national accrediting agency? If not accredited, is there satisfactory assurance that the institution will meet the accreditation standards of such an agency or association?

6.   Does the institution provide not less than a one-year program of training to prepare students for gainful employment in a recognized occupation and meet 1, 2, and 3 above?

7.   Does the college possess a charter or other form of sanction from the tribe(s) to which it offers services?

8.   Is the college being studied the only college so sanctioned by the tribe served?

9.   Is the college governed by a majority membership of Indians?

10.   What documents are used to verify the eligibility of board members?

11.   Is the college free from such affiliations with nontribal parent institutions that may limit the powers of the board to exercise full control?

12.   Do the majority of students attending this college meet the definition of Indian? (Indian is defined as a person who is a member of an Indian tribe and is eligible to receive services from the Secretary of Interior.)

13.   Is there a means in the college enrollment records to identify Indian students?

Second, the curriculum, charter, and so on, must indicate that the college is in harmony with the goals and objectives of the chartering tribe.

Third, a student records system must be in place, which has a means of identifying full- and part-time students in attendance.

Fourth, relative isolation of the college must be demonstrated. The questions to be answered are:

1. What are the distances to the nearest two alternate colleges?
2. What is the condition of the roads between the nearest two alternative colleges and the majority of the students' homes?
3. Are there any common climactic conditions that may affect commuting between the students' homes and the alternate colleges?
4. Do students have access to transportation to alternate colleges?
5. Are there any major differences in curriculum or instructional approaches at the nearest two alternative colleges that may inhibit attendance by Indian students?
6. Are student services available at the alternate colleges that would encourage Indian students to attend?
7. What are the relative costs of each school, as compared to the tribal college, in terms of tuition, transportation, boarding, and so on?
8. What are the comparative number and percentage of Indian students served by the tribal college and the nearest alternative colleges?

Fifth, the college must demonstrate that its enrollment is large enough or has the critical mass required to support a tribal college. A positive determination will be made if there has been a stable or growing student population over the last 3 years that is large enough to provide reasonable surety that:

1. The facilities can be effectively utilized.
2. A diversified professional faculty and staff can be maintained and adequate funding will be available to support the purposed program.
3. Occasional fluctuations in enrollment will not jeopardize the continuation of the program.

Determination also is made based on the responses to the following queries:

1. What is the student population? What are the size, age, gender, racial makeup, and educational attainment of the group served by the college?
2. What are the current age range and average age of students served?
3. What are the potential age range and average age of students served?
4. What is the racial makeup of the community served by the college?
5. What is the educational attainment of the community served by the college?
6. What are the trends in size, age, gender, racial makeup, and educational attainment of the group served by the college?

7. How will those trends affect the college over the next 10 years?
8. Are there enough students to support the curriculum offered? Is the current student population growing? Is the potential population growing or stable? Are there occasional fluctuations in the potential population?
9. Are there enough students to generate sufficient revenue from PL. 95-471 and other revenue sources to support the current program?
10. Are there existing facilities capable of handling the current student population?
11. Are there current and anticipated facilities capable of handling the projected student population effectively?

Sixth, the college's facilities (or potential facilities) must be sufficient to meet the needs of the student body.

Seventh, the staff of the college must be adequate to provide the services offered by the college.

Eighth, the college must demonstrate adequate financial resources that are managed in an effective and accountable manner.

Although this is a summary of the requirements that a college must meet in order to qualify under the Tribally Controlled College or University Assistance Act, it is apparent that developing a tribal college is a complicated and involved process. So given the above-mentioned criteria, what would it cost to develop a tribal college that could meet the minimum requirements of the Act? The answer to that question hinges on many variables, such as whether a tribe has existing facilities. But a plausible breakdown of costs, given the existence of minimum facilities, might look like this:

Personnel

Administrators	$ 80,000
Clerical/Student Records	$ 30,000
Student Services/Financial Aid	$ 50,000
Faculty	$200,000
Library	$ 50,000
Facilities Operator	$100,000
Business Management	$ 50,000
Other Expenses	$ 50,000
Total	$560,000

This scenario is based on the use of part-time faculty in a ratio of approximately 2 or 3 part-time faculty to every full-time-equivalent faculty, with this size of operation serving approximately 100 to 125 students.

The above-described operation is the minimal undertaking that would have to be maintained for 3 to 5 years before a Tribally Controlled College or University Assistance Act designation could be obtained and federal funds could be secured. Sources of revenue for such an operation would be, in order of availability, tribal funds, federal and state grants, foundation support, and student tuition and fees. Tuition and fees normally provide only 10% to 15% of the total revenue for the operation of an institution of higher education.

Accreditation

Accreditation is the recognition and affirmation by a regional association of colleges and universities that the degree programs offered by an institution meet standards of educational quality acceptable in that region. This is a quasi-governmental process that is approved by the U.S. Department of Education, and an institution must either be accredited or be a candidate for accreditation to receive Title IV federal student financial aid. The United States has several regional accreditation associations, with additional separate accrediting bodies that deal with selected professions and degrees such as teaching, medicine, and so on.

The regional accreditation process has two stages; candidate for accreditation and full accreditation. The time frames for these stages can vary, but generally an institution has to have been in operation for 2 to 3 years before applying for candidate status. Once candidacy is achieved, it is normally 5 years before the institution is considered for full accreditation.

Accreditation starts with a lengthy self-study conducted by the institution. At the completion of the self-study, an accreditation review team, consisting of college educators from other regional institutions, carries out a thorough and detailed site visit. The results of the site visit are reported to a commission, which then decides the accreditation status of the institution. The process is ongoing and requires reevaluation at periodic intervals.

The accreditation process has been intertwined with eligibility for Tribally Controlled College or University Assistance Act status and requires that an institution develop an ongoing operation for several years before major base funding becomes available. The question that arises is, where does the tribe find the resources to carry its institution through the initial development period?

Critical Mass

For tribal colleges to make it through the initial 3 to 5 years of development, there must be a large enough number of students—and potential students—to make this type of expenditure of tribal monies justifiable. It is also important that there is a large enough critical mass of students, over an extended period of time, to make the development of a locally controlled institution viable.

Estimating present (within a year) and future potential student enrollment has become one of the most crucial planning tasks for existing and potential tribal colleges. This task can be approached through a fairly sophisticated enrollment simulation and planning (ESP) statistical model. The following is a simplified application of ESP that can be applied to the restricted geographical areas and populations typically served by tribal colleges. The ESP model comprises three basic approaches:

1. *Environmental scanning*—This involves collecting data on the local area, such as demographics (service-area population by age, gender, ethnicity); economics (service-area employment, household income); social and cultural indicators (language/bilingual factors, social dysfunctions, literacy, high school graduation rates, and so on); present attendance at other colleges; levels of training of area workers; and availability of individual financial resources to pay for college/training. In short, in planning for a tribal college, either existing or potential, accurate, up-to-date information on the service area is essential.

2. *Enrollment market forecasting*— Once all of the demographic information is collected, the data must be analyzed and a calculated guess made for each population segment. For example, if 150 tribal students graduate from service-area high schools, potentially 50% will attend the tribal college. If the tribe employs 100 tribal members, 10% will enroll part-time to upgrade their skills. These calculated guesses will not always be accurate but can provide a baseline estimate of potential students. Colleges that have been in operation for a period of time can make more accurate forecasts based on the actual history of enrollment as it applies to the specific population niches.

Factors that the college controls also influence potential enrollment. Some of these are tuition, fees, availability of student financial aid, curriculum (including adult, vocational, and continuing education), campus sites, marketing, admissions, registration, probation, and dismissal. Some of these factors can be addressed by doing a community survey or surveys, aimed at particular groups, to determine vocational interests, course preferences, and so on.

Once baseline numbers are decided on, a forecast must be made for future years that accounts for documented demographic trends. For instance, if there are 15% more students from age 13 to 17 than there are graduating seniors in a given year, there will be 15% more potential college freshmen over the next 5 years. By analyzing all known demographic trends and extrapolating each population-niche baseline number, a projection can be made for future enrollment.

Long-term projections (5 years or more) are particularly important in determining the viability of separate curriculum offerings. For example, if 20 students need or want to be trained as welders, and there is an estimated need for 100 welders in the service area, this indicates that welding as a vocation is probably a viable curriculum.

3. *Scenario building*—A scenario is an imagined or projected vision of future events based on the existence of certain cause-and-effect variables. Two types of scenarios are important for college enrollment projections.

Baseline scenario—This scenario works from the status quo and usually reflects conservative estimates based on actual history and demographic trends.

Alternative scenario—This scenario says essentially, if conditions change in a particular way, how will this affect the baseline scenario? For example, what if the tribe builds a major casino that will provide employment to *x* number of tribal members? Obviously, this could dramatically change college enrollment, in both negative and positive ways, and could affect college operations in terms of resource availability, curriculum, and so on.

Alternative scenarios are useful in examining the consequences of manageable factors that might occur in the future. The bottom line is that it is almost impossible to develop and maintain an institution of higher education for a reasonable cost with a small number of students. At present, several tribal colleges have a marginal number of students, and these colleges are in a nearly perpetual financial crisis. On the other hand, if a tribe has the necessary resources and wants to dedicate those resources to the development of a college, it is possible, but at an extremely high cost per student served.

Alternative Models

If a tribe wants to develop a college but lacks the critical mass of students or the resources, there are alternative models that could meet standard tribal needs. If the tribe desires to offer job training or selected degree programs for specific students, or if a tribe wishes to develop, conserve, and research tribal language, history, and culture, the following two alternative models might serve those purposes.

Model 1—Through a charter, a tribe could develop an organization that would be quasi-independent of the tribe. This organization could be called an institute, a center, or some other name as desired by the tribe. This organization could have the following characteristics:

1. The organization would be chartered by the tribe(s) with specific authorities.
2. An independent board of directors could govern the organization.
3. The organization could be a not-for-profit (501 C-3) organization.
4. The organization could have a central administration.
5. The organization could be multipurpose. For example, it could contract for specific classes, courses of study, and degree programs with accredited institutions of higher education. It could provide nonaccredited training to tribal government organizations and community businesses. It could maintain a tribal language and culture division that would meet the needs of the tribe. It could administer tribal BIA higher education financial aid, track and advise tribal college students, and work with local K–12 systems.

An advantage of this model is that it is flexible, that is, services can be offered as resources become available. This would allow a variety of services to be offered without the necessity of maintaining an institutional structure, and the services would be similar to those offered by tribal colleges. This model has several advantages:

1. It offers a flexible structure that can be cost effective.
2. It can achieve major tribal higher education and cultural objectives.
3. It can be governed and directed locally.

Model 2—The tribe could affiliate with an existing tribal college. Through this arrangement, an existing tribal college (or other college) would assist with local delivery of courses based on some sort of contract. Developing institutions have made arrangements like these over the years. Such affiliations have worked well in some cases and not so well in other situations. The major advantage is that the receiving tribe does not have to maintain the infrastructure and can negotiate the contracted services to reflect local needs. The major disadvantage is that the tribe would not have control except as spelled out by the contract, and this platform may not serve to build a lasting infrastructure.

In addition to the previously described models, distance-education programs and technology are presently sweeping the United States and offer many advantages that were not previously available. Distance education can be offered through various technology platforms. Two major approaches at this time are interactive television and Internet-based web courses. Currently, several thousand courses from numerous institutions and commercial enterprises are available on the Internet. The continued development of distance-learning strategies could have a dramatic influence on the development of new tribal colleges.

There are many organizations that provide information on distance learning. Here are examples of three excellent sources for the United States; these organizations might also be able to provide referrals to similar information resources in other parts of the world:

United States Distance Learning Association. This inclusive group embraces K–12 instruction, higher education, and corporate training and education. (http://www.usdla.org)

Educause. This is the best professional group focused specifically on the use of technology and information resources in higher education. Their information includes the use of technology to deliver distance learning and to use on-campus as well. (http://www.educause.edu)

Western Cooperative for Educational Telecommunications (WCET). This is a subordinate organization to the Western Interstate Commission for Higher Education (WICHE), serving 15 states in the western United States, so its focus is primarily on the western United States, but that focus is expanding. WCET is a good source of information on distance learning and networking. (http://www.wiche.edu/telecom).

FINAL THOUGHTS

When any serious discussion of the founding of a tribally controlled college is initiated, it leads to the question: Can our community truly support a fully developed tribal college? No community that is serious about developing a tribal college can ignore such a question, but rather, should do the research necessary to answer it as honestly as possible. To put forth the tremendous effort necessary to found a tribal college and then fail because the hard questions were not carefully researched and honestly answered will deal a crushing blow to an indigenous community. If the answer to tough questions such as whether the community is able to sustain a tribal college is "no," then the honorable and intelligent course of action is to seek alternatives to developing a college. By doing so, the activists will be doing their community a great service rather then creating another failure that the community must then shoulder.

REFERENCES

Tribally Controlled Community College Assistance Act, Item 575.92 Stat. 1325 (October 17, 1978). Renamed "Tribally Controlled College or University Assistance Act," P.L. 105–244, H.R. 6 Title IX Amendment (October 7, 1998).

II

Mapping the Trail:
Charting the Future

4

The Effect of the Native American Higher Education Initiative on Strengthening Tribal Colleges and Universities: Focus on Governance and Finance

Wayne J. Stein
Montana State University
James Shanley
Fort Peck Community College
Timothy Sanchez
Teachers College, Columbia University

INTRODUCTION

The tribal college and university (TCU) movement's institutions are unique in terms of governance, organization, and finance when compared to other institutions of higher education throughout the United States. The colleges are individually chartered through the authority of tribal governments, which have much the same jurisdictional authority as state governments and relate to the federal government on a government-to-government basis. Tribal colleges are relatively new institutions, with the oldest, Diné Community College, being 32 years old. For the most part, they are relatively small institutions. From the beginning, tribal colleges have followed the example of American Indian tribes, banding together to gain strength and recognition. This banding together of the TCUs led to the formation of the American Indian Higher Education Consortium (AIHEC) in 1973, which in turn led to the development 15 years later of the American Indian College Fund (AICF).

The first section of this chapter describes the general governance and financing of the TCUs and the tribal college movement. It illustrates just how different the TCUs are from their sister institutions of higher education, yet it clearly shows that TCUs have similar goals and aspirations for their students. The second section of the chapter describes the infrastructure, development, and strengthening of two central organizations of the TCUs, AIHEC and AICF, and three important and related organizations of the TCU movement (see Figure 4.1). These three organizations are the AIHEC's Student Congress; the National Institute for Native Leadership in Higher Education (NINLHE), a new organization made up of Native American higher education student support professionals working within mainstream institutions;

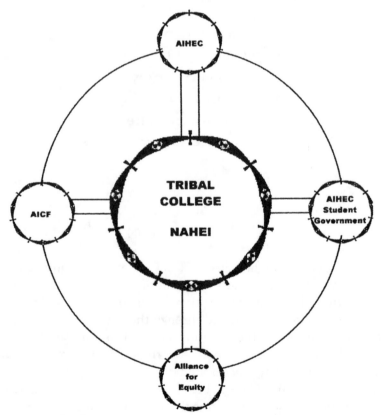

FIG.4.1.   Related Organizations.

and the Alliance for Equity, a joint organization representing the historically Black colleges and universities (HBCUs), Hispanic-serving institutions (HSIs), and TCUs. All five of these organizations have substantially supported the work of TCUs as a result of the funding and networking opportunities provided through the W. K. Kellogg Foundation's Native American Higher Education Initiative (NAHEI). The third section of the chapter explores and evaluates how several NAHEI funded projects have worked to strengthen the governance and fiscal strength of AIHEC and two tribal colleges. The concluding statements present our thoughts on the outcomes of NAHEI, its effect on the TCU movement, and the role of the W. K. Kellogg Foundation in this important educational endeavor.

FOUNDING AND GOVERNANCE OF THE TCUs

The founders of the TCU movement in the late 1960s and early 1970s understood that they were entering an educational world in which American Indian people had been denied input and, in fact, had seen an almost total eradication of all things American Indian. For several centuries, the United States government had systematically barred their communities and tribal governments from participating in the education of their children and young adults. To counteract the federal government's philosophy, which emphasized the total assimilation of their people, a small group of American Indian educators (and their non-Indian colleagues) chose the community college model of community control on which to pattern their efforts to regain control of education for their tribal communities. The founders developed a philosophy that would support a dual mission, protecting and enhancing their own cultures and at the same time embracing many of the tools of standard postsecondary education. TCU leaders recognized that they could not just prepare tribal students to be proficient in their own cultures but that they must also prepare them to be proficient in the non-Indian world that surrounds the tribal communities. Their educational institutions had to prepare native students to live in two very different cultures. It had to be that way if their people were to survive with some semblance of who they really were and are, as well as to protect what they had retained of their homelands and sovereign rights into the 21st century.

Navajo Community College (Diné College), the first TCU to open in 1968, was founded on the important principle of local community control. Its primary aim was to enhance the understanding of the Diné people's heritage, language, history, and culture. To accomplish their goal, the college founders established a clear, detailed, and powerful mission statement.

Diné College Mission Statement

- Strengthen Personal Foundations for Responsible Learning and Living consistent with Sa'ah Naagháí Bik'eh Hózhóón
- Prepare Students for Careers and Further Studies.
- Promote and Perpetuate Navajo Language and Culture.
- Provide Community Services and Research.

As the tribal college movement spread across the United States and Canada throughout the remainder of the 20th century, subsequent TCUs created similar mission statements as they laid down the foundation and governance of their colleges (Stein, 1992).

The local tribal community is the most important base and touchstone for a TCU. Once the members of the community-at-large have given their thoughts and support, the founders of a TCU can then approach the local tribal governing body for an enabling charter. The college's enabling charter must come from the local tribal government in order to legitimize the college in the eyes of the local community and the outside world. In addition to providing the charter, the local tribal government often provides some of the necessary resources needed by a fledgling indigenous college, such as meeting space for the college's early classes, funds to help defray the ever-present expenses of even the most modest effort, and land on which to build the college. The local government may also need to offer support in transactions with funding agencies and various levels of state and national government, as well as in solicitation of funds from private sources.

The college's charter would also include articles of incorporation, or a very similar set of guidelines, that describe how the college will operate as a legal entity of the tribe or indigenous community. Once the charter has been secured, a governing board of trustees for the college will be selected. Because the board of trustees will have numerous responsibilities in ensuring the success of their locally controlled college, the manner in which members are selected and the relationship they have with local governing bodies are crucial and will be defined in the college's charter (see Stein, chap. 2, this volume).

Two key factors in the success of an American Indian tribally controlled college are that its board of trustees must (a) act as a buffer between the college and the local governing body and (b) clearly set policy for the college's administrative practices. By acting as a buffer between the college and its local governing council, the board of trustees ensures that good educational practices will be maintained, rather than enacting or enabling politically charged policies because of shifting local political tensions that have nothing to do with education. In essence, an indigenously controlled college (a TCU) must be an intimate part of its local community, yet must remain administratively separate from the local governing body. What we have learned over time is that being involved in the daily business of tribal governance is a sure formula for failure (see also Boyer, 1997; Stein, 1992).

The board of trustees may be selected in a number of ways, any of which will work if the process is clear and followed faithfully by the local governing body and community (see also Stein chapter). For example, the Fort Peck Tribal Executive Board charters Fort Peck Community College (FPCC), located in Poplar, Montana. The charter created a nine-member board of directors, one of whom is the current president of the FPCC student senate; he or she is a voting member of the board. When a vacancy occurs in one of the other eight positions, it must be advertised in the local papers for 30 days. The FPCC board of directors then has the authority to appoint a replacement from the applicant pool. After the FPCC board of directors has selected a replacement for the vacant position, the charter requires it to submit its candidate for review to the FPCC executive board of directors for their review. That board can reject the recommendation, in which case the FPCC board of directors must submit a new candidate for consideration. Occasionally, the tribal executive board has rejected a name; however, in follow-up discussions between the two boards, an understanding has been reached as to the politics of the choice and its rejection. To date, this selection process has worked well for FPCC (FPCC, 1996).

In short, organizational and administrative structures vary from college to college, each reflecting its own tribal culture to some degree, yet each also reflecting the structures of Western higher education institutions. This is primarily due to regional accreditation association standards that the TCU must meet in order to receive funding assistance from the federal government and private funding agencies (see Boyer, chap. 7, this volume).

FINANCING THE TRIBAL COLLEGES AND UNIVERSITIES

TCUs have a unique foundation for financing their institutions, based on their tribal nations treaties with the United States government. Furthermore, the federal government has trust responsibilities for educating members of those federally recognized tribes that have valid treaties with it. This commitment is important for two reasons. First, most Indian land on reservations is held in trust by the federal government; hence, most tribes have not been able to develop property tax codes to support the many services, including education, that such taxes generally support. Second, state governments have no legal obligation to support tribal schools and so far, have contributed little to the TCUs' financial foundation (see also Boyer, 1997; Stein, 1992). Today, as in the past, TCUs must rely on the federal government to provide their core funding; yet the amount appropriated has not been sufficient to meet the many needs of developing educational institutions that serve tribal communities and students. Although TCUs continue to work closely with the federal government to meet most of their base funding needs, over the past several years, they have had to search for and secure other sources of funding for their developing institutions.

For example, the operating funds of a TCU come from a variety of sources, including tribal funds, state and/or local funds, and private philanthropic funds. In fact, each of these sources has contributed to the stability and longevity of the TCUs. However, because they lack sustainable support, TCUs must continue to rely heavily on limited federal funds for their core operational expenses. In particular, they depend on funds distributed through the Tribally Controlled College or University Assistance Act of 1978 (P. L. 95-471), which is administered by the Bureau of Indian Affairs. Title I of the law currently funds 25 of the colleges through a formula based on the number of Indian students enrolled (called the Indian Student Count or ISC). In fiscal year 1999, total appropriations reached $30 million. However, appropriations for Title I schools in particular have never matched the authorized funding levels originally set by Congress. The current funding of $2,964 per Indian student is now less than half the authorized amount of $6,000. Because the authorized amounts have never been fully realized, Title I tribal colleges operate with significantly less funding per student than do mainstream colleges. Estimates indicate that the TCUs will receive an average of $4,800 per full-time enrolled (FTE) student from federal, state, and local government revenues (AIHEC, 1999).

Title II of the law provides funding for core operations for Diné College. Title III provides matching funds for endowment grants and is authorized at $10 million. However, appropriations have never surpassed $1 million. Over the years, many TCUs have received multimillion dollar grants from Title III, the Higher Education Act, Aid for Institutional Development Program. In addition, funds are authorized for facility renovation and technical systems with recent total appropriations having increased slightly after remaining static in real terms for many years. Title IV is authorized at $2 million to finance local economic development projects, but the funding has not yet been appropriated.

TCUs receive funds from several other important federal sources that finance educational programs closely suited to the particular TCUs' educational missions. Two TCUs receive no P.L. 95-471 funds, but rather receive their core funding from the Carl D. Perkins Vocational and Applied Technological Act. Several other TCUs receive their core funding through separate authorizations from Congress through the Bureau of Indian Affairs. TCUs also receive minimal funding from other sources, including state block-grant programs for adult education, the Minority Science Improvement Program, environmental management grants, and other specially directed funds. TCUs generally secure these other funds through a competitive process; monies are directed specifically to areas of educational need, determined by the colleges (AIHEC, 1998, 1999).

In 1994, TCUs were given land-grant status, joining 55 state universities and 17 historically Black colleges and universities. This new designation has helped TCUs become more visible and connected to mainstream institutions by sharing projects, resources, and information with other land grant universities and colleges through equity grants of $50,000 per institution. The intention of the grants, allocated through the Equity in Education Land Grant Status Act of 1994, is to strengthen agricultural and natural resources programs. However, total appropriations authorized for all 29 eligible TCUs are about equal to the amount given to just one state land-grant university each year.

Finally, Executive Order No. 13021 concerning TCUs was implemented on October 19, 1996, by President Clinton with strong bipartisan support from Congress. The primary purpose of this order is to promote TCUs' participation in programs funded by the federal government and to bring more attention to their accomplishments as accredited higher education institutions. It will greatly assist the TCUs in their struggle to provide high-quality education and to achieve self-sufficiency.

In addition to receiving limited, yet important funds from the federal government, TCUs have received support and funding from a number of philanthropic organizations and foundations since their beginnings in 1968. Funding from philanthropic organizations and foundations has been useful over the years in helping TCUs and their national organization, AIHEC, develop specific educational programs and support the construction of organizational infrastructures that suit the particular needs of each unique community. Until recently, however, funding from foundations and philanthropic organizations was sporadic at best. TCUs often felt ignored by philanthropic organizations and foundations; and when these private institutions did interact with the TCUs, it was to tell them what tribal institutions needed rather than to ask the tribal institutions what they thought their needs were and how private institutions could best assist in meeting those needs.

In the 1990s, private foundations began to interact in a more positive and useful manner with TCUs. Several of the world's largest private foundations (e.g., W. K. Kellogg and Ford) have responded to the TCUs' desire to enter into conversations with philanthropic agencies to set the priorities that would best suit the needs of native communities. This positive response on the part of private foundations has led to a number of successful and innovative educational programs for American Indian people (see W. K. Kellogg's and Ford's Annual Reports on Projects for 1999).

Indeed, the need for an adequate and permanent funding base for TCUs is as strong today as it was in 1968. TCUs will need to continue working closely with their many federal, tribal, state, and private agencies and benefactors to ensure that the institutions are funded at a level that provides quality educational opportunities to their students.

ORGANIZATIONS THAT SUPPORT TRIBAL COLLEGES AND UNIVERSITIES

The American Indian Higher Education Consortium

AIHEC was founded in 1973 by the first six tribal colleges as the organizational focal point for the development of tribally controlled higher education. During its early years, the consortium maintained an office in Denver, Colorado, and was supported through combined monies from the U.S. Department of Education, a Title III grant called Strengthening and Developing Institutions, and several private-foundation grants. AIHEC developed a long-range strategic plan and spearheaded lobbying by the TCUs that resulted in the U.S. Congress's passage of the Tribally Controlled College or University Assistance Act of 1978 (also see Boyer, 1997; Stein, 1992).

However, because AIHEC had become dependent on short-term grants, when these funds ran out in the early 1980s, the consortium was forced to close its Denver office. Over the next 5 years, the consortium existed only through quarterly meetings of the TCU presidents, which usually were held in Washington, D.C. Membership dues and several small private foundation grants enabled AIHEC to employ a part-time, Washington, D.C.-based lobbyist by the mid-1980s. Out of necessity, the consortium evolved as a decentralized organization that existed primarily with the volunteer labor of member AIHEC presidents. The administrative functions of the organization were assigned to various colleges; for example, the AIHEC treasurers handled AIHEC finances through their colleges' business offices. In 1987, AIHEC was able to reopen its office on a full-time basis in Washington, D.C., and hire its part-time lobbyist as the full-time executive director of AIHEC. The organization then developed an aggressive legislative agenda that moved AIHEC forward as an effective advocate for TCUs. The TCUs were able to do this because they had greatly increased AIHEC membership dues to fund the base activities of the central office. Yet, in terms of governance, the board of directors of AIHEC still followed the American Indian style of decentralized management by equal, independent entities.

The aggressive strategies of AIHEC produced positive growth, which led to the founding of the AICF and the ability to purchase, in 1995, a building to house their central office in Alexandria, Virginia (this was made possible through individual investments by the tribal colleges and a grant from the Lannon Foundation). However, as with many new organizations, disagreements between the AIHEC executive director and AIHEC's executive board led to the termination of employees and a series of lawsuits that by 1997 had almost destroyed AIHEC and its subsidiary organizations. As AIHEC was rebuilding its central financial and organizational structure, it was approached by the W. K. Kellogg Foundation, which at the time was exploring the possibility of funding an initiative that would lead to the strengthening of American Indian higher education in the United States. Through discussions and collaborative efforts between the W. K. Kellogg Foundation, AIHEC's board of directors, and a host of American Indian educators and scholars, the NAHEI project was born.

Because the W. K. Kellogg Foundation recognized the importance of a strong central organization to the survival and success of TCUs, it offered, as part of the initiative funding, to strengthen AIHEC's administrative capacity. To accomplish this objective, two AIHEC projects were designed. The first was intended to build AIHEC's administrative, advocacy, and research and development capacity. The goals were:

1. To strengthen AIHEC's management and financial planning functions.
2. To strengthen AIHEC's capacity to provide technical assistance to the TCUs.
3. To strengthen AIHEC's capacity to conduct institutional data collection and policy- related research.
4. To strengthen AIHEC's capacity for advocacy and provision of public information on behalf of TCUs.

The second project was intended to support the work of AIHEC to manage the NAHEI project. AIHEC was funded to organize and deliver technical assistance to TCUs so that they could meet the goals of their individual initiatives and the overall goals of the NAHEI project. In addition to these two major efforts, AIHEC would also supervise:

1. The Hawai'i grant proposal
2. The AIHEC supplemental grant for technical assistance proposal
3. The AIHEC technology-enhancement grant proposal
4. The AIHEC cultural learning center proposal
5. The AIHEC new Meriam report proposal

The largest of these projects is the cultural learning center project in concert with the AICF, which has led to the construction of a cultural learning center at each of the TCUs.

NAHEI support has allowed the AIHEC central organization to mature within a relatively short time. Although this maturation can be attributed to many factors (including NAHEI funding), the changes are real and impressively successful. For example:

1.   Staff capabilities have been greatly enhanced.
2.   The financial position of AIHEC has been reversed from a point of near collapse in 1997 to one in which AIHEC now has substantial financial reserves. This improved financial situation allows AIHEC to perform serious long-term strategic planning and ensures protection from future funding crises.
3.   The strengthening of AIHEC's central staff has led to increased technical assistance to member TCUs and the major accomplishment of securing a White House executive order that mandates linkages between the TCUs and all agencies of the federal government.
4.   AIHEC, in cooperation with the AICF, is now able to collect data from the TCUs, which is valuable when dealing with federal agencies, the U.S. Congress, and private foundations.
5.   AIHEC has been successful in convincing the U.S. Congress and the president that funding provided by the Tribally Controlled College or University Assistance Act of 1978 and the 1994 Equity in Education Land Grant Status Act should be continually increased until TCUs gain funding parity, based on a per student basis, with mainstream institutions of higher education.

The American Indian College Fund

The AICF was established in 1986 by a formal charter of AIHEC, but it did not begin staffing and operations until late 1989. AICF was established as an organization separate from AIHEC to raise funds on behalf of the TCUs and their students by identifying and working with individuals, corporations, and private foundations interested in funding TCUs and TCU student scholarships. In the years between 1989 and 1996, AICF initiated a direct-mail campaign and allied itself with several major private foundations and corporate supporters, which resulted in raising approximately $30 million for the TCUs and their students. By 1996, the direct-mail campaign was producing about $3 million a year, and AICF was realizing an increase each year in corporate and private foundation support for TCUs (see Boyer, 1997).

The discussions that led to NAHEI's support of strengthening AIHEC were expanded to include AICF and its need for expansion as an organization that was crucial to the success of the TCUs and their students. The discussions led to a $1 million grant request to the W. K. Kellogg Foundation, through NAHEI, to develop a 3-year, $120 million capital campaign effort by AICF on behalf of the TCUs. After negotiations between the W. K. Kellogg Foundation and AICF staff members, a two-part grant was awarded to AICF in the amount of $1 million. Part one of the grant established the capital campaign effort with $500,000, which was called Campaign Si Ha Sin; part two established a $500,000 challenge grant for TCU student scholarships, which would have to be matched one for one.

AICF was given several years to meet the matching requirement in part two of the grant, but it secured the $500,000 match required for the scholarship program in fewer than 120 days. Thus, the first outcome of NAHEI was the doubling of scholarship funds available to TCU students in 1997 and growth to $5 million by the year 2000. A second positive outcome of AICF's matching the NAHEI scholarship grant funds in such a short time was national credibility with other potential contributors interested in providing scholarship funds for American Indian students in higher education. This includes the recent request by the Gates Millennium Scholarship Program that AICF administer the program's efforts to provide American Indian students with scholarships. This means that an additional $5 million in scholarship funds will be available to American Indian students in the future.

The capital campaign portion of the NAHEI grant allowed AICF to research, organize, and implement its $120 million capital campaign effort on behalf of the TCUs in 1998. Also in 1998, AICF raised an additional

$800,000 to support the planning and implementation of the capital campaign. In 1999, AICF launched its capital campaign effort, which led to a gift of $30 million from the Lilly Endowment. That gift was the largest single award ever given to an American Indian nonprofit organization and resulted in the Packard and Tierney Foundations committing an additional $3 million to the capital campaign. AICF staff have additional commitments suggesting that the capital campaign fund-raising effort would secure as much as $50 million more by early 2001.

Other positive results have occurred because of NAHEI support of AICF, such as a $17 million appropriation for TCU facility development by the federal government through such agencies as the Department of Education, the Department of Housing and Urban Development, and the Department of Agriculture. Another favorable outcome is the experience gained by AICF staff as they manage these two large programs (see AICF, 2000).

The American Indian Higher Education Consortium Student Congress

Tribal college students founded the AIHEC Student Congress in 1986 to address the academic and cultural needs of tribal college students and the economic, political, and social needs of tribal communities. The TCU student community comprises men and women whose natural abilities, personal qualities, and intellectual interests impel them to attempt to substantially improve the conditions of their communities. The W. K. Kellogg Foundation, recognizing the need for a TCU student organization that would effectively prepare American Indian students for national leadership in the 21st century, funded the AIHEC Student Congress through NAHEI in an effort to promote continued leadership and academic excellence.

The guiding principle of TCUs is to provide academic and vocational education while broadening students'knowledge and understanding of their physical, cultural, and spiritual existence. TCUs provide the means for students to apply concepts of meaning and purpose to their daily lives and also to their relationships with their communities. The TCU presidents encourage their students to participate in directing the tribal college movement. Inclusion of the Student Congress in the administrative infrastructure of AIHEC is an unprecedented administrative policy in American higher education. AIHEC recognizes the voice of its 25,000 students and values their opinions and judgments concerning issues that affect their education and communities. This inclusion develops and cultivates future leaders of Indian nations and ensures sustainability of American Indian culture and society.

The founders of AIHEC's Student Congress were concerned with the development of a national leadership organization that would work effectively and efficiently with the 33 tribal colleges in the United States. Their mission statement articulates goals, guiding principles, and values:

> We, the students, with the divine guidance of our Creator, The Great Spirit, as acknowledged by our North American and Alaska native people, do hereby establish a student organizational structure under the sanction of the American Indian Higher Education Consortium (AIHEC). Furthermore, it is our mission to provide leadership opportunities to our students; to create a sense of community between student leaders of all tribe sand nations; to promote a sense of understanding and acceptance between all people; to work for tolerance, peace, prosperity, and love across the globe; [and] to ensure longevity of native tradition, language, and culture while working together to build healthy communities. (www.AIHEC.org)

Tribal college leaders place a high value on traditional knowledge and culture in shaping the social, economic, and educational development of tribal communities. They believe that, for American Indian nations to be truly sovereign, they must be in control of their educational institutions. TCU leaders exercise self-regulation in their home higher education institutions, which is sovereignty in practice. As a result, TCUs are reviving hope and resurrecting opportunity in tribal communities by supporting traditional values of self-respect, dignity, honesty, pride, compassion, cooperation, and responsibility for the community, and by stressing that these values are equal in importance to academic excellence. It is in their students that TCU leaders see their future and the completion of the philosophical circle they started with the TCU movement. It is imperative that a responsible student congress be in place to carry on and implement the TCU leaders' philosophy of tribal sovereignty.

In an effort to continue the TCU leadership circle, the AIHEC Student Congress provides a NAHEI-sponsored program featuring valuable experience in the dynamics of leadership. The program, Leading All People (LAP), is a summer leadership institute that develops a deep understanding of the social, political, and cultural processes that exist in higher education. The Student Congress believes that leadership training, cultural awareness, and strong communication skills are essential in strengthening students' involvement and development as future tribal leaders. The LAP institute is a weeklong program in which students learn different leadership styles, examine a wide range of communication techniques, and debate the ethics of power. Delegates investigate key concepts such as self-governance and sovereignty and are exposed to different methods for bringing about social change, including tools for lobbying elected officials, navigating the legislative process, and understanding best practices in working with the media. Guiding all of these activities is an ongoing focus on self-esteem, wellness, and personal balance. A major cornerstone of the institute is the crafting of community action plans by all in attendance. Each delegate is asked to bring a specific community concern and pertinent documentation to the institute. With assistance from the group, participants develop community action plans that address their concerns. After the institute concludes, participants are charged with implementing the plans once they return home.

The AIHEC Student Congress further believes that support for tribal college students only begins with their enrollment at the TCU and must continue throughout their educational and personal careers. Funding from the W. K. Kellogg Foundation, through NAHEI, enabled one delegate from each tribal college to attend the 2000 LAP Summer Institute in Santa Fe, New Mexico. The AIHEC Student Congress has also launched its own endowment campaign to provide for its future development and continuity. Revenue from the student congress endowment will support a permanent office that develops initiatives in leadership, service, and action.

The National Institute for Native Leadership in Higher Education

NINLHE was founded by the directors of the American Indian program at Stanford University and the Native American program at Dartmouth College, based on an idea that came to fruition in 1992. Gathering a small cadre of fellow student-service professionals who also worked with American Indian students from across the United States, they put together the following working mission statement: "Members of the National Institute for Native Leadership in Higher Education are committed to sharing personal and professional experiences that cultivate Native communities through the promotion of viable and culturally appropriate support systems in higher education" (Larimore, 1992).

The founding professionals sought to improve support services for American Indian students attending colleges and universities across the country. In 1992, they submitted a proposal to Intel Corporation and received funding in 1993, that would promote the professional development of and encourage collaboration and networking between and among Native American program directors from a selected group of colleges and universities with a proven commitment to the well-being of Native American students. In spring 1993, the Intel Foundation (Corporation) funded the proposal from the group, which now called itself the National Institute for Native Leadership in Higher Education or NINLHE. The purpose of the group was to support a series of professional development institutes and create a national consortium of Native American program directors at 2- and 4-year institutions of higher education that have a demonstrated commitment to Indian education (see Larimore, 1994, Intel Corporation Grant).

NINLHE's first several years focused on the goals of developing an institute and a national consortium of major-market program directors. The institute, held during the summer months, based its programs on a theme chosen by consensus of the working governing group and featured selected participants chosen from the ranks of student-service professionals who worked closely with American Indian students. The goals of the institute were (a) to strengthen the professional personnel capabilities of institute participants; (b) to provide participants with strategic planning assistance for program development; (c) to strengthen institutional commitment to American Indian student-service programs; (d) to form regional networks of cooperation and support among American Indian student-service programs; and (e) to educate, inform, and enlist the aid of corporate, foundation, and higher education leaders in addressing American Indian educational issues and meeting the needs of American Indian students. The institute provided many of the participants with their first-ever opportunity for sustained interaction and dialogue with fellow American Indian colleagues from institutions other than their own. This interaction led to the establishment of a network of communications among the student-service professionals serving American Indian students on selected campuses across the United States (Shendo, NINLHE's 1994 Progress Report).

By 1997, NINLHE's goals of establishing a successful Institute of Professional Development and a network of professionals working for American Indian students in mainstream institutions of higher education had been met (Shendo, 1998). In meeting these goals, it became clear to the council managing the organization that, to accomplish the overall mission of better serving American Indian students in higher education, more had to be done. At that time, NINLHE turned to the W. K. Kellogg Foundation for financial support to enhance their efforts to better serve American Indian students and their student-service professionals.

NAHEI, although directed at the TCUs, also includes other major components, one of which is the strengthening of several national organizations, like NINLHE, dedicated to the improvement of American Indian participation and success in higher education. Hence, with the financial support of the W. K. Kellogg Foundation, NINLHE has identified and expanded its mission to build stronger American Indian communities through effecting lasting and meaningful change in higher education practice and policy at the individual, institutional, and national levels. To meet its objectives, NINLHE will enhance the individual capabilities of higher education professionals involved in American Indian student retention programs, strengthen the standing of American Indian student retention programs on each participating campus as a strong and lasting institutional priority, and position NINLHE as a peer with other national education organizations. NINLHE is emerging as a unique technical-support systems agent among higher education institutions.

NINHLE's membership now includes representatives from more than 50 public, private, and tribally controlled colleges and universities, as well as national native education organizations in the United States and Canada. Today, NINLHE's Institute of Professional Development provides its members an opportunity to learn about and to develop effective student retention strategies for use at their home institutions, and they also learn how to network more effectively with their peers at other colleges and universities. The institute is conducted in a collaborative manner and is a rigorous academic experience while still maintaining cultural integrity that reflects the many American Indian communities from which its participants come. Fellows selected to participate in the institute develop the conference materials from their pertinent areas of research. Topics have included principles and practices involved in helping effect healing change in those harmfully involved with alcohol; effective approaches to advising native students and families about financial aid eligibility and awards; effective methods of promoting personal, professional, and spiritual growth in leadership development; exploration of cultural and community asset-mapping and the balancing of leadership styles; and expansion of the tradition of participation. In addition, workshops in fund raising and grant writing have been conducted.

The 25 participants attending the 1999 institute stated that their expectations had been exceeded in many ways. They regarded the most valuable outcomes of the institute as the acquisition of new knowledge, the increase in their networking skills, attainment of a sense of personal renewal, the fact that a spiritual theme permeated the institute's program, and the opportunity to share perspectives with their colleagues. Participants further stated that the institute left them feeling renewed and energized to pursue the institutional changes needed at their individual campuses, in order to promote both the academic and personal success of their students. The challenge now for NINLHE is how to best support institute participants once they have returned to their individual campuses so that they can maintain their newly acquired skills and spiritual energy.

NINLHE originated as a loosely allied group of American Indian professionals in the area of student services at only mainstream institutions, but through its participation in NAHEI, the group has expanded to include TCU student service professionals. The expansion to include TCUs has elevated NINLHE's need for organizational development and strategic positioning. NAHEI financing was used, in part, to establish a series of workshops for the group's governing council, intended to strengthen organizational development. An outcome of these workshops was a 10-year strategic plan. The organization is now in the first of three stages of that plan, which is called Gathering Strengths That Sustain Organizational Life and Cultural Identity.

NINLHE has also applied for and received grants from other foundations, such as the Education Foundation of America. These grants are directed at supporting a professional fund raiser who is responsible for launching a capital campaign and an institutional membership drive for NINLHE. Other objectives of the strategic plan include (a) matching organizational functions to specific revenue sources; (b) designating other program staff and activities to be supported through grants and individual gifts; (c) establishing a professional-on-loan program, allowing the governing council to move away from direct involvement in and maintenance of programmatic initiatives; (d) diversifying funding sources to create a family of funders; and (e) developing higher education professional training modules suitable for marketing.

NINLHE is now entering its third phase of development as an organization. In phase one, founders of NINLHE worked closely with the Intel Corporation to clarify and refine its mission and purpose. In phase two of its growth, NINLHE, funded by the W. K. Kellogg Foundation, expanded its original goals to include TCUs as part of its overall mission. This required that the organization build a stronger internal infrastructure so that it could ensure its future service to scholars in both TCUs and mainstream institutions. Currently, in phase three of NINLHE's growth, funded in large part by the W. K. Kellogg Foundation, the organization is developing and instituting programs that support the scholarship of American Indian students (Larimore, 2000).

Alliance for Equity

At the American Council on Education's annual conference in Miami, Florida, the Alliance for Equity was born from a meeting sponsored by the

W. K. Kellogg Foundation and led by Dr. Hector Garza and Dr. Betty Overton-Atkins. The meeting brought together representatives from historical Black colleges and universities (HBCU), TCUs, and Hispanic-serving institutions (HSI) for initial discussions, which continued at several other educational meetings, with the continued sponsorship of the W. K. Kellogg Foundation. In June of 1999, the Alliance for Equity was officially formed and funded by NAHEI. That same month, the Alliance selected Jamie Merisotis, of the Institute for Higher Education Policy, as director of the Alliance for Equity. The three national organizations that founded the Alliance are AIHEC, the Hispanic Association of Colleges and Universities (HACU), and the National Association for Equal Opportunity in Higher Education (NAFEO). The institutions belonging to these three national organizations that make up the Alliance educate more than one third of all American Indian, Hispanic, and African-American students in the United States and also serve a high proportion of economically and educationally disadvantaged students in the United States (see Fig.4.2).

The Alliance for Equity promotes greater collaboration and cooperation among colleges and universities that serve large numbers of students of color, in order to enhance the nation's economic competitiveness, social

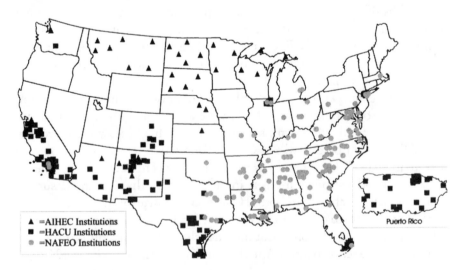

▲ =AIHEC Institutions
■ =HACU Institutions
● =NAFEO Institutions

Puerto Rico

FIG. 4.2.   Alliance for Equity in Higher Education; Minority-Serving Institutions. Note: AIHEC is the American Indian Higher Education Consortium, HACU is the Hispanic Association of Colleges and Universities, and NAFEO is the National Association for Equal Opportunity in Higher Education. Prepared by The Institute for Higher Education Policy, Washington, DC.

stability, and cultural richness. The shared values and experiences of these colleges and universities include commitment to community ideals and civic responsibility, dedication to student access and success, emphasis on teaching and scholarly excellence, belief in the power of colleges and universities to promote personal and spiritual fulfillment, devotion to the elimination of poverty and discrimination in American society, and encouragement of cultural diversity. These shared values and experiences necessitate that greater unity and coordination be established by and among these institutions. The Alliance for Equity will play a major role in convincing these college and university communities that increased collaboration is possible and will serve as a forum for shared experiences and building of agendas. The Alliance also conducts policy analysis in key areas of importance to the communities and engages in public policy advocacy on issues that are jointly supported. The Alliance's goals in pursuit of these activities include, but are not limited to, the following:

1.   Ensuring student access, success, and equal opportunity by (a) increasing student financial assistance, (b) promoting fair and inclusive college admission standards and requirements, (c) raising the number of students of color in science and technological fields, (d) expanding programs for counseling students of color, and (e) improving testing and diagnostic systems, all of which should increase enrollment and graduation rates for students of color.

2.   Enhancing teacher preparation, faculty development, and leadership by (a) strengthening teacher preparation and recruitment strategies, (b) increasing the numbers of advanced- degree recipients from underrepresented groups, (c) expanding professional development opportunities, (d) broadening K–12 linkages, (e) supporting institutional leaders, and (f) developing community leadership.

3.   Strengthening institutional development by (a) improving and expanding physical infrastructure, (b) increasing access to and use of technology, (c) raising endowment levels at participating institutions, and (d) enhancing capacity for curriculum development and innovation.

4.   Preserving and recognizing America's diversity by (a) supporting cultural values and traditions, (b) understanding the nation's richly diverse history, and (c) maximizing language abilities and skills.

5.   Exploring new opportunities for collaboration and cooperation with each other, and other groups with like interests. (Alliance for Equity, 1999)

In September 2000, the Alliance presented its first report, *Educating the Emergency Majority*, on the need for minority teachers in the United States. The report called for a minimum of $100 million to support teacher education programs at minority institutions in the United States. The report stated that the enrollment of minority students in elementary and secondary schools had increased by 73% over the last 25 years, compared to 19% for Euro-Americans students. However, minorities comprised only 16% of all students enrolled in teacher education programs, whereas 80% of students enrolled in such programs were Euro-American. This inequity is a result of substandard K–12 academic preparation of students of color, as well as social and economic factors.

The Alliance's report went on to state that the disparity between students and teachers of color adds to the overall crisis in quality and supply of elementary and secondary educators nationwide. The report then provided recommendations of ways the federal government, teacher preparation programs, governing boards of educational institutions, and researchers studying teacher education programs in the United States can strengthen teacher education programs for students of color and eliminate many of the persistent problems plaguing teacher education in the United States.

CASES OF CAPACITY BUILDING: FOCUS ON GOVERNANCE AND FINANCING

AIHEC's NAHEI Management Project

Many examples of successful, innovative NAHEI-funded projects are included in this book. Only three projects are highlighted here to illustrate how particular organizations strengthened their governing structures and fiscal capacities. The first example is AIHEC's NAHEI Management Project, a five-part project having the following basic components; (a) fiscal responsibility and management, (b) program management, (c) communications, (d) technical assistance, and (e) evaluation. In the area of fiscal management, AIHEC has further developed its own capacity to provide sound fiscal management by hiring a staff assistant, implementing strong internal controls in the central AIHEC office, closely monitoring each grantee's adherence to the project budget, and providing oversight and guidance on all budget modifications and related matters. AIHEC has also helped at least 12 of its member colleges that have requested technical assistance with fiscal management of their NAHEI projects.

In the area of program management, AIHEC has provided services to fellow NAHEI grantees by maintaining regular communications with each project director and the grantor, by providing site visits to at least six member colleges to deliver and monitor technical assistance in program management, and by assisting in the coordination of NAHEI networking conferences. In the area of communications, AIHEC was required to be a central clearinghouse for much of the communications for the overall NAHEI project. Although resources were limited, it was able to leverage other sources of funds to assist in accomplishing communications for the overall project. Its communications strategy involved making numerous telephone calls to all involved parties, making on-site visits to various NAHEI participants' home sites, holding meetings that include all stakeholders, discussing NAHEI with potential media partners, and using the *Tribal College Journal* to highlight individual member-college projects. AIHEC also made a substantial effort to reach out to the international education community by attending such events as the 1999 World Indigenous People's Education Conference in Hilo, Hawai'i.

In the area of technical assistance, which is a core mission of AIHEC, the consortium continues to provide the traditional kinds of technical assistance that it always has to its member colleges, while adding a number of new areas made possible through additional funds from NAHEI. Several of the new areas include research and data collection, fund raising, public relations, technology acquisition, and assessment. In the area of evaluation, AIHEC has developed an evaluation plan that serves as the foundation for a comprehensive assessment of the consortium's services. In the end, AIHEC has strengthened its capacity to serve a growing fleet of top-notch TCUs through programs that have required AIHEC to continually assess the programs' progress, to identify and address barriers to successful service to TCUs, and to both ascertain and achieve a clearer vision and action toward future enhancement and expansion (AIHEC, 1999).

Sitting Bull College

The NAHEI-funded project initiated by Sitting Bull College (SBC), located in Fort Yates, South Dakota, sought to achieve the following basic objectives; (a) expanding continuing education opportunities for the Standing Rock Sioux Nation; (b) developing a direct mail fund-raising campaign; and (c) developing a recruitment and retention promotional campaign and compiling, printing, and disseminating a booklet of its workshops each year that will reach the continuing education objective of SBC. In fall 1998, to meet SBC's challenge to build its programs, 420 continuing education units were provided, which in turn meant additional revenues for the college. SBC has also added economic and business workshops to its offerings and has held them in all eight districts on the Standing Rock Sioux reservation. To increase its funding stream, SBC instituted an annual direct mail campaign that has improved each year and increased its returns substantially. And, to encourage enrollment, SBC has disseminated its recruitment video to all of the area high schools and several job-training programs, such as Job Services of North Dakota and South Dakota. SBC is also presenting the video at area high schools' college night open houses and at its own annual Preview Day high school event (AIHEC, 1999).

The Southwest Indian Polytechnic Institute

The Southwest Indian Polytechnic Institute's (SIPI) project objectives were to develop its agriculture, science, extension, and technology programs. To fulfill this challenge, SIPI has undertaken a wide variety of initiatives. For example, in partnership with the U.S. Geological Survey, the U.S. Department of the Interior, and Lockheed-Martin, it has retrofitted its current greenhouse compound for joint use by its agriculture, natural resources, and environmental science degree programs. Further, SIPI has established distance-learning sites on four local Indian reservations and is also delivering Geographic Information Systems (GIS) broadcasts on topics of interest to regional Indian nations, such as the topic of implementation and protection of treaty rights.

CONCLUSION

In the end, TCUs and their partner organizations (AIHEC, AICF, AIHEC Student Congress, NINLHE, Alliance for Equity) have grown stronger through maturing and positive relationships among TCUs and between TCUs and their sister institutions (e.g., mainstream postsecondary institutions). However, there are still many challenges to be met and overcome as TCUs enter the 21st century. The funding of the many NAHEI projects must be viewed as only a beginning in the continual quest of American Indian educators to find the necessary resources to improve and increase educational opportunities for all their people seeking an education. AIHEC and the AICF have made the following recommendations to government policymakers, mainstream colleges and universities, and private-sector organizations in an effort to reinforce and solidify their help in strengthening the TCUs, the TCUs' national organizations, and the tribal communities.

1. The appropriations funding levels of the Tribally Controlled College or University Assistance Act, which funds the base operations of the TCUs, should be increased at reasonable rates.
2. The Equity in Education Land Grant Status Act should be fully funded at the authorized levels approved by Congress, which would allow the TCUs to further develop and build on their programs in agriculture, natural resources, and nutrition.
3. Faculty development for TCUs faculties must have increased financial and strategic support, as this is an area that requires continuous effort.
4. Teacher education programs housed within the TCUs must be strengthened and given additional resources to improve the participation and success of American Indians in these programs.
5. American Indians need the TCUs to increase their research efforts in the areas of health and nutrition; this can be done by continuous support of the new National Center for Research on Minority Health and Health Disparities.
6. Opportunities must provide for TCUs to have more interaction with early education intervention programs such as TRIO and Head Start, which will lead to greater success of American Indian youths as they pursue their educational futures.
7. More collaboration between TCUs and K–12 institutions should be promoted by providing innovative funding opportunities for collaborative programs; this will lead to a smoother transition from K–12 to higher education institutions, thus ensuring greater success of students.
8. Traditional values, histories, art, languages, and many other valued parts of American Indian life and culture should be preserved and expanded by supporting private-sector initiatives, such as tribal cultural and learning centers.
9. Federal funding of TCUs' technology grants should be increased so that the TCUs can leverage private-sector investments, which will expand and strengthen their information- technology infrastructure.
10. By increasing resources to a TCU, aimed at encouraging cooperative agreements, all funding agencies, public and private, will promote and support partnership development and collaboration with other TCUs and mainstream institutions.

The W. K. Kellogg Foundation has shown how a private philanthropic organization can make a substantial contribution. It is providing the leadership within its own circle that can be replicated by other philanthropic organizations, as well as public agencies, in the creative funding and support that

American Indians desire for tribally controlled educational institutions. It is the NAHEI project model, emphasizing cooperation and partnership among all stakeholders, that has made such a successful difference in AIHEC and the TCUs' efforts to build stronger and better-financed institutions.

REFERENCES

Alliance for Equity. (2000). *Educating the emerging majority.* Washington, DC: Author.
Alliance for Equity. (1999). *Grant to the W. K. Kellogg Foundation.* Washington, DC: Author.
American Indian College Fund. (2000). *Annual report.* Denver, CO: Author.
American Indian Higher Education Consortium. (1999). *Annual report.* Alexandria, VA: Author.
American Indian Higher Education Consortium. (1998). *Annual report.* Alexandria, VA: Author.
AIHEC. (2001). www.AIHEC.org
Boyer, P. (1997). *Native American colleges: Progress and prospects.* Princeton, NJ: The Carnegie Foundation for the Advancement of Teaching.
Ford Foundation. (1999). *Annual report.* New York: Author.
Fort Peck Community College. (1996, October). *Evaluation committee report: Fort Peck Community College.* Poplar, MT: Northwest Association of Schools and Colleges Commission on Colleges.
W. K. Kellogg Foundation. (1999). *Annual report.* Battle Creek, MI: Author.
Larimore, C. (2000). *At the crossroads: The path to sustainability. A proposal to the Kellogg Foundation.* Berkeley, CA: Author.
Larimore, J. (1992). *A collaborative proposal to the Intel Corporation.* Stanford, CA: National Institute for Native Leadership in Higher Education.
Larimore, J. (1994). *A report to the Intel Foundation.* Stanford, CA: American Indian Program, Stanford University, and Native American Program, Dartmouth College.
Shendo, B. (1994). *National Institute for Native Leadership in Higher Education progress report.* Albuquerque, NM: National Institute for Native Leadership in Higher Education.
Shendo, B. (1998). *Annual progress report to University of New Mexico.* Albuquerque, NM: National Institute for Native Leadership in Higher Education.
Stein, W. J. (1992). *Tribally controlled colleges: Making good medicine.* New York: Peter Lang Publishing.
U.S. Department of Education: White House Initiative on Tribal Colleges and Universities (Executive Order No. 13021, October 19, 1996).

5

Tribal Colleges and Universities Building Community: Education, Social, Cultural, and Economic Development

Jack Barden
(formerly) North Dakota Association of Tribal Colleges

INTRODUCTION: A COMMUNITY FOCUS

Perhaps more than any other educational institution, tribal colleges and universities (TCUs) are creatures of their communities. Hence, community building is a primary feature and goal of the current 33 TCUs in the United States and is the focus of this chapter. The mission statements that guide TCUs stem from their unique native/indigenous communities' history and cultural traditions; consequently, the activities supported by TCUs are aimed at meeting their communities' varied needs. A brief look at tribal colleges' mission statements confirms this and reveals that not only are the TCUs designed to serve their communities, but they also define their communities and propose to serve them in different ways.

After nearly 30 years, TCUs have expanded the communities that they serve. The multilayered communities that today's TCUs are challenged to serve are shown in Fig.5.1. Their first responsibility is to their local, native community. Over time, individual TCUs have learned that certain things (e.g., language immersion programs, economic development initiatives, access to funding sources) can be achieved more effectively and at less cost if TCUs combine their efforts to achieve common needs and goals. In so doing, they have created the next level of community, serving a broader population of Native American Indian tribes. These coalitions have taken different forms, ranging from formally incorporated associations to ad hoc collections of colleges. In addition, their focuses have varied from a single purpose to longer lasting, long-term associations centered on a number of common issues. They are usually geographically grouped, serving tribes that have similar cultures and often share kindred interests. More recently, the TCU community catchments has expanded, at least in some measure through the use of technology, to national and international educational communities.

Their mission statements attest to the fact that community, in some form, is important to TCUs.[1] Many indicate that it is central to their purpose to provide educational experiences to their local community. Chief Dull Knife College in Montana, for instance, expresses in its mission statement that it is "an open-admission, community based, comprehensive, tribally controlled community college and land grant institution designed to provide affordable, quality educational opportunities to residents of the Northern Cheyenne reservation and surrounding communities." Fort Berthold Community College in North Dakota states that it "strives for pragmatic and holistic approaches to higher education and focuses on providing and improving individual competences relevant to the individual and to the community."

Other TCUs maintain that they have a responsibility not only to provide educational services to local communities, but also to serve them in a number of economic, social, and cultural ways. For example, Oglala Lakota Col-

FIG. 5.1.   Communities served by TCUs.

---

[1]The mission statements that are included in this discussion can all be found through links to the colleges on the AIHEC web site—www.AIHEC.org/

lege in South Dakota states that part of its mission is to "assist with the determination of development needs of the reservation districts and communities and to assist the reservation districts and communities in achieving their goal." Turtle Mountain Community College in North Dakota includes as part of its mission, "to establish an administration, faculty, and student body involved in exerting leadership within the community and providing service to it." More specifically, Turtle Mountain has a goal of "cooperating with local Indian-owned businesses and stimulation of economic development for the service area."

There are also a number of colleges not located on reservations whose missions include service to a broader community. For example, five tribes whose jurisdiction is wholly or partially in North Dakota operate United Tribes Technical College in that state. A central component of its mission is "to provide an intertribal forum and special projects aimed at the perpetuation of tribal rights and the economic progress of American Indians." Additionally, the mission of the Southwestern Indian Polytechnic Institute, located in Albuquerque, New Mexico, is to serve a broad population of native students "throughout the national Indian community."

To better understand how TCUs have met the challenges of serving a number of communities, as well as the challenges they have met and those that have perplexed them, this chapter is focused on the nature of their commitments at each of four identified levels; (a) the local tribal community, (b) regional partnerships that serve broader communities, (c) national consortiums, and (d) international partnerships that serve a more global movement. In addition, examples are provided of initiatives that have supported community building.

LOCAL COMMUNITIES

At the local level, a community usually means a geographically identifiable place that is occupied by a number of people and that has social, kinship, and governmental ties that hold it together. These local places are usually within or near the boundaries of reservations. In at least some cases, these communities are the continuation of "camps" or villages that were traditional places where certain families or clans lived. With the coming of the reservation system, and, in particular, the coming of the Indian Reorganization Act in 1934, which established governments similar to those found in the rest of the country, these communities were made permanent. The governing structure defined by this Act often is not how native communities would govern themselves.

These local communities are different from mainstream communities in that they are founded on traditional native values that are often contrary to those of their neighboring communities. The local communities often suffer the consequences of oppression, such as chemical abuse, health-related illnesses, teen pregnancy, gang violence, and high unemployment. On reservations where TCUs are located, for instance, the percentage of the labor force that was not working in 1995, was 42%. This compares with 6% unemployment across the U.S. population at the same time [American Indian Higher Education Consortium (AIHEC) & Institute for Higher Education Policy (IHEP), 2000].

Economic Development Initiatives

To address both social and economic issues that native communities face, TCU leaders have long considered education as a major priority in empowering their communities. However, many educational leaders also realize that educating citizens for jobs that do not exist requires that they work with their local community governments to support economic development projects. To support economic development planning, however, has long been thwarted by the community's geographical remoteness (e.g., long distances require expensive transport of manufactured goods to market). Therefore, a current focus on e-commerce has emerged, and much attention has been given to building technological infrastructure (e.g., cable and satellite).

Tribal economic development is a complex topic and is beyond the scope of this chapter. Suffice it to say, that even though a great deal of effort and money has been expended on trying to improve the economic condition of reservation residents, the need to do more continues. In some measure, the reason that there is still a need to put more effort into tribal economic development is that past efforts have focused on getting industries to move onto the reservation. In some cases, this strategy has been successful. For example, the Spirit Lake Reservation in North Dakota established a manufacturing enterprise called Dakota Sioux Enterprises in the 1980s. With defense contracts, the plant has employed substantial numbers of people over the years and has manufactured several products, ranging from camouflage netting to helmets. Similarly, the Turtle Mountain Band of Chippewa, also in North Dakota, established Turtle Mountain Manufacturing. Also contracting with the U.S. Department of Defense, the plant at Belcourt produced the water tanks that were used in the Gulf War. These are examples of instances in which tribes and their colleges have worked together to develop industries and to train people to work in them. However, given the remoteness of many reservations and their distance from markets, this strategy will not work everywhere.

On the whole, many of the economic development strategies that were employed in the past were the creations of external entities and did not result in real, lasting change (see AIHEC & IHEP, 2000). As a result, TCUs are working with their local tribal communities to create economic development programs that are designed in-house (by community members) to meet cultural principles and local needs, and to ensure long-lasting sustainability. For example, some years ago, business and tribal leaders on the Turtle Mountain Reservation in North Dakota incorporated Uniband, a data-entry firm. Currently, the company has contracts with major federal agencies, including the Immigration and Naturalization Service, to enter data and then transmit those data electronically to national databases. The college is providing the necessary training for company employees. Although data entry is low-end information technology work and has the disadvantage of being relatively low paid, it has the advantage of employing large numbers of people and, although turnover is high, of having a steady supply of labor. The following vignette further describes TMCC's effort to support economic development activities in their community.

Vignette One: Center for New Growth and Economic Development at Turtle Mountain Community College

NAHEI funding has allowed Turtle Mountain Community College in Northern North Dakota to participate in a meaningful way in Tribal Economic Development. The Center for New Growth and Economic Development is the realization of a dream—the founding of a sustained effort, which includes both service and education to improve economic conditions on its reservation. The Center has produced a list of accomplishments among which are:

1. Participating in the development of an application for Empowerment Zone status, which resulted in the reservation being designated a Champion Community, a designation that provides preferential treatment in certain federal applications. There are only three such designations in North Dakota.

2. Cooperating with North Dakota's Small Business Administration in funding a Small Business Development Center for people wishing to start, expand, or maintain a business.

3. Working with a Vocational Rehabilitation (VR) Program to develop a Center at which VR clients are prepared to enter into small business ventures.

Among its other accomplishments, the Center is developing processes for the collection, storage, and analysis of data related to the communities and economic conditions on the reservation and making these data available to community entities that are moving toward developing businesses.

A significant feature in all this activity is the ongoing stress on sustainability. The College and its Center have concrete plans to be able to continue their services into the future.

Another economic development strategy that has the potential to strengthen the community is telecommuting. In particular, TCUs that have information technology programs have the potential for serving their local communities in this way. Many large companies hire well-qualified people for a variety of positions and allow them to work at a distance from their home offices. Still other companies are seeking locations in which there are numbers of workers who are skilled in the high end of information technology, for example, programmers and systems analysts, who can perform highly skilled tasks. IBM Corporation, for instance, has been involved in discussions with a number of TCUs at the national level. A programming operation is planned, and IBM management wishes to try such a venture on a reservation. TCUs that are positioned to provide the kinds of personnel who are needed for this type of operation will have an opportunity to provide high-level assistance to their local communities. Further, if it is successful, this model of providing both education and employment opportunities for national corporations may prove workable for other companies.

There are instances in which TCUs actually "do" economic development. For example, Salish-Kootenai College has founded and is operating an environmental testing project. Sitting Bull College owns and operates a construction company. Both of these business ventures are operated by the colleges and are connected to a degree-bearing academic program. In addition, the intention of the colleges is to eventually sell the businesses to private individuals. Both of these business ventures are successful and may be a model of a kind of "incubator" that allows businesses to have start-up time and an opportunity to mature before being completely taken over by private individuals. These ventures have potential, with the emerging interest in electronic commerce. Particularly given the climate in which many web-based businesses are losing money and even having to close, it will be important for colleges to either start e-businesses themselves or to provide incubation time and facilities as the businesses mature.

The Ford Foundation, in partnership with the American Association of Community Colleges and the American Council on Education, has also entered the economic development arena. The Rural Community College Initiative includes six TCUs—Blackfeet Community College, Ft. Belknap College, Ft. Peck Community College, Salish-Kootenai College, Sinte Gleska University, and Sitting Bull College. This initiative concentrates on reservationwide planning, involvement of communities in economic development, and development of infrastructure. Project evaluations have tended to indicate that some "culturally conscious" small business development is occurring on reservations (Eller, et al., 1998).

No discussion of economic development in Indian country would be complete without mention of tribal gaming. Casinos have been established on at least eight of the reservations where Tribal Colleges are located. These casinos have experienced varying degrees of success in making a profit for their tribes. In almost every case, colleges have been involved in the success of these enterprises in at least two ways; (a) most gaming tribes rely on their colleges for training new employees and for preparing a skilled management workforce, and (b) at least some of the colleges receive distributions of varying sizes from the casino profits.

Initiatives That Build Social and Cultural Capacity

Along with the effort that is being expended on economic development to strengthen communities, concomitant social and educational development is needed. There is often a vicious circle operating in communities. Economic development can help break the cycle of poverty and, with education at its core, bring prosperity to local communities and eliminate some of the dysfunctional elements that currently exist. But, things like poverty, chemical abuse, and resultant poor work habits prevent much of the development from taking place. The social conditions that economic development is designed to improve can also inhibit economic prosperity.

Projects that seek to change dysfunctional social conditions tend to take both a cultural and a social direction. At Fort Peck Community College in Montana, a project called the Family Education Model is being put to work in improving communities (see Ortiz and Heavy Runner, chap. 11). The model is based on the premise that the social conditions that inhibit economic development are the same ones that make things difficult for at least some students as they pursue degrees at the college. The project focuses on four areas; family life skills, family cultural activities, family-based mentoring, and student/family counseling. Although this model was begun at Fort Peck, it is now being used by a number of regional, national, and international (Canadian) tribal and indigenous institutions of higher learning.

In Indian country, it is axiomatic that, in order to heal communities, culture must be involved. What is not as explicit is what culture means. Basically, the divisions are between the "old culture"—that which existed in the beginning—and the "modern culture"—that which exists now. The everyday reservation culture differs somewhat from traditional culture. It now includes elements that were once useful to communities but that have become, in some measure and under some circumstances, dysfunctional, for example, gossip and reliance on employed family members to share income with unemployed members. At one time, gossip served as a means of social control; now it simply creates difficulties. At one time, sharing goods allowed the entire community to survive; now it can be a disincentive to "getting ahead."

The point is that if social change is to be effected, both of these aspects of culture need to be taken into account. The Learning Lodge Institute at Little Big Horn College in Montana is an example of community development with culture in mind. The institute serves both the local community and other communities in Montana. The project includes all seven TCUs located in Montana and concentrates on integrating native languages into the college curriculum. Implicit in this activity is that the healing process must begin through the strengthening of cultural and language bonds. Reports on the project indicate that, at one site, 3- and 4-year-olds are being taught the native language using Montessori methods, whereas their parents are studying the language at the college level. At another site, staff members are preparing information on traditional plants and their medicinal and ceremonial uses. Although this kind of activity may not, at first glance, appear to be related to social aspects of community building, the connection with the traditional cultures of the communities is important in improving the quality of life in these communities (see also Benham and Mann chapter). Vignette two captures a program that focuses on language and culture.

Vignette Two: Learning Lodge Institute at Little Big Horn College

All seven of the tribal colleges in Montana are involved in the NAHEI funded Learning Lodge Institute. The stated purpose of the Institute is to revitalize tribal languages on reservations and to embed these languages in the curricula of the colleges.

Since by its very nature the project focuses on the uniqueness of tribal communities, the project fosters collaboration by requiring that each site, although focusing on its own language, work in partnership with at least one of the other sites. And in order to ensure that language-related material is embedded in the everyday curriculum of its college, language activities must be tied to the content of at least three commonly offered courses.

A wide variety of approaches to language revitalization have been tried with varying degrees of success. Two of the colleges have chosen "immersion camps" in which only the language is spoken; another has tried one-on-one language mentoring, with a native speaker being paired with a non-speaker. On one campus, the language is being offered to 3- and 4-year-olds using Montessori methods while their parents also study the language in college classes. Two of the sites are doing projects that relate to the native names of places on their reservations and on local plants that are used medicinally and ceremonially and merging this information into college classes.

Although traditional culture, such as that expressed in the Learning Lodge Institute (Vignette Two), is an important aspect of community development, there is another culture that is alive and flourishing in 2001. And for reservations to develop, knowledge of this culture is also highly important. At Sinte Gleska University, the Sicangu Policy Institute applies this kind of knowledge for social and economic development on the Rosebud Reservation in South Dakota.

Vignette Three: Sicangu Policy Institute at Sinte Gleska University

At Sinte Gleska University in South Dakota, the need for a policy and planning center was the cornerstone of its NAHEI project. Designed to develop grass roots, reservation-based initiatives, which are appropriate for change in tribal government, programs, and tribal communities and in the university itself, the project is involved in a wide range of policy and planning efforts:

1. Established a non-political arm of the tribe—the Rosebud Economic Development Corporation
2. Conducted an inventory of land on the reservation and worked on the development of a land-use planning process
3. Studied existing policy related to social issues, e.g., teen pregnancies, substance abuse, and youth health issues, and are involved with improvements in those and other areas
4. Moved beyond reservation boundaries to host meetings on enrollment policies and water rights

In addition, the Institute has sponsored and participated in community forums on subjects including a controversial hog farm proposal, management of the tribe's casino, teen pregnancy, and marketing of local contractors' services.

The project has also sponsored an internship program in which a number of interns have had the opportunity to study such things as the effects of welfare reform on the SGU community, working with Habitat for Humanity, and taking various roles in the water resources area.

Less remote communities have many of the same conditions that exist in the more remote communities. In addition, there is the issue of relations with a non-Indian community that is the dominant community. At Fond du Lac Tribal and Community College in Northeast Minnesota, the Institute for Objective Human Understanding focuses on improving the relations of the tribal community with its non-Indian neighbors.

Vignette Four: Institute for Objective Human Understanding at Fond du Lac Tribal and Community College

With funding from NAHEI, Fond du Lac Tribal and Community College has been able to work directly with its non-Indian neighbors by providing diversity education to promote cultural understanding in surrounding communities. The accomplishments of the project, which have a direct effect on the surrounding communities, include:

1. Sponsorship of community events such as the Giving Thanks Feast, which drew 325 people last year, approximately one-half Native American and one-half non-Indian.

2. Collaboration with both the Racial Bias Task Force of the Sixth Judicial District and the Fond du Lac tribal government in sponsoring a conference to combat racism and discrimination. Approximately 300 people attended this conference.

At a more general level, the college, which has 150 students enrolled in its law enforcement program, has used NAHEI funding to bring on a part-time coordinator specifically dedicated to graduating culturally educated police officers for a diverse community. The college currently is not able to offer all that is needed for certification of these culturally aware police officers and under the auspices of the NAHEI grant is working toward developing the course work that will allow full certification. Further, the project seeks to promote cultural inclusion in all its workshops and in all curriculum development projects.

Improved Access to Higher Education

It is difficult for those with urban backgrounds to understand the remoteness of reservations and to comprehend the way people think about the sizes of communities. On the Standing Rock Reservation in North and South Dakota, for instance, there are eight communities. One of these, Fort Yates, is considered the major community because the Standing Rock Sioux tribal headquarters is there, as is the Standing Rock Agency of the Bureau of Indian Affairs. Fort Yates, with a population of 1,500, is 75 miles from Bismarck, North Dakota, and 50 miles from Mobridge, South Dakota. These are the two nearest city centers for groceries, entertainment, and other business. People go to Fort Yates to conduct their business as they would any national capital. The seven outlying communities range in population from fewer than 100 people to 500 people. The outlying communities are some 50 to 100 miles from Fort Yates. Distance, coupled with harsh climate and inadequate roads, makes coming to Fort Yates, where Sitting Bull College is located, a challenge, especially when poverty forces most people to drive "res cars," which may or may not withstand the trip.

Although this information can be viewed as an isolated "reservation horror story," it is not unusual. Each TCU has a similar story. Distances and climate may vary, but the basic issues of poverty, remoteness, and lack of access to higher education present important challenges to each of the TCUs. It is to be expected, then, that delivering classes and programs to remote communities would be a priority of the TCUs. In many cases, the colleges have established "centers" in their distant communities, but this solution is costly. Because class sizes in these off-campus sites are also small, it is difficult to pay a teacher for travel there. Yet, the community mission is so strong that most TCUs continue to provide some form of this service to their communities.

There are a number of variations on this theme. Sitting Bull College, for example, using the philosophical tenets of the personalized system of instruction (PSI), developed courses that are similar to correspondence courses. However, these courses are designed so that students can do most of the course work on their own, with the assistance of a mentor who regularly visits the remote communities to assist students with their work, give tests, and conduct other assessment activities. That the concept was successful in the beginning is attested to by the fact that college enrollment rose by nearly 100 students when the PSIs were first introduced. This was one way to try to avoid the high cost of delivering of a broad array of courses to small numbers of people. A disadvantage of the PSIs is that they require continuous revision and monitoring. Although Sitting Bull College still delivers PSIs, fewer are offered now than in the beginning. Sitting Bull College has begun to convert the PSIs to courses that are delivered via the Internet. However, taking the next step to provide online instruction has been slow going as the college awaits improved electronic access.

Although many TCUs have limited access to the Internet, they continue to develop their expertise and capability to deliver course work to their communities using electronic means. Efforts to increase access to higher education also affect other, more specific programs. Welfare to Work programs, for instance, often require that welfare recipients take training. TCUs are working hard to provide the needed instruction via the Internet in light of poor transportation and child care, as well as the lack of telephone lines and computers to deliver distance education. As part of this effort, TCUs are trying to locate funding to improve their electronic infrastructure and are pursuing solutions with their local telephone companies in an effort to increase penetration. Others are pursuing wireless solutions for delivering video, data, and telephony.

Even if connectivity improves, there remains the issue of access to computers in remote communities. K–12 schools in these communities often are minimally networked and rarely are available during hours beyond the normal school day. TCUs are approaching this issue in a variety of ways, most notably by establishing community technology centers located in convenient places and open for a substantial part of the day. Fort Berthold Community College, which in the past has made efforts to deliver courses to remote communities, has established learning centers in each of its outlying communities. Each of the centers is equipped with computers that have access to the Internet through a telephone modem. The resultant low-speed access is often frustrating to students. Hence, the college, in concert with its tribal government, is exploring wireless access so that band-width issues will not present barriers in the future. Another problem that they are currently working to resolve is managing and funding staff members to keep the centers open throughout the day.

Ensuring that Indian students in remote areas have access to higher education is a top priority of TCUs (for more information on technology programs see O'Donnell, Mitchell, Anderson, Lambert, Burland, and Barber, chap. 13, this volume). In addition, they are acutely aware that, to make the extension of access to higher education useful, they must pay particular attention to providing support services to their students in remote locations (see Ortiz and HeavyRunner, chap. 11, this volume). Given the challenges of reservation life, many TCUs are still struggling to locate effective and efficient methods of reaching out across the broad geographic expanse of their communities.

REGIONAL COMMUNITIES

In recent times, TCUs have extended their definition of community service to include aggregations of communities that are not geographically proximate. In essence, these regional communities began as loose alliances of tribal colleges that initially were formed to facilitate funding and to educate state legislatures. One early example of tribal colleges banding together for funding was Project DISCOVER, a project comprising five TCUs in North Dakota that was established to fund vocational education. The project was coordinated by the United Tribes Technical College and existed for some 5 years. As another example, several tribal colleges met periodically to develop tools and strategies to inform their respective state legislatures about the work of TCUs and the need of significant numbers of Indian students who receive virtually no financial support. These limited-purpose coalitions achieved varying degrees of success. TCUs also have worked with nontribal colleges in their states or regions to achieve specific purposes. In Montana and North Dakota, for instance, projects designed to prepare teachers for Indian reservations were undertaken in the late 1970s and continue today.

These networks of colleges came and went as their purposes were achieved or as it became clear that those aims would not be realized. However, in many cases, significant outcomes were achieved. Vocational education is now a staple in North Dakota's colleges, and there are now many Native American teachers on reservations. (More information on the connections that TCUs have formed with mainstream institutions can be found in the Nichols and Monette chapter and more on TCU teacher preparation programs is contained in the Pavel, Larimore, and VanAlstine, chap. 10, this volume.) Perhaps the most significant outcome of these early alliances to achieve special purposes was the realization that there were numerous issues that could best be approached by a group. In many cases, these early partnerships formed the basis for the more permanent collaborations that were to come.

During the 1990s, these associations of tribal colleges have grown to include such things as shared course work and degree programs, continued collaboration for funding, and development of community-based social and community programs.

Vignette Five: Intertribal College Partnership, The North Dakota Association of Tribal Colleges

The six TCUs that are wholly or partially in North Dakota are all part of a formally incorporated association—The North Dakota Association of Tribal Colleges. Beginning with NAHEI funding, the Association began work on the Intertribal College Partnership, a project of the Association that is designed to (a) facilitate course sharing and (b) develop a means of delivering third- and fourth- year course work so that North Dakota's TCU students and graduates will be able to pursue work at the baccalaureate level without having to leave their homes and families.

Because of the work that the NAHEI funding allowed it to do, the Association was able to leverage this grant into a much larger grant from the Learning Anytime Anywhere Partnerships, a grant program of the U.S. Department of Education, which is dedicated to asynchronous learning on the World Wide Web.

The project currently has some 30 courses online and is beginning to develop course work at the bachelor's degree level. In large measure, faculty members at North Dakota's TCUs are developing these upper division courses. This approach makes use of the existing talent found in the colleges. It is based on a model that has a strong cultural component focused on the areas of specialization that students choose, e.g., students who concentrate in business will master a substantial amount of material related to traditional economies and the way that those economies are currently expressed. An important aspect of this culturally based curriculum is that, although all tribes had some means of producing and distributing goods and services, they were expressed in a variety of ways. Therefore, these important elements of the curriculum are being locally developed.

The TCUs that became involved in the earliest regional community projects entered into those arrangements to provide greater and more focused service to their local communities, consistent with their missions. Now, they also deal with some of the community dysfunction noted earlier, as well as economic development that can be facilitated by partnership across tribal colleges.

Regional collaborations have resulted in long-term TCU partnerships based on geography and have focused on the cultures of the partnering tribes. For example, the Great Lakes and Woodlands partnerships are composed of colleges in Minnesota, Wisconsin, and Michigan, which are largely Ojibwa institutions. Similar groupings have developed in Montana and North Dakota. Another variation on the regional theme is that some

TCUs now serve other tribes in their regions that do not have a tribal college. Bay Mills Community College in Brimley, Michigan, for instance, serves all of the bands in the State of Michigan, using interactive video and the Internet. Northwest Indian College in Bellingham, Washington, serves more than 20 smaller tribes in the state of Washington, using the satellite-based AIHEC Network. And Fond du Lac Tribal and Community College in Cloquet, Minnesota, serves two remote reservations in the very northernmost part of that state, using both the Internet and interactive video.

Colleges that are not located on reservations can and do serve local as well as regional and national communities. Most commonly, this service is provided by regional coalitions built around particular topics; these coalitions are made up of area tribal colleges. One such coalition combining an emphasis on economic development with deeply held tribal traditions is the Northern Plains Bison Education Network.

Vignette Six: United Tribes Technical College, Northern Plains Bison Education Network

The purpose of this network is to help TCUs in the Northern Plains to develop curriculum on raising bison in a culturally relevant way, to develop short courses on bison management, and to develop herds for research and for training on range improvement. This NAHEI-funded project has nine tribal college partners in North and South Dakota and Nebraska.

Since its inception as a "bison as livestock" project, the network has changed its emphasis so that now the mission reflects the sacred connection among bison, land, and people.

The project has completed a classroom guide and is working to expand this document into a text for use in classes. It is hoped that it will evolve into a model for culturally sensitive curriculum development related to bison husbandry and that it will be used in all TCUs whose tribes have a cultural connection to bison.

The change in focus from bison as a purely economic commodity to the spiritual connection among bison, land, and people is an important shift that recognizes the uniqueness of individual tribal communities in that each tribe or band had a unique relationship with the bison. That is being continued.

For the most part, the project has been a focal point for the activities of the nine communities involved. The use of the term "network" is appropriate in that the people at the sites make the decisions about their own connections to bison.

NATIONAL COMMUNITIES

The most obvious example of a national community that has emerged from the tribal college movement is AIHEC. This organization was formed in 1973 when there were only six tribally controlled institutions in existence (see Stein, Shanley, and Sanchez, chap. 4, this volume). That number has grown to 33 in 2001 and most likely will continue to grow as more tribes develop their own colleges. AIHEC has been instrumental in building a professional community among the TCUs. It provides annual forums for national discussion of issues and provides a focal point around which the colleges can rally.

In more recent times, a major part of the consortium's work, on the national level, has been to manage a national technology initiative designed to improve connectivity and provide content for use on the Internet. Other major initiatives that focus on the national American Indian community include working with the Strengthening Developing Institutions Program of the U.S. Department of Education, which funds institutional development projects; developing programs with the National Science Foundation (NSF) to initiate opportunities for instructional improvement in the critical areas of science, mathematics, engineering, and technology; and working with the White House Initiative on Tribal Colleges and Universities to influence policy decisions in a number of federal agencies.

An example of AIHEC's national efforts is their work to establish a technology initiative in 1997. As part of its work, the Technology Initiative has sponsored a Prosperity Game™, which will result in a national framework for technology development in TCUs. One component of the national framework that has the potential to influence the community-serving aspects of TCUs is a web-based collaboration system called a collaboratory. Such an entity is being developed on a national scale to allow all of the colleges to collaborate with each other on various projects. When the national collaboratory is developed, it will be possible and feasible to spin off many regional or local, smaller, collaboratories. In fact, even without the collaboratory, a good deal of free software (webex, egroups, groove) is available to allow all or some colleges and communities to work on projects together and generally to "stay in touch."

Vignette Seven: AIHEC, Technology Initiative

AIHEC is a participant in a number of technology-related efforts. One is a grant funded by NSF. EDUCAUSE, a major national organization that works to improve education through technology, holds the grant named the Advanced Networking with Minority-Serving Institutions Project, for three minority communities; Historically Black Colleges and Universities, Hispanic Association of Colleges and Universities, and Tribal Colleges and Universities.

The project is involved in a number of areas including networking technology, executive awareness, remote technical support, and wireless solutions. The project focuses solely on infrastructure development and involves the leadership of all three of the minority communities served. This stance is in keeping with the conviction that outside agencies and large aggregations can provide certain services but that the direction of these services is best determined by local communities or collections of these communities.

The W. K. Kellogg Foundation through the Alliance funded a second project for community technology at the University of Michigan. This project is placing Virtual Library web pages at TCUs that wish to participate. A database devoted to Native American information available in full-text format is being developed to facilitate searching and keeping the network updated. Eighteen TCUs currently have the library page running, and another 10 colleges have indicated that they wish to make use of the service. Training on the database was conducted in the spring of 2001 so that TCUs would have control of the database and would be able to add, change, or remove links as they desire.

Whereas AIHEC has done a prodigious job of bringing together TCUs to participate in nationally important initiatives, there are many other examples of collaborative work among TCUs that have a national reach. For example, a small number of TCUs are not located on reservations. Haskell Indian Nations University, the Institute of American Indian Arts, and the Southwest Indian Polytechnic Institute all grew out of needs in the Indian community nationally and were founded by federal entities. United Tribes Technical College is also national in scope; it was founded by North Dakota's tribes in response to a need for vocational training and has grown to the national entity it is today. Each of these institutions is mandated by its charter to serve Native Americans throughout the United States. These are some of the oldest institutions of higher education in Indian country, predating the more general formation of TCUs. United Tribes is the newest institution with a national mandate. It was founded in 1968.

A large number of tribal colleges are extending their service to both their local (on or close to the reservation) and other K–12 schools in the region. The Tribal College Rural Systemic Initiative (TCRSI) is a national effort to improve science and mathematics education on 20 reservations in six states. It works directly with K–12 schools to bring about systemic change in education.

Vignette Eight: Tribal College Rural Systemic Initiative

TCRSI is an NSF-funded program whose purpose is to improve science, mathematics, and technology teaching and learning. It is part of a larger effort by the NSF to encourage systemic reform. The grantee for the project is Turtle Mountain Community College, which is operated primarily through subcontracts to participating schools. The subawards were made primarily to some 20 tribal colleges in Montana, North Dakota, South Dakota, Nebraska, Minnesota, and Wyoming. Each site is operated on its own within certain basic guidelines.

All of the projects began with efforts to gain the support of their own communities for systemic reform. At the same time, the project offered professional development opportunities for teachers identified by their own communities and worked toward placing standards-based curricula in the schools.

In order for the results to stay in place after the 5-year term of the project, a good deal of effort was put into changing policies so that the changes would be permanent. The project officially ended in October 2000; however, an extension was granted to allow the projects to continue until May 2001.

A second phase has now begun, with some significant differences. The operation of the project is no longer vested in one college; rather, the colleges that were sites under the TCRSI were made eligible to become grantees on their own in the second phase. Ten colleges were successful in the competition for funding, and another four colleges received "development" funding that would allow them to participate in implementation grants beginning in October 2001.

One of the key elements in the betterment of education is the improvement of teaching. In keeping with the basic philosophy of tribal colleges that the direction that changes take is best determined by people who know the local situations, a number of efforts have been undertaken to improve the training of teachers (see Pavel, Larimore, and VanAlstine, chap. 10, this volume).

THE INTERNATIONAL COMMUNITY

Currently, TCUs have made only tentative forays into the international arena. Contact has been made at a number of levels with Maori people from New Zealand to open discussions about what they might do together as indigenous people. That this is a serious effort is attested to by the fact that the

AIHEC board of directors, made up of presidents and board members from all member colleges, directed at both its October 2000, and July 2001 meetings, that contact with the Maori be continued. As a result, several presidents and AIHEC staff members visited with a number of Maori educational leaders during summer and fall 1999 and spring 2001, and visited New Zealand in summer 2001. Each meeting focused on the development of an educational community. As an outgrowth of this effort, relations have been initiated with other indigenous groups in Canada, Central and South America, Norway, and Finland.

NEXT STEPS FOR RESEARCH

Although the missions of TCUs, like those of most community colleges, generally do not include a research function, there is a great need for studies conducted by local people to provide more specific knowledge about their communities. These research efforts can focus on a single, short-term activity, but in order to be valuable, they need to be ongoing efforts to building communities' capacities to serve multiple groups. Several kinds of studies are needed that relate specifically:

1. Studies that define more carefully the exact populations of the communities including disaggregating by age, gender, and the ethnic makeup of these communities.
2. Studies that attempt to determine the degree to which the traditional cultural values of communities remain a major force and the extent to which contemporary values are embraced.
3. Studies that assess the potential for various kinds of economic development activities in native communities.
4. Studies that investigate the relationship between higher education and success in economic development.
5. Studies that test the relationship between colleges' intervention in community social development and improvements in social conditions.

Data on many of these issues already exist, so some of the work that needs to be done will involve collating the results of existing studies. A significant change from past practices is that the TCUs and AIHEC should conduct the research and interpret their findings. This is not to say that other colleges and universities cannot play a role in this research process, but rather that the management, control, and interpretation of data be primarily the responsibility of native tribal communities.

Most of the activities described are geared toward bringing about real changes in the way both TCUs and tribes operate. Thus, it is imperative that ongoing research be done on the effects of these changes on economic and social development efforts and the cultures of college communities. By engaging in research, TCUs will be able to determine and explain the influence that their work has had in bringing about specific improvements and, at the same time, contribute to the knowledge base about change on reservations.

CONCLUSIONS

This brief review of some of the activities that are currently taking place at TCUs in their work to build communities' capacities to address their needs revealed a vast variety of approaches. Tribal colleges, by virtue of the fact that they are local and are attuned to the contemporary and traditional cultures of their reservations are in a position to make significant contributions to social and economic development in their communities. The Northern Plains Bison Education Project, the Learning Lodge Institute, and the Sicangu Policy Institute are instances in which TCUs have brought their knowledge of these cultures to bear on improving their reservations.

However, TCUs have not always enjoyed cordial relations with their tribal governments. In some cases, the colleges are seen as intruders in an arena that rightly belongs to tribal government. It is not uncommon for tribal governments to believe that colleges ought to work in areas that are related to education and not become involved in actual economic and social development. One major outcome of projects involving the local community and college is that roles are being clarified. The Center for New Growth and Economic Development, for instance, has established a significant role for itself as the aggregator of data that can be used to bolster economic development efforts by both the tribe and the college itself. This clarification of roles, which at least in some measure has been brought about by NAHEI funding, is an important result of the projects and will make a major contribution to the long-term economic development of reservations.

More frequently, TCUs collaborate with one another. A number of NAHEI projects involve groups of TCUs working together to achieve a common goal. Lead institutions in these collaborations tend to play a coordinating role, with individual colleges taking the lead for their unique communities. The Northern Plains Bison Education Network, the AIHEC Advanced Networking with Minority-Serving Institutions Project, the Learning Lodge Institute, the Family Education Model, the Intertribal College Partnership, and the Oglala Nation Educational Leadership Project are all examples of projects in which one college or organization takes a leadership role that consists of providing opportunities to other colleges to improve conditions in a variety of areas based on their own goals and their own knowledge of how to proceed.

In addition to intra and intertribal partnerships, collaborations with external entities have been fostered by NAHEI projects. For example, whereas some TCUs have had long-standing collaborations with mainstream colleges and universities in their areas, others have followed this example and benefited from these efforts. Now TCUs are dealing with small business administration centers in their states and with other organizations such as EDUCAUSE to achieve their missions in service to their communities. Although the work that is being done in concert with outside groups is significant, TCUs in large part remain focused on influencing the direction of the work, using the knowledge they have of their tribes to guide their work.

The projects described in this chapter are aimed at bringing about deep, systemic change. They are not meant to produce "band aid" fixes for reservation conditions. Rather, they are aimed at changing the way that business as usual is defined. Ranging from involving communities in the education of college students to changing reservation policy to increasing the amount of business that is done electronically, these projects are making fundamental changes in the ways that reservations and colleges operate and serve their multiple communities.

REFERENCES

American Indian Higher Education Consortium & the Institute for Higher Education Policy. (2000, February). *Tribal college contributions to local economic development.* Alexandria, VA: Author.

Dull Knife College. (2001). www.dkimc.cc.mt.us

Eller, R., Martinez, R., Pace, C., Pavel, M., Garza, H., & Barnett, L. (1998). *Rural community college initiative: Economic development.* Washington, DC: American Association of Community Colleges.

Fort Berthold Community College. (2001). www.fbcc.bia.edu

Indian Reorganization Act, 41 Stat. 984 (June 18, 1934).

Oglala Lakota College. (2001). www.OLD.edu

Southwestern Indian Polytechnic Institute. (2001). http://kafka.SIPI.TCC.nm.us

Turtle Mountain Community College. (2001). www.Turtle-Mountain.cc.nd.us

United Tribes Technical College. (2001). www.unitedtribestech.com

6

Linking Tribal Colleges and Mainstream Institutions: Fundamental Tensions and Lessons Learned

Richard Nichols
Nichols & Associates
Gerald "Carty" Monette
Turtle Mountain Community College

INTRODUCTION

From their inception, tribal colleges have been linked with mainstream institutions of higher education. Indeed, their very existence came about because existing systems of higher education were failing large numbers of American Indian students. As Boyer (1997) noted:

> Especially since [enactment of] the GI Bill and the Higher Education Act, the federal government, as well as individual colleges and universities, had encouraged Indian students to enroll. But as more did, it became clear that access did not guarantee academic success. The dropout rate for American Indians remained at 90 percent or higher at many institutions. (p. 25)

A case in point was the experience of the Navajo Nation, which had established a higher education scholarship fund in 1957, and discovered in 1959 that more than half of the scholarship recipients were dropping out of college by the end of their freshman year. Thus, when the Navajo educational leaders began talking about establishing a tribal community or junior college, representatives of state universities and community colleges were invited to participate in these deliberations. The last such public meeting, in May 1968, before Navajo Community College was chartered, involved representatives of Arizona State University and the Arizona Junior College Board. Such involvement "alleviated public criticism of the [tribal college] idea by state higher education institutions" (Stein, 1992, p. 11). In fact, Arizona State University has remained an ally of the Navajo college, renamed Diné College in 1997, and is helping that college establish its first baccalaureate program, with assistance under the W. K. Kellogg Foundation's Native American Higher Education Initiative (NAHEI).

Similarly, other tribes brought colleges and universities from their own as well as other states into the initial planning for chartering their own tribal colleges. By the late 1960s, on the Pine Ridge Indian Reservation, the University of Colorado, Black Hills State College, and the University of South Dakota were offering courses that were eventually consolidated, in 1971, under the name Lakota Higher Education Center (now Oglala Lakota College) as the tribal college for the Oglala Lakota Nation. On the Rosebud Sioux Reservation, the tribe's educational leaders sought support and assistance from institutions as diverse as the University of South Dakota, Notre Dame University, and the University of Minnesota in establishing the tribally chartered Sinte Gleska College (now University). In 1971, these first two tribal colleges in South Dakota negotiated with various state institutions and the South Dakota Board of Regents to offer courses on their reservations and to confer associate of arts degrees in conjunction with accredited state institutions of higher education (IHEs; Stein, 1992).

Similarly, local educational leaders of several tribes in North Dakota were pursuing mainstream institutions in their state to provide support and assistance in establishing higher education centers on their reservations. For example, one reason for the establishment of Turtle Mountain Community College was to coordinate all of the higher education and continuing education opportunities that were coming to the reservation from mainstream colleges like the University of Colorado and the University of Utah. Nearly all of these arrangements were noncredit courses, were not intended to count toward a degree, and were of little or no use to tribal members.

Because of the nature of these arrangements, these early tribal colleges sought assistance from other Indian organizations and among themselves. In the early 1970s, the Coalition of Indian Controlled School Boards, located in Denver, established a relationship with Turtle Mountain Community College to provide funding that was intended to serve individual

Indians who were pursuing teacher education. The small grants allowed two Turtle Mountain Chippewa tribal members, who had already earned a teaching degree through the Future Indian Teachers Program, to earn master's degrees in special education. Just as important, the grants helped Turtle Mountain Community College build its fiscal capacity, which later helped the college secure other grants.

These first tribal colleges relied on a variety of funding sources to establish their first course offerings and to staff their fledgling operations. These sources included a hodgepodge of various federal programs [e.g., Office of Economic Opportunity, Bureau of Indian Affairs (BIA), and Volunteers in Service to American (VISTA)] as well as foundations. In the early 1970s, the federal Strengthening Developing Institutions Programs (Title III of the Higher Education Act) became the focus of funding for tribal colleges as other tribes in North and South Dakota, Montana, and Washington approached nearby mainstream institutions to enter into "bilateral agreements" to apply for Title III funds, essentially to establish extension campuses on their reservations. Through these agreements, the assisting mainstream institutions provided accredited course offerings on the reservations, sanctioned the instructional staff of the reservation learning centers, and, by extending their accreditation to these centers, extended eligibility for reservation-based students to apply for federal financial aid. Often, these institutions also offered their own staffs as instructors and administrators to assist the reservation-based educational leaders in institutional planning and curriculum development. Additionally, for almost a decade, the American Indian Higher Education Consortium (AIHEC), established in 1973, maintained a technical-assistance staff to provide these early colleges with help in accreditation, institutional planning, and curriculum development, among other things.

FUNDAMENTAL TENSIONS

Although these bilateral agreements provided for assistance in establishing the tribal colleges, certain fundamental tensions arose in the relationships between tribal colleges and the mainstream higher education system. For example, in 1971, Turtle Mountain tribal officials seeking accreditation under Title III approached the North Dakota Board of Higher Education. Because board officials thought it was humorous that an Indian tribe wanted to establish its own college, it passed the TMCC application to the smallest and weakest state institution. Although this link was not the best, the tribal college maintained this bilateral agreement until it earned candidacy for its own accreditation in 1978 to 1979. The tensions in this relationship were both qualitative and quantitative; that is, they involved both attitudinal and fiscal factors. The mainstream institution did not always sanction the courses or instructors that reservation-based leaders sought. Educational leaders at the reservation-based centers often thought that the assisting institution took an unnecessary amount of overhead for providing assistance under Title III and other federal grants.

This experience mirrored other instances in which assisting institutions did not approve of the fact that these unaccredited tribal institutions were providing "dual credit" for the courses offered by the mainstream institution. Although IHEs had entered into agreements with TCUs, many of the mainstream institutions did not fully appreciate the important role they played to incubate and nurture the tribal college(s) so that they could earn accreditation status from their respective regional accreditation association, thereby establishing themselves as legitimate institutions of higher education.

An essential requirement for gaining accreditation status was to have achieved a degree of financial stability, which often meant not relying solely on various federal grants. Some of the tribes recognized this and through Snyder Act authority, established the college as a funding priority in the BIA tribal budget. The Snyder Act funding served the purposes of establishing stability and demonstrating tribal commitment. Further stability was provided in 1978 by passage of federal legislation providing for basic operational support of tribal colleges under the Tribally Controlled College or University Assistance Act (PL 95-471).

In summary, the purposes of these early linkages were perceived differently by the mainstream IHEs and the emerging tribal colleges. The mainstream IHEs viewed these linkages as a way of extending access to higher education students in reservation communities and gaining additional revenues through sponsorship of federal programs, such as Title III, as well as from Indian students' tuition. However, the tribal colleges saw these linkages as a way to locate funding sources that would help them begin institutional planning efforts that would lead to their independent development. This difference in perspectives can be framed in the lens of the times, that is, the 1960s and early 1970s. The mainstream IHEs viewed their role as providing for minority community development by extending higher education opportunities on to the reservation. On the other hand, the tribal colleges' leaders viewed these linkages as a temporary strategy for gaining Indian self-determination.

REMAINING TENSIONS IN TCU
AND MAINSTREAM IHE LINKAGES

Despite several successful collaborations, which are described later, there remain serious tensions between TCUs and mainstream IHEs. At the root, these tensions reflect the fundamental inequities in funding and other resources that exist between these two distinctly different higher education institutions. Some of these remaining tensions are now discussed.

Equity Versus Competition for Partnership Resources

TCU and mainstream IHE partnerships can be hampered if there is competition for the resources that either type of institution receives or if there are perceived inequities in distributing shared resources. Overhead rates and other administrative costs of mainstream IHEs are often substantially larger than those of the partner TCU. When entering into cooperative agreements or other contractual arrangements, mainstream IHEs must realize that "it is not business as usual" and make arrangements for bringing equity into these shared costs. Otherwise, the TCU will not reap the full benefit from the partnership. Furthermore, salaries at nontribal institutions are often higher than those at TCUs. Thus, when entering into agreements for sharing instructional resources, such as through distance learning, those inequities can be problematic.

Distribution of Power: Losing/Sharing Authority

Another tension experienced in partnerships between TCUs and mainstream IHEs concerns the degree of authority exercised by either party. As mentioned earlier in this chapter, in the early partnerships or bilateral agreements entered into by the developing TCUs and their assisting institutions, the latter imposed conditions that the nascent tribal colleges found restrictive. Some of these had to do with approving individuals proposed as tribal college instructors, granting accreditation for proposed courses at the tribal college, and approving syllabi. These types of restrictions can still hamper development of cooperative relationships between TCUs and mainstream institutions and are a factor in choosing appropriate partners. The experience of Diné College in developing its first 4-year program, the Diné Teacher Education Program, is an example of how collaboration works. In seeking a four-year institution to provide accreditation for its teacher education program, the staff of Diné College canvassed all state universities in New Mexico and Arizona as potential partners. However, only one university, Arizona State University (ASU), did not impose restrictions on who could be approved as the instructional staff or on the proposed course of study. Because of the university's many years of previous collaborations, ASU staff had trust in the TCU and allowed the tribal college staff to determine what were appropriate qualifications for instructional staff, based on tribal cultural values. Similar identification and deferment of institutional bias by mainstream IHEs can help them build better relationships with TCUs (Diné College, 1996).

Which Institution Benefits From Indian Student Enrollments?

Interinstitutional partnerships between mainstream IHEs and tribal colleges often provide for mainstream IHE courses to be offered at local TCUs. Credit for these courses is also often provided by the mainstream IHE. These linkages often end up in roadblocks caused by the question of which institution will benefit from the revenue generated by Indian student enrollments. If tribal colleges were funded according to need and not by credit hours generated, as is currently the case under the Tribally Controlled Colleges or University Assistance Act, there would be less emphasis on who benefits from student enrollments. To secure funding for operational purposes, tribal colleges must hold on to every credit that is generated. This necessary practice creates a tension between tribal colleges and mainstream institutions, where enrollment also counts and where it may be decreasing.

Furthermore, other tensions exist in nonacademic program areas where programmatic competition results, especially in going after shared federal program funds. These types of programs provide services to tribal members and help defray overhead costs for the tribal colleges. Many tribal colleges supplement operational funding with overhead and indirect cost benefits that come with nonacademic grants and contracts. Thus, if a linkage results in programmatic funds being shared between the two types of institutions, there is tension over which institution can collect the overhead and indirect costs provided through the federally funded program.

Inequity in Resources

Passage of the Tribal Controlled College or University Assistance Act in 1978 provided greater stability for all eligible tribal colleges, at least at a minimal operational level. However, 20 years after the Act was signed into law, the colleges are still underfunded in that appropriations under the Act have only recently reached the 50% level of authorization. The colleges continue to be funded at approximately half of the amount that mainstream colleges receive per student. The needs of tribal colleges have never been met adequately in all this time, and this inequity in resources has led to ongoing tensions between TCUs and mainstream IHEs.

Differences in Providing or Accepting Cultural Contexts

Ideally, a tribal college student obtains foundational knowledge about native culture, history, and language. Upon transferring to a mainstream IHE, the student uses this knowledge as a source of strengthened identity, which helps him or her succeed in the mainstream IHE. Mainstream IHEs thus benefit from the cultural context provided to these transfer students. Furthermore, mainstream IHEs can build on their Indian students' cultural knowledge, but are hesitant to do so. Mainstream institutions have difficulty accepting the culture of one particular group, such as Indians, and would rather focus on diversity. However, because culture matters to Indian students, this focus on group and culture rather than on individual achievement can create tension with non-Indian staff and students at mainstream universities.

Differences in Academic Missions, Especially Regarding Native Students

Some researchers have found that tribal colleges prepare more successful Indian people than do other IHEs (Boyer, 1997). For example, an Indian student has a better chance of succeeding at a mainstream institution if he or she attends a tribal college first. This is because tribal colleges are uniquely positioned and charged with serving *all* tribal students. Tribal colleges are educating a pool of people who have not enjoyed full access to equal educational opportunity, that is, nontraditional students who would normally have difficulty being admitted to or remaining in mainstream IHEs. Furthermore, tribal colleges draw students from an educational system that has often failed native students. High school dropout rates on most reservations are well over 50%. Indian students often do not get the courses in reservation high schools that serve as gateways for success in mainstream institutions. Also, as a whole, Indian students' standardized achievement test scores are far below the national averages. Poverty conditions on the reservations, at Depression-era levels on some reservations, add to the problems students normally have in achieving a higher education. Therefore, TCUs often have to upgrade students' basic educational skills as part of their higher educational missions.

Thus, tribal colleges are serving students who would not normally attend mainstream IHEs and are succeeding at it. However, despite their success, TCUs continue to struggle to gain the financial footing that would allow them to retain faculty and other resources. Dependent primarily on federal programmatic resources, TCUs continue to justify their existence as the political landscape changes after each election, whereas mainstream IHEs easily access state funding on a continuing basis. This discrepancy remains an ongoing tension.

NAHEI-FOSTERED LINKAGES BETWEEN TRIBAL AND MAINSTREAM INSTITUTIONS

In 1995, the W. K. Kellogg Foundation made a major commitment, through NAHEI, to assist tribal colleges. This commitment of $30 million was to assist tribal colleges to strengthen their institutional infrastructures, as well as to develop new and necessary programs to meet the needs of their respective tribes or Indian communities. In addition, the NAHEI commitment was meant to foster or build on relationships between tribal and mainstream institutions to improve higher education for Native American students in general. Thus, among the purposes of the initiative were to:

1. improve the success rates of Native Americans in mainstream education institutions;
2. increase the pipeline of potential Native American faculty for Native-controlled and mainstream institutions; and,
3. build coalitions and partnerships among Native American-controlled and mainstream institutions in order to facilitate student access and resource and knowledge sharing. (W. K. Kellogg Foundation, 1997)

A total of 15 collaborations between TCUs and mainstream IHEs were funded. Most of these were funded under a provision of the grant that sought to foster "collaborative partnerships between and among tribal colleges and with mainstream colleges and universities." These partnerships involved a total of 23 mainstream IHEs and 27 TCUs. These partnerships serve a variety of purposes among which are:

1. Strengthening TCU infrastructure (Little Priest Community College and Wayne State College).
2. Enhancing TCU student services (Fort Peck Community College and six other Montana TCUs with the University of Montana).

3. Broadening academic coursework offerings at TCUs (Lac Courtes Oreilles Ojibwa Community College and the College of the Menominee Nation with the Universities of Wisconsin-Superior and Green Bay, and Fond du Lac Tribal and Community College and Leech Lake Tribal College with the University of Minnesota-Duluth).

4. Conducting research to develop new curricula/programs (D-Q University with Humboldt State University, Sinte Gleska University with the University of California-Los Angeles, Leech Lake Tribal College with the University of Minnesota-Duluth, and Crownpoint Institute of Technology with six mainstream IHEs[1]).

5. Providing faculty development opportunities (the four New Mexico TCUs with New Mexico State University, and Haskell Indian Nations University with Kansas State University).

6. Developing new baccalaureate programs (Diné College with Arizona State University, and Northwest Indian College with Washington State University and Western Washington University).

7. Developing new master's degree programs (Oglala Lakota College and other South Dakota TCUs with The University of South Dakota and Chadron State University).

8. Increasing native student transfer/access to mainstream IHEs (Leech Lake Tribal College with Bemidji State University, and the four New Mexico TCUs with New Mexico State University).

9. Providing technical assistance (Bay Mills Community College with Michigan State University, and Turtle Mountain Community College with The University of North Dakota).

10. Sharing courses via new technologies (the North Dakota Association of Tribal Colleges, a nonprofit organization of North Dakota's tribal colleges has an established relationship with the state university system that allows the tribal colleges to offer and receive interactive and Internet courses to/from other tribal colleges and the state university system).

The range of these partnerships provides an ample example of the ways in which TCUs and mainstream IHEs can assist each other in improving higher education opportunities and in impacting American Indian students nationwide. Furthermore, the W. K. Kellogg Foundation initiative also funded the following types of TCU and mainstream IHE coalitions[2]:

---

[1]Colorado State University, Iowa State University, The University of Georgia, The University of Pennsylvania, The University of Tennessee, and Tufts University.

[2]Another three NAHEI partnerships involve exclusively TCUs; two partnerships are between a TCU and Indian communities/organizations; one other partnership involves a mainstream IHE and Hawai'i Native community organizations.

1.   Improving native student services: The National Institute for Native Leadership in Higher Education (NINLHE) includes representatives from more than 50 public, private, and tribally controlled colleges and universities as well as national native education organizations in the United States and Canada. NINLHE's goal is to effect lasting change in higher education practice and policy through enhancing the individual capabilities of student affairs professionals who are native and whose work (a) supports native students' goal of graduation, and (b) strengthens the standing of native student retention programs as lasting institutional priorities.

2.   Developing equity in higher education resources (Alliance for Equity in Higher Education[3]).

These new and/or developing coalitions show promise for providing equity in access and opportunity for native students across the nation. They are linking TCUs and mainstream IHEs to provide for the critical pipeline of Indian students and professionals both into the world at large and back into native communities.

MODELS FOR REPLICATION

Several NAHEI-initiated partnerships can potentially serve as models for other TCUs and Indian communities. Below are highlighted three TCU and mainstream IHE partnerships that have been successfully implemented and have resulted in impressive impacts to date. (Note: Many other partnerships, not mentioned in this chapter, are also worthy of highlighting, but because of space concerns, they are not discussed here.)

Culture Matters: Project HOOP, Sinte Gleska University With The University of California Los Angeles

The purpose of this project is to establish native theater as an integrated subject of study in TCUs and American Indian communities. Project HOOP (Honoring Our Origins and People) combines academic and artistic program delivery in native theater with community cultural development. The project is developing a series of six models for 2-year programs that involve curricula, artist-in-residence opportunities, and a culminating com-

---

[3]An advocacy organization formed in 1999, the alliance comprises of the AIHEC, the Hispanic Association of Colleges and Universities, and the National Association for Equal Opportunity in Higher Education. The alliance is coordinated by the Institute for Higher Education Policy in Washington, DC.

munity theater festival/performance. Project HOOP is totally culturally based and, moreover, is grounded in a community-based model approach. Progress to date includes:

1.   As of 2001, eight new theater courses were developed and taught at Sinte Gleska University. These courses focus on both performance traditions in a theater context (examining storytelling, song, dance, and games) and contemporary performance methods, as well as developing a group theater piece for performance (including teaching individual performance style synthesizing traditional and modern techniques).

2.   The project has compiled the *Stories of Our Ways* anthology, and the *American Indian Theater in Performance: A Reader*. These two works have been published by UCLA's American Indian Studies Center. (These publications showcase the works of native playwrights and also provide academic and artistic support for teaching native theater. Another anthology will be published as part of the Center's new Native Theater series.)

3.   Having retained 100% of Sinte Gleska's first-year theater students, the project expanded its recruitment efforts in 2000 and 2001, collaborating with the university's teacher education, art institute, and Lakota studies programs.

4.   In 2001, Project HOOP staff were working with local Indian Health Service personnel to raise awareness about diabetes by having theater students produce a video on diabetes for use as a teaching tool with community members.

Students Matter: Leech Lake Tribal College With Northwest Indian College, Sinte Gleska University, and Bemidji State University

The purpose of this project is to increase student enrollment and improve retention at Leech Lake Tribal College and Bemidji State University by developing opportunities for students to complete 4-year degrees on site at the TCU. The main strategy employed is to share resources through distance learning (e.g., interactive TV and the Internet), thus increasing student choices and providing higher quality learning opportunities. Progress to date includes the following:

1.   As of 2000, upper level elementary education courses were offered at Leech Lake Tribal College through an agreement with Sinte Gleska University. Twenty-two students were enrolled, 10 of those in

their third and fourth year of study. The teacher education program was developed in response to Leech Lake Tribal Council's *Strategic Plan*, which cited education as a needed "critical profession." These teachers will increase the pool of native teachers in the seven schools serving Leech Lake Ojibwa students.

2. A new partnership with Bemidji State University and Northwest Technical College allows Leech Lake Tribal College students to enroll in Northwest Technical College's Associate-level licensed practical nursing program and then transfer to Bemidji State's baccalaureate-level nursing program.

3. Leech Lake Tribal College students now have access to Bemidji State's extended learning and self-directed programs delivered over the Internet and ITV.

4. Bemidji State University's Indian student enrollment increased from 142 in 1996 to 1997 to 197 in 1999 to 2000, a 38% increase. Furthermore, there has been a 200% increase in Leech Lake Tribal College degreed students enrolled at Bemidji State and a 300% increase in the Leech Lake Tribal College students earning baccalaureate degrees in 1998 to 1999.

5. Since the new NAHEI-funded Indian mediator/counselor position was created at Bemidji State, early withdrawal by Indian students decreased by 50% in the spring and fall 1999 semesters and has held at this rate.

Community Building and Tribal Sovereignty Matter: OKSALE Teacher Education Program, Northwest Indian College With Washington State University

The OKSALE Teacher Education Program, a NAHEI-established partnership between Northwest Indian College and Washington State University, has led to the development of a new relationship between the two colleges, as well as with K–12 native students, native communities, and tribes. This partnership resulted in Washington State's receipt of a $10 million 5-year grant from the U.S. Department of Education. This grant, which includes subcontracts to Northwest Indian College and public/tribal schools serving native students in the state, is intended to enable the various stakeholders to ensure that the educational needs of Indian students in the state are better met by providing, among other supports, native teacher training and training and technical assistance to public school staff and teachers.

Of significance is that this partnership also includes tribal governments in the state. Tribal chairpersons will serve on Washington State's new tribal advisory board, which is intended to advise the university not only on the U.S. Department of Education project but also on issues pertinent to the entire institution.

Other Linkages

The W. K. Kellogg Foundation's NAHEI project is also indirectly assisting in developing other linkages to mainstream colleges. For example, six tribal colleges in Minnesota, North Dakota, and Wisconsin and the University of Minnesota have formed a partnership called *Woodlands Wisdom* whose purpose is to create a culturally specific nutrition education program for the colleges. The project combines tribal history, food production, food preparation, and practices of the woodland tribes. Although still in its infancy, the project has gained national recognition.

Turtle Mountain Community College, working with the University of North Dakota, has its students applying geographic information systems/global positioning system (GIS/GPS) technology in order to map the extent of diabetes on the reservation, where more than 2,000 households have at least one resident with some level of diabetes. The mapping project, in addition to other benefits, will lead into a 9-1-1 emergency telephone system for the reservation.

LESSONS LEARNED FROM AND ABOUT MAINSTREAM IHE AND TCU LINKAGES

In examining the linkages among tribal colleges and mainstream IHEs fostered through NAHEI and other initiatives, we have identified four central "lessons learned" that are important to maintaining and strengthening supportive relationships among these two types of institutions. These lessons learned are now discussed.

Establish Explicit and Strong Linkage Agreements

One lesson learned is that types of contractual arrangements that have been used [e.g., essential elements of articulation agreements, memoranda of agreement (MOA) must explicitly state partners' expectations and responsibilities. For example, the UCLA/Sinte Gleska partnership that resulted in Project HOOP involves an MOA that specifically details the obligations, commitments, and expectations of both partners. (Note: Such

specificity does not exist in all the NAHEI-funded collaborations.) Another partnership involves seven North Dakota mainstream institutions
and four North Dakota tribal colleges (excluding United Tribes Technical
College). In May 2000, these institutions signed an MOA for the dual admission and transfer of undergraduate agricultural students among the participating state and tribal colleges. Students may apply to any two
institutions and be assured of dual admission status; each college will consider students as though they had entered as freshmen, bringing all of the
benefits of each institution to the student. An essential element of this
MOA is explicit academic-progress criteria.

Develop Shared Decision Making

When a tribal college works with a well-established mainstream IHE, there
must be some assurance that each institution will maintain institutional integrity. Each institution must answer how this is done. Often, a mainstream
institution may view itself as having more expertise and may view the tribal
college as only a feeder institution. However, the tribal college is also aware
that mainstream institutions historically have not served tribal members
well. Both types of institutions must recognize their individual strengths
when forming a partnership and must be willing to provide for shared decision making within the partnership.

Provide for Flexibility in Partnerships

The key to the success of any partnership is to make sure that the interest of
each partner is protected. The developmental nature and characteristics of
tribal colleges in areas such as tribal control, governance, academic preparation of the student body, massive poverty in its service area, lack of resources, inadequate facilities, and so on, are often in contrast to those found
at mainstream colleges. Yet, a good partnership linkage can happen only
when both types of institutions find a way to protect their institutional interests while meeting the needs of tribal members. As simple as it may seem,
building trust among institutional representatives is an important factor in
developing this flexibility. When institutional representatives trust and understand each other's interests and motives, they will then act to advocate
within their respective institutions for flexibility in bending institutional
rules. Often, shared interests, previous experience, and a history of successful partnerships are fundamental to building this trust. Shared interests and
previous experience may be as basic as having a history of serving the same

pool of tribal students. Thus, state universities that have students from TCU reservations may be more willing to enter into partnerships to better serve those students.

Expect Institutional Change to Be Difficult and Slow

As the previous examples indicate, successful partnerships evolve over time. When partners have realistic expectations based on explicit responsibilities stated in interinstitutional agreements, the partnership is more likely to result in the trust and shared decision making that will provide a foundation for ongoing or new relationships. When starting out, partners should expect a parrying of institutional interests, which may jeopardize the partnership. However, explicitly stated agreements can help bridge the tensions resulting from brokering institutional interests and can help foster the types of behaviors, shared decision making, and trust necessary for the linkages to succeed.

REFERENCES

Boyer, P. (1997). *Native American colleges: Progress and prospects.* Princeton, NJ: Carnegie Foundation for the Advancement of Teaching.

Diné College. (1996, February). *Proposal Addendum for W. K. Kellogg Foundation support of Navajo Community College.* Tsaile, AZ: Author.

W. K. Kellogg Foundation. (1997, January). *Native American Higher Education Initiative: "Capturing the Dream" Request for Proposals.* Battle Creek, MI: Author.

Stein, W. (1992). *Tribally controlled colleges: Making good medicine.* New York: Peter Lang Publishing.

7

Building Tribal Communities: Defining the Mission and Measuring the Outcomes of Tribal Colleges

Paul Boyer
Pennsylvania State University

INTRODUCTION

The first tribal colleges represented something entirely new in American higher education. Few people knew they even existed, and those who did—some federal bureaucrats and state education officials, among others—were not always supportive. In their early years, some colleges also faced opposition within their own communities, from tribal members who distrusted higher education or doubted that Indians could create a "real" college.

In this climate of low expectation and disapproval, success of the tribal college movement in its first quarter century of life could be defined simply as *survival*. To be imagined, created, and sustained was, itself, a major accomplishment for the early institutions. Considering the overwhelming poverty and isolation of many Indian reservations, as well as the long history of failed government initiatives, it seemed to many that the establishment of a college was, at best, a quixotic enterprise.

But as the years pass and the institutions grow, mature, and gain legitimacy both within and beyond their communities, survival is no longer in doubt. The colleges are part of the landscape of more than 30 reservations and Native American communities. Funding is still low, but hard-won federal legislation and increased private-sector support provide a degree of security.

All of this is reason for celebration. However, the tribal colleges have now entered a new and equally challenging era. Although few people now question the legitimacy of the movement, it is no longer sufficient to say that the colleges succeed because they have survived. Instead, success is being measured in more rigorous ways. Yes, tribal colleges have a right to exist, but, beyond this, challenging questions are being asked: Are they making a difference? If so, where is the proof? And, in either case, how can they become even better?

TRIBAL COLLEGES AND THE NEW ACCOUNTABILITY

These questions are not being asked of tribal colleges alone. All of American higher education has come under increased scrutiny over the past two decades. A preoccupation with institutional efficiency and student outcomes now shapes much of the debate over higher education policy. Both consumers and policymakers want to know that their investments of time and money are worthwhile.

This era, dubbed the new accountability, emerged in the early 1980s and reflected, among other things, a suspicion that colleges were not well managed and "a vague but growing conviction that [higher education] had lost sight of its original public charge" (Ewell, 1999, p. 149). The result has been a growing focus on assessment by accreditors, state legislatures, and federal agencies.

At its best, this new accountability has been a boon to tribal colleges and other nonelite institutions by, in effect, democratizing the definition of quality in American higher education. When the emphasis is on the measurable outcomes of a college education, tribal colleges and other nonelite institutions have an opportunity to prove their worth. More traditional measurements of quality based on institutional resources, reputation, and selectivity still matter to a great many people, but they are no longer the only way to define a "good" college.

However, this focus on accountability also presents multiple challenges to the tribal colleges. Tribal college leaders are used to being examined, critiqued, and criticized, and some worry that common approaches to institutional assessment will be used only to find fault—by, for example, revealing only what students do not know on standardized tests or spotlighting retention and graduation rates that are lower than selective 4-year institutions.

In a larger sense, however, tribal college leaders may also feel that these approaches to assessment are intrusive and distracting because they impose Western definitions of quality on institutions grounded in non-Western traditions. "We are being evaluated against standards and expectations foreign to our tribal environments and needs," former Sinte Gleska University Vice President Cheryl Crazy Bull charged in a 1994 critique of the regional accrediting bodies (p. 25). At the time, she proposed development of an alternative accreditation process led by the colleges.

However, it is difficult and risky to turn away accreditors and others who can confer legitimacy and provide resources to the colleges. "To be accredited," acknowledged Crazy Bull, "meant 'official' recognition by the other educational institutions, government agencies and even by students. It also meant participation in federally funded programs, such as student financial aid and the opening of doors for private and foundation resources" (p. 25).

What is needed is an approach to assessment that satisfies the needs of accreditors and others who evaluate the work of American higher education. But it must also allow the tribal colleges to demonstrate their strengths. Most important, it must be a process that makes the colleges stronger and better able to fulfill their mission statements. This, in fact, is the real purpose of assessment.

ACCOUNTABLE TO WHOM? A CONCEPTUAL MODEL FOR SELF-ASSESSMENT

The discussion of accountability within the tribal college movement, up to this point, has suggested that the only solution is to make compromises—to accommodate *either* the tribe *or* the expectations of evaluators and accreditors. But there may be another way to approach the issue of accountability. In a culturally based model offered by Fort Peck Community College President James Shanley, accountability is about a great deal more than providing data, on demand, to accreditors and public agencies. Instead, it is more about recognizing that there are many layers of accountability. It begins with a sense of personal responsibility, an awareness that the strength of an institution is built on the thoughts and actions of the individuals who participate in the work of the college. It is impossible to have an accountable college when those who are part of the college do not feel accountable to themselves or to its mission.

From here, like ripples in a pond, accountability reaches out to embrace others—family, friends, relatives, a clan, the tribe, the surrounding non-Indian community, the state, accreditors, foundations, and the nation as a whole. It is important also to recognize that responsibility exists not only to people, but also to the natural world. Nor is accountability only for the living; there is also accountability to ancestors and to generations yet to come. This sense of inclusiveness is one of the great strengths of Native societies.

When individuals and communities become accountable for themselves and each other, they strengthen both culture and sovereignty. They are acting out of their own convictions, building on their own visions, remaining focused on the missions of their own institutions. There is nothing to compromise. But they also recognize that they are not isolated from the rest of the world. Colleges are made stronger and students benefit through articulation agreements with mainstream institutions, when funds are available for programs that support social and economic programs. Further, tribal colleges have an opportunity to share their knowledge and the knowledge of their tribal nations with others. But accountability at these levels is put in its proper place. It is allowed to support, not control, the mission of the college.

ACCOUNTABLE FOR WHAT?
THE CENTRALITY OF MISSION STATEMENTS

Accountability does not begin with standardized test scores, student portfolios, or survey instruments; it begins with an examination of the college's mission statement. It is from this document that a college develops the standards by which it is judged. The 1987 Carnegie Foundation report on undergraduate education declared:

> Measuring the outcome of a college education, in the end, is an assessment of the institution. And only as we gain greater clarity about the mission of the college—about the purpose that the functions are to serve—will we have the standards against which to measure our procedures. Only as college leaders clarify goals will they have the confidence to proceed with any form of evaluation. (Boyer, p. 262)

In the case of tribal colleges, most stress what is often called a dual mission. On the one hand, they are expected to provide students with training for immediate employment, as well as academic preparation for continued learning at mainstream institutions. With a degree and a set of skills, graduates can expect to enjoy greater economic and social mobility, either on or off the reservation. In this sense, they are much like the mainstream community colleges upon which tribal colleges were modeled.

On the other hand, tribal colleges are *also* expected to reflect and strengthen the cultural knowledge of the tribe or tribes they serve and, by using culture as their frame of reference, address the social and economic needs of their communities. In this way, the colleges must provide an opportunity for the individuals who enroll while also strengthening their tribal societies as distinct and sustainable communities. In a very real way, the function of tribal colleges is to help ensure the survival of indigenous peoples in America.

Janine Pease Pretty on Top, former president of Little Big Horn College, powerfully expressed this part of the tribal college mission some years ago when she called her college "the Harvard of the Crow Nation." She meant that Little Big Horn served the unique needs of the Crow people in the same way that Harvard reflected the values, traditions, and needs of the United States.

This dual mission is complex, often poorly understood, and challenging to implement. Difficult questions are still being asked within the movement: How, exactly, are tribal colleges different from mainstream institutions? What contribution do they make to the landscape of American higher education that cannot be made by any other institution? What, in the end, does it means to be a *Crow* college, a *Lakota* college, or a *Turtle Mountain Chippewa* college?

The growing focus on assessment in higher education only heightens the urgent need of tribal colleges to understand and explain their unique visions, both to themselves and to others. When the mission is not clearly understood, or when it is not clear how a college can fulfill its mission and provide evidence of success, then a college can, indeed, be diverted. Goals become muddled and forgotten amid the myriad competing expectations of tribal constituents, evaluators, funders, and critics, each with their own notions of what a good tribal college is, or should be.

TOWARD A DEFINITION OF EXCELLENCE
IN AMERICAN INDIAN HIGHER EDUCATION

There are several ways to define quality, or "excellence," in higher education. But not all of them fully reflect the vision—and mission—of tribal colleges. The first is what Astin (1999) called the reputational approach, which is "based on the idea that the most excellent institutions are the ones that enjoy the best academic reputations" (p. 158). Simply put, the best is the best because it is the best. The logic is maddeningly circular, yet as stated earlier, it remains a powerful force for prospective students and parents who inundate a handful of Ivy League institutions with applications every fall.

However, such logic does have merit in the sense that it is self-reinforcing. Schools believed to be the best do attract the students, scholars, and resources needed to reinforce their elite reputations. But it is very difficult for nonelite institutions to gain status when playing by these rules, although many colleges and universities are attempting to prime the pump of reputation by aping Ivy League institutions. They hire a few academic stars, promote research over teaching, and become more selective in their admission process. These are questionable tactics and, in any case, are not options for poor and nonselective colleges.

The focus of the new accountability, in contrast, attempts to get beyond reputation and resources, in part by tracking institutions' ability to make a difference in the lives of students. Data regarding retention and graduation rates, student scores on standardized examinations, and trends in postgraduation employment are among the indicators that allow consumers to compare institutions and encourage colleges to monitor performance and develop strategies for self-improvement.

This approach has merit. That is to say that students enroll in college hoping to graduate with a degree and get a job. A college should be able to demonstrate that it can help them reach their goals. Yet, these particular measurements of outcomes cannot fully define excellence in higher education. This approach runs the risk of measuring only what is most easily measured, not what matters most in higher education. Alfred and Carter (2000) warned, for example, that a focus on such performance indicators "limited the terrain for interpretation of institutional performance." "All too often," they added, "these substitutes for direct experience drive accountability expectations although they may have little or nothing to do with the mission of the institution or its performance" (p. 4).

Other long-time observers of assessment trends have agreed. Astin (1999) forcefully argued that affective outcomes are no less important than cognitive outcomes. They are, in fact, central to the mission of most institutions of higher education in America. "Most of us are inclined to shy away from assessing affective outcomes because we think they are too 'value-laden,'" Astin acknowledged.

> But if you read through a few college catalogs, you begin to realize that colleges claim to be concerned about a number of "affective" things such as good judgment, citizenship, social responsibility, character and the like. Indeed, most descriptions of the "liberally educated" person sound at least as "affective" as they do "cognitive." (p. 169)

Thus, a college of quality must be at least as concerned with a student's ability to become a responsible citizen as it is with his or her academic standing and employability after graduation.

This richer understanding of how higher education shapes lives leads to another way to conceptualize excellence. It, too, focuses on students and learning, but it more adequately captures the fullness of most tribal college mission statements by stressing the importance of connections, service, and community. This vision of excellence was expressed in a 1988 report entitled *Building community: A vision for the new century*, developed by the Commission on the Future of Community Colleges (American Association of Community and Junior Colleges, 1988). It declared that community colleges must live up to their name, not only by serving a community, but also by strengthening a *sense* of community. It explained, "We define the term 'community' not only as a region to be served, but also as a climate to be created," that "in its broadest and best sense, encompasses a concern for the whole, for integration and collaboration." Community, the report continued, is built in the classroom, across campus, and, ultimately, beyond campus. "As never before," it affirmed, "the nation needs institutions that recognize not only the dignity of the individual but also the interests of community" (p. 9).

The continuing vitality of this vision is expressed in the more recent vocabulary of "engagement" in higher education. The Kellogg Commission on the Future of State and Land Grant Universities (2000), for example, urged land-grant universities to return to the vision of their founders by becoming "engaged institutions" committed to interdisciplinary scholarship and "greater faculty involvement with their surrounding communities" (p. 21).

Whether discussed through the language of "community" or "engagement," this approach to quality is one that most closely matches the stated mission of most tribal colleges. It also validates President Shanely's vision by reminding educators that accountability must be generated internally, not imposed externally. When the focus is on the strengthening of community, tribal colleges have a mandate to examine the needs of their students and reservations. The task of assessment, then, is to measure a college's ability to both serve a community and build a community.

BECOMING ACCOUNTABLE: ASSESSMENT OF TRIBAL COLLEGES

Assessment, to be meaningful, must help an institution become more accountable to the community it serves. It must not be viewed as an externally imposed obligation—to be done grudgingly, if at all—but part of an open and ongoing conversation among all tribal college constituents—students, faculty, administrators, tribal leaders, and all members of the reservation community. To be meaningful, it must make room for both self-criticism and self-improvement.

The culturally based model of accountability proposed earlier not only provides a rationale for assessment, but also hints at some possible approaches to assessment. President Shanley proposed, for example, that accountability begins with the self and grows to encompass larger and larger communities. So, too, should institutional assessment address different and progressively more inclusive notions of community? In the following discussion, I will draw on both the recommendations of the *Building Community* report and interviews with faculty and administrators at several tribal colleges.

First, and most fundamental, is a sense of individual accountability to the college's core—the mission statement. Are all members of the college community—faculty, staff, *and* students—familiar with the statement? How often does it appear in college publications? How often is it discussed in public forums, faculty meetings, and board conversations? When was the last time it was reviewed and revised?

These exercises can be superficial and perfunctory. But Brian Palaceck, assessment coordinator and faculty member at United Tribes Technical College, argued that, at its best, a discussion of the mission statement provides an opportunity for deep personal reflection and professional renewal. This awareness of the mission helps a college—especially poor and isolated tribal colleges—focus on opportunities, not limitations. Palaceck argued that appreciation of the mission statement encourages members of a college community to look beyond a lack of institutional resources and focus instead on the strength of the college's vision (personal communication, June 14, 2000).

From here the scope of accountability widens to include the classroom experience. Here the focus is on student learning. To be accountable at this level requires a college to ask: How has the student grown both intellectually and emotionally? What has he or she actually *learned*? Beyond traditional forms of written examination, colleges are helping to answer this question by asking students to demonstrate progress through responsive essays, portfolios, presentations, or, in the case of at least one automotive class at United Tribes Technical College, becoming "manager for a day."

Beyond the classroom, there is also accountability to the larger campus community. A tribal college of quality will work to create a climate for learning where students can achieve their educational goals. Here, it is appropriate to track overall patterns of student enrollment, retention, graduation, and employment. Broad general education objectives, such as the development of proficiency in writing and oral expression, can also be effectively assessed through exit examinations or "capstone" courses.

Cultural outcomes should also be assessed if they, too, are part of the general education objectives of a college. Turtle Mountain Community College in Belcourt, North Dakota is breaking new ground by encouraging faculty to integrate the Seven Teachings of the Ojibwe—wisdom, love, respect, bravery, honesty, humility, and truth—throughout the curriculum, including vocational courses. Annual surveys of students provide an opportunity to assess how well cultural knowledge is integrated into courses and how it is being applied by students outside the classroom.

Next, accountability reaches out beyond the campus to the wider tribal community. People frustrated by the social, economic, and political realities of their tribal communities created tribal colleges. Thus, it is appropriate to ask how the colleges, as models of "engaged institutions," are able to strengthen tribal communities. Assessments may incorporate data on the reservation's standard of living, including levels of individual income and outside investment. But while these numbers do matter, it also is important, especially in the poorest and most isolated communities, to find ways of tracking the prerequisites for change, such as an emerging sense of hope or a willingness of tribal leaders to take responsibility for change.

Again, culture matters. Accountability means the college embraces its responsibility, not only to build wealth, but also to reflect and rebuild cultural knowledge. Is the college helping restore traditional values and skills to the fabric of daily life? This is a difficult mandate, but one that many colleges have given themselves. These institutions are working to keep languages alive, maintain a place for cultural celebrations, and validate traditional values, such as respect for elders and the natural world. Finding ways to measure, both formally and informally, the long-term influence of the college on the community is a crucial aspect of assessment.

At each level of assessment, it is important to remember that findings are meaningful only if they indicate weaknesses as well as strengths and generate proposals for change. Institutions will grow stronger and become more accountable only when they act on the information they receive. Turtle Mountain Community College President Carty Monette observed that assessment can be uncomfortable, and even destabilizing. Assumptions will be challenged and uncomfortable truths exposed. What if it is found that students are earning As but not gaining necessary skills? What if it is discovered that the college's effect on local economic development is negligible? An accountable college will find itself repeatedly engaged in open discussions, looking for new approaches, and returning again and again to the mission statement.

Finally, there is yet another level of accountability—to communities beyond the reservation, including the regional accrediting associations, federal agencies and philanthropies that support the movement. By now, the colleges have already gathered for their own use much of the data needed to satisfy the inquiries of those who monitor America's colleges and universities. Through self-assessment, the tribal colleges have become more than a group of outlying institutions and should serve as models for all of American higher education and the nation.

RECOMMENDATIONS

This chapter argues for the importance of assessment in tribal colleges and proposes that assessment can help colleges fulfill their mission statements and become models of excellence in higher education. Ultimately, assessment makes tribal colleges more accountable to students, the tribe, and the wisdom of their cultural heritage. However, there is a need to take this discussion to the next step by systematically investigating how tribal colleges are responding to the assessment movement. Turtle Mountain Community College and United Tribes Technical College are cited here. Their work deserves more careful scrutiny. As well, creative approaches at other tribal colleges deserve to be spotlighted. Most critically, tribal colleges need to develop and share alternative approaches to assessment, both within and outside the classroom.

REFERENCES

Alfred, R., & Carter, P. (2000). Contradictory colleges: Thriving in an era of continuous change [Issue Paper No. 6]. In New expeditions: Chartering the second century of community college. Washington, DC: The American Association of Community Colleges.

American Association of Community and Junior Colleges. (1988). Building community: A vision for the new century. Washington, DC: Author.

Astin, A. W. (1999). Assessment, student development, and public policy. In S. J. Messick (Ed.), Assessment in higher education: Issues of access, quality, student development and public policy (pp. 157–175). Mahwah, NJ: Lawrence Erlbaum Associates.

Boyer, E. L. (1987). College: The undergraduate experience in America. New York: Harper & Row.

Crazy Bull, C. (1994). Who should pass judgment? Tribal College Journal of American Indian Higher Education, 5(4), 25–28.

Ewell, P. T. (1999). Assessment of higher education quality: Promise and politics. In S. J. Messick (Ed.), Assessment in higher education: Issues of access, quality, student development and public policy (pp. 147–156). Mahwah, NJ: Lawrence Erlbaum Associates.

Kellogg Commission on the Future of State and Land Grant Universities. (2000, March). Renewing the covenant: Learning, discovery, and engagement in a new age and different world. Battle Creek, MI: Author.

III

Nurturing and Advocating Spirit and Voice

8

Native Leadership: Advocacy for Transformation, Culture, Community, and Sovereignty

Valorie Johnson
W. K. Kellogg Foundation
Maenette K. P. Benham
Michigan State University
Matthew Jason VanAlstine
Michigan State University

INTRODUCTION

A prevailing view of education in native/indigenous communities is that it is a vehicle to empower individuals and groups to have more control over their own affairs (White House Conference on Indian Education, 1992). In fact, in the space of three decades, Native Americans have progressed from having their education determined for them to having more control over the cognitive and pedagogical course of their education (Benham & Cooper, 2000; Noley, 1992). This movement toward self-determination has been attributed to a variety of educational interventions, including shifts in federal legislation and public policy, targeted funding, and the growth of alternative educational institutions at both the K–12 and postsecondary levels. These and other educational interventions have been instituted because of committed Native American leadership at the local, tribal, state, and national levels (Tippeconnic, 1992). Unfortunately, limited research has been conducted on how native leaders have catalyzed efforts to change education, or how these leaders describe their own leadership development.

Although there is a paucity of literature focusing on effective Native American leadership, the literature that does exist supports the need for greater numbers of highly trained leaders in all fields who are knowledgeable about their culture and secure in their identity. In the field of education, Lynch and Charleston (1990) noted that American Indians, both male and female, are relatively new to educational administration and other types of formal leadership positions. In their article "The Emergence of American Indian Leadership in Education," they stressed that in order to understand American Indian leadership, one must first understand the context in which the entry of Indian people into administrative positions finally became a reality. Lynch and Charleston noted that it was not until the late 1960s that the relationship between the federal government and Indian nations began to change and Indian communities began to exercise control over their educational systems. At the beginning of the 2000s, there are many strong individuals who are leading change in education, yet the supply of qualified leaders has not yet met the demand. Without greater numbers of more highly trained Native American educational leaders in administration and teaching who can continue to lead change in education and who can contribute an understanding of the needs of native students, the educational gains made in the past 30 years may be lost, and the disparity between the educational outcomes of Native American and nonnative children will increase.

Therefore, it is important to understand native leadership and how it has been influenced by social, cultural, and historical contexts. One of the finest examples of native leadership in the history of Indian education can be found with groups of individuals who have been involved in advancing the tribal college movement over the last 30 years. In this chapter, we have chosen to examine this form of leadership because such knowledge is critical not only to our common growth and development as a nation, but to the growth and development of future educational leaders.

The purpose of this chapter is to present a beginning discussion in which we attempt to answer the questions: What appear to be the grounding elements of native leadership that moves educational policy, practice, and change among current and past tribal college leaders? What practical skills enhance the work of tribal college leaders? What challenges and opportunities do native leaders of tribal colleges face? What steps can be taken to ensure greater numbers of highly trained native educational leaders?

FRAMING LEADERSHIP

With the growing prominence of literature on culture-related leadership, the focus has begun to shift from a centralized perspective of leadership to one that is decentralized (see Reyes, 1993; Wheatley, 1994). This move recognizes the values of collectivity and community in Native leadership thought and practice. For example, Belasco and Stayer (1993) created an image of decentralized leadership with their metaphor of a flock of geese in which leadership changes repeatedly and responsibility is shared. De Pree (1989, 1997), using the Native American water carrier as a metaphor, suggested that leadership emerges from a fundamental principle; that everyone, regardless of position, is responsible for nourishing the good of the community. Within a tribal context, every person has a role to play, and each person's role is important to the whole (Arden & Wall, 1990; Bray 1996). The total of individual contributions results in a dynamic whole that includes many voices.

This recent explosion of "new" views of leadership is not so new to native communities. Leadership, as it has been practiced for generations among the native people of the Americas, is grounded on the principles of community, shared responsibility, and cultural appropriateness. Western theories of leadership are embedded in institutional structures that lend themselves to more hierarchical relationships and autocratic ways of leading. That is, leadership tends to focus on individuals in positions of power influencing followers to pursue organizational or societal goals. Native ways of leadership are built on fluid relationships and shared leadership. Such leadership is focused more on a community of skilled individuals involved in a process that contributes to the good of the community. Edward Benton-Banai, Ojibwe spiritual leader, stated: "A native leader is not known for what he has done for himself, but rather what he has done for his people" (1975, p. 1).

Don Coyhis (1993), founder of White Bison, in "Servant Leadership: The Elders Have Said Leadership is About Service," pointed out that leadership in a Western "separated" system is about individuals competing for power and control, whereas leadership in a native "interconnected" system is about cooperation, relationships, humility, patience, and sharing. Coyhis referred to a chart developed by Joann Sebastian Morris, that shows contrasting views of leadership according to Indian and non-Indian values (see Table 8.1). Coyhis concluded that differences between Euro-American and native perspectives of leadership require new models of practice that incorporate diverse experiences and worldviews.

Table 8.1
Contrasting Views on Leadership

Traditional Indian Values	Non-Indian Values
Cooperation	Competition
Group emphasis	Individual emphasis
Modesty	Self-attention
Passive	Active
Patience	Aggressiveness
Generosity/sharing	Saving
Nonmaterialistic	Materialistic
Work for current need	Work for the sake of work
Time always with us	Use every minute
Orientation to present	Orientation to future
Pragmatic	Theoretical
Respect for age	Respect for youth
Harmony with nature	Conquest over nature
Spiritual/mystical	Skeptical
Nonverbal	Verbal
Religion as a way of life	Religion as a segment of life
Indirect criticism	Direct criticism

Created by Joann Sebastian in 1980. Permission given to reprint.

Johnson (1997) developed a model of leadership that focuses on the type of leadership exhibited in the work of tribal college leaders. Entitled the *Osah gan gio* model, it focuses on native leaders as weavers of change. Johnson presented a contemporary understanding of a polyvocal, cooperative, context-rich view of native ways of practicing leadership. The metaphor for leadership, basket weaving, suggests that the weaver is the facilitator of a group whose purpose is to weave a basket that is both functional and aesthetically pleasing, and carries in its designs respect for tribal history and culture. The model emerged from a critical analysis of interviews with native educational leaders. It became evident that leaders emerged from the critical interplay of values and commitments; cultural, social and historical influences; and personal events that motivated and mobilized their actions, yet there appeared to be critical elements that were common among the native leaders who were interviewed. Five themes emerged as a common thread that guided both their ways of living and leadership, as they firmly believed that the two were interconnected. The five themes are as follows:

1. Leaders shared a commitment to serving their community by creating positive social change.
2. Leaders learned to claim their voice, to develop the courage to take risks and action, not only for themselves, but also for their people or their community.
3. Leaders demonstrated and modeled ways that education is key to cultural survival and self-determination.
4. Leaders traveled across boundaries to understand and bridge relationships with others who were different from themselves, and in the process, motivated and strengthened others' abilities to look out to the broader world and envision new possibilities for the future.
5. Leaders continually nurtured their inner spirit and sustained their soul in order to maintain a sense of balance in their lives and awareness that their life and work had meaning and purpose.

A Commitment to Serving the Community

Commitment to serving one's tribal community is a fundamental value of Indian life and leadership. Although native communities today continue to grow in their diversity, willingness to serve is an attribute that many tribal college leaders share. This strong sense of responsibility to use one's strengths, talents, and education to make a difference in the lives of individuals and families often originated in their childhood and came from several sources, including a caring family mentor, personal experiences, and their "school" and university education. In several cases, tribal college leaders indicated that one or more of their family members loved them deeply, encouraged them in positive ways, and played an instrumental role in instilling an attitude of service. Many leaders told remarkable stories about family and tribal members who modeled a strong conviction for and acted proactively to ensure equity and self-determination for Indian communities.

For many Native Americans, the effects of oppression and discrimination, often due to attendance at boarding schools or relocation (onto reservations as well as into urban centers) have translated into powerlessness, poverty, and pain. The hopelessness that breeds in these situations often has led to drug abuse, domestic violence, and health problems (to name only a few social ills). The educational leaders who were interviewed drew on their powerful experiences of living with these problems in ways that helped them shape policies and programs that provided an opportunity for individuals, families, and communities to support their own courses of action to achieve a better quality of life. Each leader could share an example of how these personal, often painful experiences played a powerful role in shaping his or her core values that motivated people to act.

Many leaders believed that serving their community was a tremendous responsibility that not only benefitted others, but also gave meaning to their lives. To serve their community "in a good way," many leaders sought the guidance of a spiritual and cultural elder or mentor who helped the leader think about his or her work as being greater than a single individual. Given the individualistic and materialistic world of the 21st century, it was often difficult for them to construct their lives as "giving of oneself for the good of others." This sometimes required relinquishing all ego, for example, by not making significantly more money than the janitor or the bus driver, and not being the "buck stops here" person. Instead, it meant holding sacred the covenant that decisions are often made by a community of people, not an individual. In addition, the cultural and spiritual elder or mentor could teach appropriate protocol, and many leaders cited instances in which these teachings helped them connect successfully with others in their community. The elders or mentor also taught them ways to nurture their inner strength so that they could more effectively deal with adversity and maintain their commitment to community during difficult times.

The Emergence and Claiming of One's Native Voice

The theme of loss of culture and language as well as native identity pervades Indian country and has led tribal college leaders to carry the torch for cultural revitalization and community healing. To do this work, tribal college leaders have developed a strong spirit (and a tough skin). For many of the interviewed leaders, the journey to claim one's native voice was filled with rich stories of challenges they faced in both the mainstream and Indian communities, personal and professional difficulties resulting from the effects of oppression and colonization, as well as family and community successes that made the journey worth traveling. Overall, tribal college leaders shared the importance of finding, claiming, and using one's native identity as a means to act for community. One former president of a native-controlled higher education institution shared her story regarding the importance of voice and her responsibility to train emerging native leaders:

I now serve as an advisor for a program that has been developed for emerging native leaders. One of their first activities in this program focuses on helping young natives with a tremendous potential to find their [native] voice. Those of us who advise have already learned through our own experiences that an individual must be aware of her own strengths and be able to assume responsibility for herself before she can lead and share responsibility for our community. One of the first activities that a spiritual leader gets them involved in is identifying and understanding where their source of "medicine" is and being able to articulate it to others.

Some of them already know the answers and are firmly grounded in who they are. For others, this ends up being a very personal journey of searching their roots, their family and tribal history, meeting relatives, and learning cultural ways. The whole group acts as a source of support by helping each individual begin where she is and then helping her move further along on her journey. In this journey, she learns to take risks, to act for herself and complete the search. For some, this means grieving the loss of language and culture and then healing, while for others, it means recognizing and giving thanks for the gifts of medicine that they were fortunate to receive in their growing-up years. You just see self-knowledge, self-esteem, and confidence grow in all of them as they find that their culture wasn't totally lost. Rather, it was inside them all along, waiting to be tapped into. Their competence as a leader definitely increases. It's proven to be a very powerful leadership development strategy, not only for these emerging leaders, but also for those of us who serve as advisors.

We look at these young leaders as "diamonds in the rough" who may need to spend some emotional energy looking for their strength. There are lots of competent people out there who are not empowered because they do not yet believe in their own competence. Unfortunately, too many of us [Native Americans] have had bad experiences with other national leadership programs that see us as troubled, disadvantaged, or dysfunctional from the moment they meet us. To them, we are just another rock that they throw back onto the reservation when we do not "sparkle," act or lead in the ways they think we should. (Personal Communication, Oct. 12, 1996)

Whether or not tribal college leaders grew up speaking their mother tongue and practicing their tribal ceremonies, all believed strongly in the importance of having a native spirit, voice, and identity. To many, this self-knowledge and cultural knowing required a commitment to lifelong learning through which they actively searched out opportunities to strengthen their personal awareness, their own inner strength, or as some described it, their own "medicine."

Claiming one's voice means developing the courage to take action, not only for oneself but also for the community. For the interviewed leaders, it meant developing the skills and knowledge needed to challenge the status quo, such as community mobilization, conflict resolution, communication, problem solving, and advocacy, as well as less tangible skills such as sustaining hope and inspiring action.

Education as Service is Key to Cultural Survival and Self-Determination

Although education is important, it sometimes is met with suspicion in native communities. Just possessing a college degree does not make one a leader in a native community. Instead, one's acts of service, demonstrated in tangible ways and with results that benefit the community, guide one to a leadership role. In speaking to the scholars who were charged to write this book, Dr. Dave Warren (Personal Communication, September 27, 2000) of the Santa Clara Pueblo, told a story about his son who had earned a graduate degree at a prestigious university and was returning to the pueblo. He shared, "My son, who I am proud of, will take his place at the back of the line. Regardless of his degree, he will need to learn his place in our community. He will have to use what he learned out there in ways to serve our community. Remember this, it is not your degree that makes you a leader, it is your service."

This message of service beyond the "degree" has been essential to the success of many tribal college leaders (many of whom hold graduate degrees). Green (1990) wrote:

> Leadership is validated and uniformly informed in our communities, by the invisibility of things that are associated with leadership in mainstream communities. Degrees, lists of achievements, lists of high-powered jobs, the wearing of power suits are nothing. What counts is how much we give to our communities ... This leadership can be given in various forms. You can be a peacemaker, an artist, a diplomat, a storyteller, an auntie, a grandmother, and a sister. You do not assess if you are a leader, the community does. (p. 66)

Many of the interviewed leaders indicated that they were often challenged to find ways to demonstrate to their communities that their higher education could serve as a valuable tool. They often demonstrated this in tangible ways, but the example given by all those who were interviewed was that of writing proposals and securing funding for programs that were greatly needed in the community. One leader pointed out:

> Once the elders could see that I was able to secure resources for them to be involved in protecting cultural ways, I could often count on their support for

other activities promoting education in our community. Being opposed by the elders because you're one of "those degreed Indians" can often be a major barrier to creating change. From my perspective, re-securing their support after I returned from college to my community was a major success.

Travelers Across Boundaries

This theme has dual meanings in both physical and spiritual dimensions of traveling. For example, many tribal college leaders have had the opportunity to travel to different reservations, college campuses, and communities to experience diverse cultures (both native and nonnative). These travels have broadened their global view and have shaped the ways in which they think about and practice leadership. Many of today's tribal college leaders travel to New Zealand to learn with the Maori who are successfully maintaining their language, culture, and sovereignty; to Hawai'i to visit with Native Hawaiians and other indigenous people to learn more about creating educational sovereignty (World Indigenous Peoples Conference on Higher Education, 1999); to Africa to meet with indigenous groups who are working to protect their land and resources; and to Australia to meet with peace advocates and to talk deeply about issues of race.

The dynamics of leadership influenced by this travel assists native educational leaders to become skilled in crossing cultural boundaries and to promote understanding across differences. Tribal college leaders become cultural brokers. Szasz (1994) indicated that, "the fluidity of their cultural movement is almost unconscious. They persist because the two or more worlds are important to them; each helps to define who they are; and each has a claim on part of their identity" (p. 10). These travels result in building relationships with other communities (native and nonnative) that foster successful, new educational programs, protection of tribal sovereignty, and the perpetuation of language and culture.

In the early 2000s, tribal college leaders formed a relationship with the Maori college leaders of the Wananga in New Zealand to cross cultural boundaries and promote understanding. Both groups planned to visit each other's land, communities, and institutions to share their educational solutions and challenges, and organizers hoped that their trip would lead to new alliances, as well as other exchanges among students, faculty, artists, political leaders, performers, and other groups that had not yet connected. Initially, each of the "culture brokers" leading this particular boundary crossing encountered and responded to opposition and resistance to the travel within their respective groups, yet the leaders persisted in enlisting others in this vision because they all shared a determination to help their respective group learn about other cultures, see the world as an extended community, and more effectively prepare their community members for life in an increasingly global society and international marketplace.

The spiritual rewards of travel varied across tribal educational leaders. Some said that traveling had offered them opportunities to see the world through a multicultural lens. Knowing that their Indian community existed within a living and ever-evolving global system of differences, a multicultural lens that supported self-sovereignty as well as global understanding was an asset. Currently, there is a need for leaders who are aware of changing global conditions and who have skill and experience in traveling across boundaries. In the near future, there will be a greater demand for leaders who can work across boundaries of race, culture, and faith to foster change by mobilizing communities to take action.

The Spirit and Soul of Native Leadership

There is no one model of native leadership, just as every basket has its own peculiar warp and weave, each reflecting the history, culture, and language of a community of people. However, at the core of these ways of knowing about leadership are the values and guiding life principles that connect the physical to the spiritual, the spiritual to the emotional, and the emotional to the intellectual, in an entwined, ever-evolving circle. The soul of native leadership is grounded on principles that reflect an inner strength, a meaning and purpose in one's life to make a difference in one's native community. This awareness is often referred to as spirituality.

Spirituality is recognized as an important component of leadership in many cultures, and should not be confused with religion. Lorraine Matusak (1997), a noted scholar on leadership, believed that a good leader possesses not only effective leadership skills, but also an inner strength or spirituality. In her book *Finding Your Voice*, she described spirituality as "the need to center and strengthen inner well-being and to maintain a sense of balance so as to effectively and ethically make an impact on our environment" (p. 35). She asserted that leaders must possess inner strength before they can transcend their own personal boundaries to support and serve others. Matusak's premise that effective leadership should be based on integrity, honesty, love, and respect for all humanity—with service as the primary motivation for the action—is in harmony with native ways of knowing about leadership.

The metaphor of the weaver brings together these five principles. As in basket making, leadership is a process that begins with a strong core and builds up and out in a holographic sense, with a circular, spiraling effect.

Like the weaver, the leader begins with a strong personal base that is deeply rooted in the spirit of his or her native history. Much like the basket maker, the tribal college leader is passionate about her or his art and the possibility of creating something new. Just as the artist organizes the dynamic process of weaving, the leader catalyzes the process of leadership by forming strong relationships with people and communities, refining and sharing visions that see people living a quality and self-determined life, empowering others to use their talents and skills to enhance the process and work together to generate change, and managing the tensions associated with the process. For the artist, the outcome is the basket that she or he wove. For the leader, the outcome is the social change that she or he mobilized.

PRACTICAL SKILLS: LESSONS LEARNED FROM TRIBAL COLLEGE LEADERS

In their monograph, Robbins and Tippeconnic (1985) identified characteristics of effective Indian educational leaders that affirm the five principles of *Osah gan gio* (Weavers of Change). The characteristics they noted are as follows:

1. A leader must be able to recognize that differences between native and nonnative people exist and are often incompatible. An effective educational leader will share information with both the native and the nonnative community in ways that promote respect, rather than contempt, for cultural differences.
2. A leader must possess skill in cross-cultural communications. She or he must be able to exchange ideas and convey concepts through such means as public speaking, writing proficiently, and serving as an ambassador for native concerns with groups such as educational administrators, congressional representatives, university representatives, and government officials.
3. A leader must be able to translate theory into practice so that formal educational experiences may be of practical benefit to the native community. This is particularly important for natives who are college graduates and want to return to their communities to improve social and economic conditions. Translating what they have learned in college into culturally acceptable practice is often a difficult task.
4. A leader must maintain a positive attitude toward and a deep commitment to the education of, by, and for American Indians. The commitment to education for Native Americans implies a respect for na-

tive heritage, cultures, and values. Oftentimes, the issues are so complex that it requires great strength for a leader not to become discouraged.

5.   A leader must have creativity and vision. Effective leaders must be able to develop new and innovative approaches to education and not be hampered by previous attempts to do what seems impossible. They must have a vision of how life could be better and plans to achieve that vision.

6.   A leader must demonstrate patience and tolerance with regard to various opinions and positions. Creating positive change can sometimes be very frustrating, especially when leaders must deal with various levels of bureaucracy, bureaucrats whose values are very different from those of the native community, and community members who are negative about any change.

7.   Finally, a leader must possess self-confidence and pride in being a Native American. This attitude is exhibited through care and concern for self but, more important, for family and the tribal community.

In the past 30 years, when contributions of leaders have been assessed in terms of how they have influenced the fiber of this country, the vast contributions of Native American educational leaders have gone largely unnoticed. As a result, Native American educational leaders often have been invisible or misrepresented. This not only adds to the misinformation about and stereotyping of native peoples that has been generated over the years, but also continues to diminish their humanity today (Bowker, 1993). As a result, a potentially rich source of information about leadership has been overlooked. This oversight contributes to the continuing denial of the dignity of native leaders, including their history, experiences, contributions to contemporary society, and distinct ways of approaching life and leading educational change. Listening to the stories of native educational leaders provides a means to determine how they define and enact leadership, as well as how they develop their leadership competencies.

THE CHALLENGES
FOR TRIBAL COLLEGE LEADERS

Many native leaders recognize the need for tribal colleges to be active participants in developing leaders who are skilled at addressing the complex issues facing Indian communities and educational institutions in the 21st century. This challenge requires tribal colleges to strengthen their capacity to mentor, educate, and provide leadership opportunities for their students, staff, and faculty in both the institution and in the community. Additionally, tribal colleges must work to develop partnership programs with other tribal colleges, postsecondary institutions, and nonprofit organizations that focus on strengthening leadership, management, and administrative skills.

Such partnerships require that mainstream postsecondary institutions participate actively in building their own capacity to educate larger numbers of Native American students. These institutions must work more effectively to (a) increase access and graduation of Native American students at all levels, (b) provide excellent scholarly programs that are culturally relevant, (c) develop learning communities that encourage and provide assistance for professional and personal growth, (d) support scholarship that advances indigenous knowledge, (e) increase the number of native faculty and staff, and (f) increase the institutions' understanding of and respect for Native American cultures.

Whereas both tribal colleges and mainstream postsecondary institutions must work to strengthen their programs that promote leadership development, national leadership development programs must also begin to recognize the value of the Native American voice. They must understand that the new voices at the table will include not only those that have been overlooked, but also the "different" voices, those voices that will challenge the status quo and traditional organizational structures by pressing for communities to participate in decision making. Investing in the development of new leadership voices will require enhancing individuals' capacity to participate more effectively in policymaking discussions that affect their lives, and assist them in becoming positional leaders, if they so desire. As leadership development programs invest in developing new leadership voices, they will face a number of challenges, such as entrenched prejudices and inequalities, the need to continually renew and expand new leadership voices, institutional and policy barriers that make it difficult to engage new voices, and the resistance of existing leaders. To eliminate these barriers, programs may need to broker relationships, provide technical assistance and resources, and recognize that these new efforts will take time and persistence.

An important feature of leadership development models should be an intergenerational focus. Providing opportunities for seasoned elders and scholars to share their knowledge with emerging leaders is an essential part of native ways of learning. Intergenerational programs should be built around purposeful activities through which group members can learn skills they will need to be leaders in their native communities. For example, a gathering could bring together current tribal college leaders and emerging leaders to learn more about shared visioning, team building, decision making, and conflict negotiation. These gatherings could also provide diverse opportunities to test one's courage and take risks in a safe and encouraging environment. Leadership development seminars should also provide opportunities to share wisdom, celebrate successes, and learn how to integrate native ways of thinking into one's own leadership practice.

Finally, a challenge for both tribal college leaders and native scholars is to be ever vigilant in recording the wisdom of elder leaders by creating respectful opportunities for them to share their gifts. Sharing their rich knowledge of native ways of leadership and the strong bonds between action and the spirit of one's lineage is one way that native elders can give to their community. In a major initiative focused on Native American higher education in the late 1990s, leaders of both tribal and mainstream colleges met annually to network, share successes and challenges, and strengthen their leadership skills. At every meeting, elders were invited to share their reflections on the work that was in progress. Through the use of storytelling, readings, songs, poetry, jokes, dance, and ceremony, elders praised, scolded, encouraged, educated, challenged, inspired, teased, and goaded participants to pursue their goals. In every evaluation of the networking conference, elder reflections were rated as the most beneficial portion of the conference. In appreciation, the participants highly respected, loved, and frequently honored the elders.

IMPLICATIONS FOR FUTURE STUDY

There are a number of activities that tribal colleges, mainstream colleges and universities, and other institutions can do to support leadership development in the native community. However, because of a lack of understanding regarding native ways of leadership, further study is needed. First, native scholars should continue to use native leaders' life stories as a methodology for studying native ways of leadership. It is through the telling of the story that the wisdom of elders is best captured. And it is through the multiple and rich interpretations of these stories that we can better understand the synergistic interrelationships among the individual, the community, and the cultural/spiritual core that define living and leadership.

This approach to gathering and presenting native ways of leadership can be further enhanced through exploring how cultural values and spiritual principles construct native ways of living and leadership. The approach might begin with Native American leaders but can be extended to embrace the leadership of First Peoples in Canada, Native Alaskans, Native Hawaiians and other people of the Pacific, and other indigenous groups. Building a foundation of literature that explores and seeks to understand indigenous ways of leadership will establish a knowledge base that is critical to supporting commitments to self-determination, native-community building, and revitalizing language and culture.

A CONCLUDING STORY

Current research and study of native leadership in tribal colleges have affirmed that knowledge and enactment of leadership are shaped by social, historical, and cultural experiences. Tribal college leaders, drawing on their depth of self and cultural identity, have become skillful and passionate "basket weavers." Many have overcome many obstacles (e.g., economic, political, structural, and human resources) as they labor to gather the tools and materials they need to provide the best possible educational opportunity for native people. To honor those who have gone before us, our families and friends who are here now, and the generations yet to come, we share a story passed on to Dr. Valorie Johnson by her grandfather, David Owl.

One time there was a leader who had four children. There came a time when the father had to choose one to be the leader in his place. He couldn't decide which one was the most able. He knew they could do all these other things. They were good protectors and caretakers; he could not make a decision from these things. He wanted to find out what was in their hearts.

This man's children had grown into fine young adults. The time came when the father needed to select one of the children to take his place as leader of the family. It was not always the oldest child who took the father's place; more often it was the one that showed the most ability. The time came to put them to a test to determine which one would take his place. It would be a simple test, but one of endurance and perseverance.

Early one morning the father called his children together. He was dressed in his most elegant clothing so they would remember how he looked and would be impressed with the importance of the leader's role. He said, "I want you all to go to the top of the mountain and bring me back a gift." The children had the same upbringing and were instilled with the same ideals. They all started out. Their father watched them until they were out of sight, and then returned to his lodge, where he rested and waited.

Early in the afternoon, the first child returned. She brought back a beautiful stone. It was perfectly smooth, an unusual shape, and was a beautiful color. She said, "My father, I picked this stone up at the base of the mountain. It is beautiful, and I thought you would like it." Her father thanked her and accepted the gift.

A short time later, the second child returned home. He brought back a pine branch, taken from a tree that stood tall and stately on the tree line. "Oh father, I have brought this from high on the mountain. I would like you to have it. It has been a long journey." His father thanked him and accepted it.

The third child returned some time later. He had with him some moss he gathered from up on the snowline. It was green, soft and thick. "My father, far up on the mountain I found this moss. I thought you would like it." His father thanked him and accepted the gift.

The fourth child returned after sunset. She walked with a buoyant step, and her face was radiant. "My father, I bring nothing in my hands as a gift. Today I stood on the top of the mountain. I gave thanks to the Creator for all that he has given to us—the wind, the plants, the animals, our warriors. I looked in one direction to the east and saw the place of the rising sun, the sign of a new day. I looked to the south and saw a clear blue lake beyond the mountains. I turned to the west and stood there for a long time watching the place where the sun disappears, watching the beautiful colors change as the day disappeared into night. I then turned to the north and saw the snow of the north-country and felt the cold wind blowing on my face. Today I have seen a beautiful world that we must care for. I bring you this." Her father thanked her and accepted the gift.

To his children he said, "Tomorrow, I will give you my answer." The next day, he called his children together. "The child who brought me no gift at all in her hands is the one that will be the next leader. She has brought me the greatest gift of all. She went to the top of the mountain as I instructed and witnessed and recognized the qualities of the four directions—the east, the south, the west, and the north. She has a keen mind and a good spirit. She is sharp and perceptive. She has a heart that is strong, steadfast, and loving. She has connected her heart and mind to view, understand, and give thanks for the boundless wonders of the Creator. She will serve us well and make a good leader.

REFERENCES

Arden, H., & Wall, S. (1990). *Wisdomkeepers: Meetings with Native American spiritual elders.* Hillsboro, OR: Beyond Words Publishing, Inc.

Belasco, J. A., & Stayer, R. C. (1993). *Flight of the Buffalo: Soaring to excellence, Learning to let employees lead.* New York: Warner Books.

Benham, M., & Cooper, J. (Eds.). (2000). *Indigenous educational models for contemporary practice: In our mother's voice.* Mahwah, NJ: Lawrence Erlbaum Associates.

Benton-Banai, E. B. (1975). *A history-coloring book of the Ojibway Indians, Book No. 1: The Ojibway Creation Story. A Mishonis Book.* St. Paul, Minn.: Author.

Bowker, A. (1993). *Sisters in the blood: The education of women in Native America.* Newton, MA: WEEA Publishing Center.

Bray, M. T. (1996, November). *Contrasting American and Native American views of leadership*. Paper presented at the annual meeting of the University Council for Educational Administration, Louisville, KY.

Coyhis, D. (1993). Servant leadership: The elders have said leadership is about service. *Winds of Change, 8*(3), 23–24.

De Pree, M. (1989). *Leadership is an art*. New York: Doubleday.

De Pree, M. (1997). *Leading without power: Finding hope in serving community*. San Francisco: Jossey-Bass.

Green, R. (1990). The Pocahontas perplex: The image of Indian women in American culture. In E. C. Dubois & V. Ruiz (Eds.), *Unequal sisters: A multicultural reader in U.S. women's history* (pp. 15–21). New York: Routledge.

Johnson, V. J. (1997). *Weavers of change: Portraits of Native American women educational leaders*. Unpublished doctoral dissertation, Michigan State University, East Lansing, Michigan.

Lynch, P. D., & Charleston, M. (1990). The emergence of American Indian leadership in education. *Journal of American Indian Education, 29* (2), 1–10.

Matusak, L. (1997). *Finding your voice: Learning to lead … Anywhere you want to make a difference*. San Francisco: Jossey-Bass.

Noley, G. (1992). *Educational reform and American Indian cultures*. Palo Alto, CA: American Institutes for Research in the Behavioral Sciences.

Reyes, R. C. (1993). *Community organizing: Strategies for recruitment and retention*. Washington, DC: National Institute for Literacy.

Robbins, R., & Tippeconnic, J. W., III. (1985). *American Indian education leadership*. Tempe, AZ: Center for Indian Education.

Szasz, M. C. (1994). *Education and the American Indian*. Albuquerque, NM: University of New Mexico Press.

Tippeconnic, J. W., III. (1992). The education of American Indians Policy, practice and future Direction. In D. E. Green & T. V. Tonnesen (Eds.), *American Indians: Social justice and public policy*. Milwaukee, WI: University of Wisconsin, Institute on Race and Identity.

Wheatley, M. J. (1994). *Leadership and the new science: Learning about organization from an orderly universe*. San Francisco: Berrett-Koehler.

White House Conference on Indian Education. (1992). *Final report of the White House Conference on Indian Education*. Washington, DC: Author.

World Indigenous Peoples Conference on Education. (2002). www.fnahec.org/wipce2002.

9

Culture and Language Matters: Defining, Implementing, and Evaluating

Maenette K. P. Benham
Michigan State University
with
Henrietta Mann
Montana State University

INTRODUCTION: WHY LANGUAGE AND CULTURE? WHAT WE KNOW

The crisis of Native American languages can be summarized as follows: unless current trends are reversed, and soon, the number of extinctions seems certain to increase. Numerous tongues—perhaps one-third of the total—are on the verge of disappearing along with their last elderly speakers. Many others are not far behind. And even among the most vigorous 10 percent, their hold upon the young is rapidly weakening. In short, Native American languages are becoming endangered species.   (Crawford, 1995, p. 21)

Language and culture identify a cohesive set of worldviews, such as, values, concepts, and beliefs, that are essential to the life of human beings. Language, through its many texts, embraces the human agency of competencies and potentialities as it embodies the meaning, knowledge, and intellect of a community of people. Indeed, their language forms the actions of people, illuminated in their cultural practices, such as, chants, dances, rituals, beadwork, basket weaving, pottery, and farming. Because language and culture are the lifeblood of a people, they must be visible; otherwise, they will die. It is, therefore, the responsibility of native institutions of education and the communities they serve to create a safe place for native languages and cultures to survive and thrive (see also Crawford, 1995; Yazzie, 1999). Tribal colleges have taken up this daunting charge, working with their communities not only to validate both their native knowledge and worldviews through language and culture, but also to integrate contemporary knowledge and worldviews into the learning experience. It is our purpose in this chapter to discuss the work around language and culture, present an overview of the work across tribal colleges, and in light of multiple challenges provide ideas for next steps.

THIS IS A POLITICAL STAND
AND, MORE IMPORTANTLY, A SPIRITUAL JOURNEY

Children are not speaking Crow today. Why? Because of the media, cable TV, economic factors, lack of institutional settings, isolating elders in nursing homes. Education is mainstream; it doesn't value our language. Because of the lack of resources, there has not been a coordinated effort to bring together language and language instruction ... But more than that, we still need to address the real problems that led to the loss of language. There needs to be a great awakening. [Cultural] identity happens over time only when we learn the psychology of our culture. (Dr. Lanny Real Bird, personal communication, March 27, 2000)

The Flathead Reservation's fluent tribal language speakers recently produced the following list of local obstacles that still mitigate against tribal language renewal: lack of interest, poor self-image among many Indians, no consistency between classes at the various age levels or between the few schools that even offer such classes, limited language practice in the home, low pay for teachers, few Indian teachers, difficulty of maintaining immersion standards, and little parental assertiveness toward getting Indian languages included in reservation school curricula. (Brod & McQuiston, 1997, p. 153)

Advocating for native languages and cultures as the ontological, epistemological, and pedagogical foundation of learning and teaching has become a political movement that has been challenged by both native and nonnative alike. Boyer (1993) pointed out that, over time, native people have been entrenched in fear and disengagement from their native languages and culture because of a blanket of "capitalistic economy, corruption of traditional spirituality, as well as Christianization" (p. 15). The internal barriers that Boyer went on to identify appear between those who are literate and fluent in their mother tongue and those who are not, thereby developing a two-tier system within the community. Advocates of language and culture instruction confront the desires of native parents and students to be fully assimilated into a mainstream western language and worldview. At the same time, some people believe that language and culture should be taught at home, not in schools. Indeed, the concern of colonized people (globally) appears to lie in the ambiguity and uncertainty of the purpose, meaning, and benefits of language and culture instruction.

Over time, social policy toward American Indians has sought to isolate, acculturate, and amalgamate native communities in an effort to solve the "Indian problem." School policy, which assigned native children and youths to mainstream settings, served to deepen attitudinal chasms within native communities through the introduction of social identifiers to include new values of individualism, pragmatism, and materialism (Crawford, 1996). Furthermore, the influence of demographic shifts (due to migration and isolation in urban settings), economics, and mass media and pop culture has complicated these tensions. Although empirical research now indicates greater student success in educative programs that are grounded in native language and culture, supporters of these programs continue to face attitudinal and economic challenges (see Estrada & Vasquez, 1981; Rosier & Holm, 1980; Troike, 1978; Trueba, 1988; VanHamme, 1996).

In light of these challenges, advocating for language and culture becomes a political stance because it means that one believes that native sovereignty matters, that native people have the right to engage in matters that are directive and purposeful, and that native communities are empowered to act on important matters. That all indigenous people have the right to selfdetermination and governance, something that has been systematically denied them, is at the core of this movement. Taking this stand is a firm statement against an external monolingual language education that places the control of native language and culture in the hands of nonindigenous governing institutions. Hence, native communities have the right to own their culture and language "in the sense that it denotes a system of symbols by means of which a people impose meaning and order in their world" (Ortiz, 1990, p. 5). This idea is grounded in the rich and complex stories that reveal the interconnectedness of language and culture and is the "picture of the way things in sheer actuality are, their concept of nature, of self, of society" (Geertz, 1973, p. 127).

When I was 30 years old, I made the statement in a speech I was delivering in Minneapolis that my generation is the last generation that speaks Ojibwe fluently. When I was 40, I made that same statement in a lecture before a class at the University of Minnesota at Duluth. I'm 52 now and I just made the same statement a couple of weeks ago in another lecture. I don't want to be saying it when I'm 60 or 70 years old.

(Larry Smallwood, as cited in Hinkle, 2000, p. 14)

Given that all people have the right to define their worldviews, valuing native knowledge and intellect engages human agency in an action of acknowledging that one's language and culture are endangered, and then committing to doing something about it and knowing that something can be done. The Native American Languages Act (NALA), passed in 1990, marked the beginning of federal recognition, but it is a belated policy that has had only a small impact on the needs of native people. Engaging in activities that place language and culture in the center requires that individuals and institutions come to know, value, and practice the depth and richness of their unique heritage and the dynamics of their culture (e.g., values, norms, and behaviors through ritual and ceremony). In addition, valuing mother tongue and culture recognizes the unique needs of diverse native communities as well as their strengths, independence, and interdependence. The power of diversity across native communities must be respected; after all, native people of the North and South American continents were diverse long before the arrival of westerners and have remained so despite many efforts to homogenize them. It is through building a foundation of diversity and respect of native languages and cultures that empowerment of both the individual and the community can be actualized (see also Reyhner & Eder, 1992; Schorr, 1989; Tozer, Violas, & Senese, 1998).

My mother had several names, one was Crow Woman. Why? Because she was born at Crow Agency in 1893. My grandfather was a chief, Hollow Horn Bear. He went to Crow Agency in 1893 to make peace. He said, "We're all fenced in and unless we work together we'll all die." During the meeting, my mother was born. My mother didn't encourage me to go to school. I was the youngest. My grandfather died in 1913, a result of jealousy from another tribe. Poisoned. We forgave them. Simple statement. We have these stories, every tribe and every nation, how we are related. All our languages were invaded just as our land were invaded and controlled by the government. Our language is a different culture, different philosophy, it has a religion. We learn new things today, new words. We debate words. We meet twice a week, sit down, and say here's a word. How do you define it? Where did it come from? Who taught you it? We have subcultures in our language. We have to do what we need to do not what others think we should do. At a meeting like this, a Hopi gentleman spoke. He said his tribe has similar problems (defining a lexicon). Most recent problem is talking to tourist. They ask to take our pictures, come to our village. One fellow was sitting on the ground and a tourist jumped out of his car and took his picture. The tourist said, "Sir, are you brown from the sun?" The old Indian guy said, "No ma'am, I'm Jim from the earth."   (Albert White Hat, March, 2001)

Empowerment and engagement are powerful concepts that press individuals and communities to define their own direction and use of resources (e.g., land, human, and cultural). Taking control of how resources are distributed in educational institutions is a powerful and promising step for native communities as they define their sovereignty. However, as Van Hamme (1996) noted, "unfortunately, in many other instances, the process has been hampered by reservation poverty, inconsistencies in federal financial support, and interference by the BIA [Bureau of Indian Affairs]" (p. 23). What we are learning through the work of tribal colleges, in their respective communities, is that economic development plans that address these issues, but are also grounded in the native communities' spiritual and cultural values, can be a significant educative force.

In chapter 5, which focuses on community building, Jack Barden gives examples of how tribal communities can improve their economies and quality of life without relinquishing control to an external group (for example see, The Sicangu Enterprise Center at Rosebud Reservation, organized by Sinte Gleska University, and the Mazaska program at Pine Ridge Reservation, developed by Oglala Lakota College). At the forefront of this work are the tribal colleges (Houser, 1991). These examples, coupled with the successful revitalization of the Hebrew language and culture in Israel, teach us many valuable lessons about our own political struggle. Perhaps a primary lesson is that language and culture are the foundational elements that can support a principled direction for community building toward a new polity that is native control.

> First, we need to pray to establish a spiritual focus. Education is a sovereign right and language is the key; it is the lifeblood of a culture. So we must study indigenous thought and ways to preserve, revitalize and maintain who we are as Native peoples. Tribal governments need to be serious about the education of our youth; we need to teach the babies the language of our people.
> (Dr. Henrietta Mann, personal communication, March 29, 2000)
>
> There is no divide between the spirit and education.
> (Dr. Norbert Hill, personal communication, March 29, 2000)

To achieve and sustain sovereignty, engagement, and empowerment through the daily and natural use of native language and culture will take

the commitment and energy of individuals and communities to contem-
plate what has passed and, with reverence, to move forward. The one dynamic that will bind together this fragile and complex set of goals is the
spirituality and sacred covenants passed to native people through the
mother tongue and cultural practices. This unity of spirit is rooted in the
ways of knowing that are embedded in every aspect of native life and is
deeply respectful of and concerned with the interconnections among family, kin (extended family), clan, tribe, intertribal bonds, and external allies
of native communities. Keeping our indigenous knowledge alive in a contemporary world ensures that what is instructive and what promotes life is
respectful of native people's living history and ceremonies, the health and
well-being of both people and communities; the cognitive, affective, and
cultural education of children and youth; and the economic stability and
self-governance that identify a sovereign people.

THEORIZING OUR PRACTICE

Over a hundred years ago, our life connection was taken away. The bison was
an essential part of many native people, socially, economically, and spiritu-
ally. Extermination of the bison was an assault on native people. For over a
120 years we've been disconnected from an essential part of our culture.
Some have said bring the buffalo back. Questions were raised: How do we reconnect with something taken away for 120 years? We have our stories about
how the buffalo came. We talked to presidents of the tribal colleges. Lots of
politics. We agreed it had to be done as started with four universities. Then
six more said they wanted in. Our goal was to bring the buffalo back. The issues: Whose land? How do you sustain it? How does this compare to the cat-
tle industry?

It (the buffalo) is our foundation. We've done traditional kills, you have to be
there to understand the ceremonies. Some things have to be told in our language. Our next step is to bring back the bison to our diet. Nutrition is important because diabetes is rampant. We're going to do a full court press on
wellness. Through the buffalo we will reconnect to our relatives, they will
take care of us once again. We don't need legislation in congress to do this, we
are going to take care of our own. (Phil Baird, March, 2001)

What we have learned through the Native American Higher Education
Initiative (NAHEI) and other language-immersion programs is that just in-
troducing (in a celebratory, folkloric, festival manner) one's mother tongue
to the learning and teaching environment will not work! The process must
be coupled with other improved features of the learning and teaching expe-

rience. Current language-immersion initiatives have taught us many important lessons, one of which is that a model of learning and teaching should be grounded in the principles of the native community (see Benham & Cooper, 2000). For example, Genny Gollnick (2000), Oneida, described a philosophical foundation of learning that comes from the teachings of the Peacemaker, which forms the universal laws of the Longhouse. This message is presented through the use of a tree metaphor, which speaks to peace, stillness, well-being, and power. At the Fort Peck Community College Montessori School, traditional and contemporary learning is grounded on Assiniboine spiritual respect for the Tree of Life traditions. Theorizing the language and cultural practices of NAHEI-funded programs, then, suggests forwarding a native epistemological model that defines native/indigenous worldviews of ways of being and regarding knowing.

The model presented here is founded on three principles that emerge across the Initiative's programs. The key principles include:

1. Learning that leads to sovereignty, engagement, and empowerment begins with an individual's spiritual and cultural, emotional, physical, and cognitive strength and self-esteem.
2. An individual's learning must embrace interrelated disciplines, including the humanities, professions, social sciences, and natural sciences; thereby, learning is balanced, equitable, and develops high ethical standards in natives for living in a contemporary world.
3. The learner, with a strong inner core, can then be challenged to design solutions or actions that address social, political, cultural, and economic issues that affect wellness, the family and tribe/clans, and the land, water, and natural resources that sustain life.

The model can best be presented in three dimensions, perhaps using the metaphor of a basket or a clay pot. The concentric circles of the model illustrate the principle that learning begins with a strong "learner/self" that can then reach out to extended family members, tribal/indigenous communities, land and water (and other natural resources), and regional, national, and global communities. Understanding the interrelatedness of these important elements of community leads to respect for people and culture, action, well-being, and nature represented in the four poles (see Fig. 9.1).

The directionality of these poles symbolizes the cyclical nature of a woven basket as it moves from East to South and onward to the West and North, and back again to the East. In the East, one learns respect for people and art, and it is here that we begin with learning our mother tongue and

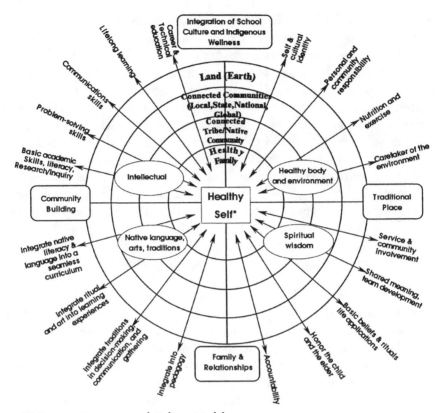

FIG. 9.1.   Language and Culture Model.

the origin of our ceremonies and stories (humanities). The East is the beginning. Moving to the South, one learns respect for doing good work through vocations (professions). This is where we learn the skills that will help us meet the challenges of climbing the mountain. In the West, we learn respect for the health and well-being of ourselves and our communities (social sciences). It is here that we shed our baggage, the colonial mindset and effects of boarding school education, and become committed to the good works of building relationships and community grounded on traditional truths. As we turn to the North, we learn to respect and be the stewards of nature (natural sciences). This is the illumination of our sacred covenant to sustain life, where we serve, and where we begin our journey to learn more.

This journey illuminates the principle that learning must embrace the academic disciplines of the humanities, professions, social sciences, and natural sciences. And it suggests that the learning journey includes both native traditional knowledge and contemporary knowledge as it weaves a strong community basket. This is revealed in each of the four quadrants that cut across each concentric circle. Within the spiritual, a person learns the stories, ceremonies, and art of her or his lineage that are passed through mother-tongue instruction. This spiritual strength defines a way of living that supports a native cultural identity and integrity, which builds a strong sense of affective balance. The spiritual and affective balance of self can lead to expressions of communal wholeness and stewardship expressed in the concentric circles of the model. In the third quadrant, physical health and well-being links the importance of a healthy mind, body, and spirit. Both native and nonnative language and cultural norms need to be balanced in this quadrant as individuals and communities work collectively to govern fairly and inclusively. The final quadrant, the cognitive (intellectual growth), honors a diverse knowledge base that supports an individual's fluency across social venues.

Using this model, educational scholars, teachers, leaders, and policymakers can think more broadly, more inclusively, about the content of and the approach to learning experiences. In addition, the model takes into account each unique community's circular and cyclical ways of viewing the world. In many cases, the articulation of this model must begin with the oral-narrative truth, for example, beginning with elders and storytellers/poets, as well as with the family unit, and moving onward to the clan, the tribe, and the whole community. The first step is to think deeply and thoroughly about the philosophical and spiritual constructs of one's culture and language, thereby preparing the language to be taught and to be the medium of instruction in a formal school or learning setting. Begin by clearly articulating the guiding principles for learning that is grounded in the community's unique native language, history, and culture. Ask the question: What is essential about our native way of knowing and being that must be illuminated in both the pedagogy and curricular materials? The following are two programs that exemplify the model.

Brigham Young University—Hawai'i

The focus of the work at Brigham Young University—Hawai'i has been to support the development of the Center for Hawaiian Language and Cultural Studies. The aim of this center is to collaborate with Native Hawaiian language and culture experts (community members and elders) to create a Native Hawaiian studies major and to network Native Hawaiian language and culture teachers. A lesson learned about creating this major project within a traditional, mainstream university setting was the amount of time and energy project directors committed to building relationships with Native Hawaiian language and culture scholars, as well as community *kupuna* (elders).

At the same time, project directors spent a good deal of time nurturing relationships within the university (e.g., with department faculty and chairpersons, college deans, and university administrators). Taking the time, early on, to be inclusive and informative has proven to be a successful strategy. After careful program and course development, two new language courses were introduced, which used materials from traditional Native Hawaiian epics that were compiled in 1902. In addition, a course on Hawaiian culture, a course on the importance of caring for the land with a unique hands-on lab experience, and a course (with a lab) on traditional practices for nurturing and caring for the ocean were introduced. This last course is unique in that it is intended to help students understand the important links between the land and the sea.

This initiative illustrates the native epistemological model forwarded in this chapter. A primary aim of the Center's 3-year program is to support the development (or recovery) of Native Hawaiian identity through language and cultural ceremonies. This learning process not only recognizes the need to begin with the individual, but also to include family and community in the journey. The courses reveal a respect for the humanities, the teaching profession, the social sciences, and the natural sciences as they reach across the academic disciplines to include study of art and culture, education, and natural resources. Finally, the work of students to actively participate in their communities to be stewards of the land and sea, to teach language and culture, and to be role models appears to be having an effect. In the second year of this program, the Center and its students conduct and teach Hawaiiana protocols and cultural ways. In the third year, the Center supports local K–12 and elder learning experiences, and has linked with other indigenous Pacific Island groups.

Project HOOP

Dr. Duane Champagne, Hanay Geiogamah, and Dr. Jaye Derby lead the Project HOOP (Honoring Our Origins and People through Native Theatre, Education, and Community Development). This program is a collaboration between The University of California, Los Angeles (UCLA) and Sinte Gleska University. The program presents a dynamic process that illuminates the elements of the epistemological model and values of community building. Project HOOP is an academic and artistic program that is delivered through the medium of native theatre. Its goal is to present opportunities and experiences that build community cultural awareness and knowing.

In its first 2 years, Project HOOP developed adult theatre programs and a summer youth theatre camp (in collaboration with the American Indian Relief Fund). Using rich talking circles with community members, important collaborations were formed with tribal health departments that have resulted in a video series, theatrical performances, and written information about diabetes. The project's effort to develop course materials that integrate native theatre into learning has resulted in the publication of *Stories of our Way: An Anthology of American Indian Plays* (1999) and *American Indian Theatre in Performance: A Reader* (2000). The project includes cultural scholars and native artists in residence, as a means of engaging youths and community members in learning their own language and culture. The program staffs at both UCLA and Sinte Gleska University are developing academic curriculum tools, with an interdisciplinary focus, that can be shared across the disciplines. The Project HOOP Manual will contain descriptions of course work, syllabi, and potential funding sources to sustain and further develop an arts-in-education curriculum. In 2000, Project HOOP received a Fund for the Improvement of Post Secondary Education (FIPSE) grant to continue and expand its work to the College of Menominee and the Institute of American Indian Arts (IAIA), and to publish a third anthology of native plays.

HOW A NATIVE EPISTEMOLOGICAL MODEL IS TRANSLATED INTO EFFECTIVE POLICIES AND PRACTICES

Educational policies and practices that enhance learning and student success built on a native epistemological model of mother-tongue language and native culture must include; (a) preparation of mother-tongue bilingual teachers and teacher aides, (b) leadership of cultural experts, including tribal and community elders, (c) thoughtful planning and dissemination of effective and quality teaching tools, (d) critical development of evaluation and assessment tools to measure accountability and academic achievement, and (e) a community learning model that involves adults and families in the education process. Tribal colleges, because of their sovereign status (see Stein, chap. 2, this volume) and because "more than any other single institution … [they] are changing lives and offering real hope for the future" (Boyer, 1995, p. 2), should, and in many cases have, become a nurturing venue for language and culture instruction.

Preparation and Certification of Native Teachers

Because D. Michael Pavel and his coauthors present a thorough and thoughtful chapter on teacher preparation in this book (see chap. 10, this volume), suffice it to say here that preparing native/mother-tongue bilingual teachers and teacher's aides (including nonnative staff) is essential to reviving and engaging mother-tongue instruction. Pavel, Larimore, and VanAlstine argue that teachers must be certified (at both native/tribal controlled and mainstream postsecondary institutions) in both their academic/disciplinary area *and* their native/mother-tongue. (See, for example, the American Indian Language and Culture Specialist Certification, Chief Dull Knife College, Lame Deer, Montana; Oneida Teacher Certification—Wisconsin; Native Hawaiian Teacher Certification at University of Hawai'i—Hilo, Hawai'i; and College of the Menominee Nation, Keshena, Wisconsin). This certifying mechanism not only values the mother tongue, but also links teacher learning and preparation to national academic standards (see, Chester, 1997; LaPlante & Carlson, 1992; Sianjina, Cage, & Allen, 1996).

Recent studies of American Indian educational programs that integrate language and culture into the curriculum provide helpful pedagogical guidelines to teachers (see Pavel, Larimore, & VanAlstine, chap. 10, this volume). For instance, teachers should learn to recognize the need for students to develop an understanding of self and to develop a positive self-image, learn how to help students understand and deal with issues of racism, and learn the relevancy of traditional aspects of language and culture to contemporary life. For example, at Chief Dull Knife College, language and culture specialists have been charged to develop the Northern Cheyenne curriculum and certification rubric for Montana State's American Indian Language and Culture Specialist Certification (Class 7 Certification).

Prospective teachers need to be recruited and supported during their college experience and throughout their professional careers. An example of this approach is the Diné Teacher Education Program at Diné College in Tsaile, Arizona (formerly Navajo Community College). This program has been growing and evolving over the last 12 years, and is funded by a number of private, federal, and tribal resources. Their efforts have produced a coherent elementary teacher education program across an A.A. (first 2 years of their program) and a B.A. degree (the last 2 years of their program), and have partnered successfully with Northern Arizona University, Fort Lewis College, and the University of New Mexico—Gallup. In 1999, they had 19 graduates, 18 of whom are teaching. Evaluators noted that most of these students had transferred to Diné from other institutions (rather than transferring out of a tribal college) to participate in this program. An attribute of the program is its attention to native student-related issues, including recruitment, counseling, apprenticeship, and assessment. For example, Diné currently admits between 13 and 16 cohort students each fall (they were into their fifth cohort in fall, 2000), and in partnership with the Navajo Department of Higher Education, teacher education students can receive scholarships.

Not only does the Diné program attend to the needs of its students, but the cultural integrity of the program is kept to a high standard through oversight from the Diné Educational Philosophy Committee. Although the Diné Teacher Education Program Curriculum Center is still under construction, faculty have worked hard to integrate cultural aspects into the entire teacher education program. Students begin their program with an orientation ceremony and learn more about Navajo history and culture through similar ceremonies and classroom work. Currently, Diné is creating professional development modules to ensure that current teachers can remain true to Diné language and culture in their daily teaching practices. Additionally, graduates are often encouraged to pursue a master's of education degree, offered at Diné (accredited by Arizona State University) during the summer months.[1]

Preparation of Native Educational Leaders (K–12 Schools)

In addition to preparing and certifying teachers in native languages, tribal colleges are focusing on developing educational leaders who have both the vision and the management skills to lead native educational institutions into the 21st century. In chapter 8, Johnson, Benham, and VanAlstine present examples of leadership preparation programs for youths, community leaders, and elders. The authors suggest that tribal colleges, in partnership with tribal government, community service organizations, and cultural leaders, must build into the college experience multiple opportunities for strengthening leadership in areas of policy analysis, policy development and implementation, assessment, and communication skills. Examples of successful programs at mainstream institutions of higher education include those at Pennsylvania State University under the guidance of Dr. Gerald Gipp and Dr. John Tippeconnic, III; Montana State University under the leadership of Dr. Wayne Stein; and the National Institute for Native Lead-

---

[1]There are several excellent examples of teacher education programs (e.g., OKSALE at Northwest Indian College, and Haskell University) that are enhanced by their continued development of instructional tools and strategies. They are discussed further in the chapter by Pavel, Larimore, and VanAlstine.

ership in Higher Education (NINLHE), currently housed at the University of New Mexico, under the guidance of Benny Shendo, Jr.

Many innovative programs have been instituted at tribal colleges and universities. For example, at Oglala Lakota College, a goal has been to increase the number of Native American administrators in K–12 schools. Throughout current collaboration with the University of South Dakota, a Lakota leadership master's degree in educational administration/leadership has been developed, with a focus on elementary and secondary school certification. As a result, in February, 1999, 31 native students were enrolled in this program. The start-up for the program was funded in part by the W. K. Kellogg Foundation, with in-kind contributions from both Oglala Lakota College and the University of South Dakota. Oglala Lakota College will continue to resource (budget and planning) this collaboration and degree program.

Programs to support leadership development for people of all ages require more thought and engagement by many levels of education and community groups. At a recent networking meeting of tribal colleges and universities, much of the discussion focused on the need to build leadership development programs across the life span, beginning with elementary school children. Leaders of the American Indian College Fund and the American Indian Higher Education Consortium Student Congress supported this agenda. The group suggested that, at the elementary school level, curriculum and instruction should provide native youths with an opportunity to learn to value their cultural values and traditions, speak their native language, and understand the spiritual foundations of their heritage.

At the middle school level, youth should be given opportunities to create a vision for themselves, their families, and their communities. They should be taught the value of collaborating and being responsible for themselves and their brothers and their sisters through experiential learning (e.g., Upward Bound). During the high school years, student leaders should begin to situate their learning and vision within their native community(ies) and more globally. Having an opportunity to visit with students from other tribes, from other states, and from other countries (diverse races/ ethnicities) would encourage student leaders to go beyond racism and toward understanding. TCUs are committed to provide the structure and academic balance to support the dreams of native youths. Many of the participants spoke highly of internship opportunities for college-aged students in a variety of venues, both local and national.

Although there was a good deal of focus on the K–12 and college-age years, discussion soon turned to building leadership development opportunities for individuals midcareer, people returning to school in their 30s and

40s, and elders. Mana Forbes, a Maori leader from Te Wananga O Aotearoa (an institution similar to tribal colleges), reminded the group that everyone in the community plays a leadership role, hence, everyone should have the opportunity to fine tune her or his skills and to learn new ones. Although it has become cliché, the Iroquois philosophy, "It takes a village to teach one child," has deep meaning in light of community efforts to build leadership learning opportunities.

Leadership of Cultural Scholars

Cultural scholars (including elders and tribal/community leaders) must take leading, teaching, and mentoring roles on both postsecondary and pre-K–12 instructional faculty and staff remembering, however, that for some communities, certain traditional subjects can be taught only by appropriate people and at appropriate times. Integrating traditional culture is self-validating for native students, and knowing how native knowledge has contributed to the overall well-being of mainstream society can enrich students' self-identities. For example, native students must learn that agricultural knowledge (Jaimes, 1991), pharmacology (Weatherford, 1988), and democratic governance exemplified by the Iroquois Confederacy (Butterfield, 1983; Jaimes, 1991; Weatherford, 1988) have their roots in native ways of knowing. Van Hamme (1996) wrote, "Pre-European contact American Indians also originated the mathematical concept of zero, developed a calendar extending with great accuracy 500 years into the future, and possessed a body of astronomical knowledge far superior to that in use at the time in Europe" (pp. 30–31). Educators, therefore, must work with cultural scholars to locate respectful ways of presenting traditional knowledge with contemporary world education (see the Cradleboard program that integrates technology and culture).[2]

Little Big Horn College's Learning Lodge Institute is an example of a partnership with community elders and cultural scholars. The initiative's work to revitalize 11 Native languages in Montana, partners seven tribal colleges; Little Big Horn College, Blackfeet Community College, Chief Dull Knife College, Fort Belknap College, Fort Peck Community College, Salish-Kootenai College, and Stone Child College. The thrust of the Institute's work has been to promote the involvement of community elders,

---

[2]Cradleboard is a cultural and language based-program that links native and nonnative students and their teachers around substantive learning experiences. Much of the work is done by means of computer technology (e.g., web-based work), with opportunities for site visits. The program is led by Buffy Saint Marie and is partially funded by the W. K. Kellogg Foundation.

scholars, teachers, and students in developing and piloting curriculum materials and immersion programs/camps. For example, the Blackfeet hosted two immersion camps and one immersion retreat in which 250 people participated (100 were scholars and consultants and 150 were elders, teachers, and students). Chief Dull Knife College also held language-immersion camps, which involved tribal elders and educators from local schools.

Because of the diversity of languages and cultural practices across the seven institutions (Assiniboine, Blackfeet, Chippewa, Cree, Crow, Gros Ventre, Kooteni, Nakoda, Northern Cheyenne, Salish, and Plains sign language), direct partnering around curriculum development has been difficult. However, lessons learned regarding immersion (what works and what does not), inclusion of elders and cultural scholars as teachers and as teachers of teachers, and linking learning to social activity that addresses community problems has led to many successful language and culture-based activities. For example, Fort Belknap works hard to develop mentoring activities that match a native speaker with a learner to increase the amount of time spent in an immersion setting. At Fort Peck, native language and culture is being taught to 3- and 4-year-olds while their parents take lessons in their college classes. Little Big Horn has developed a course on Crow music, and Salish Kootenai has developed language materials to be used at their site and others. Connecting to natural resources, Stone Child has developed lessons about the medicinal and ceremonial value of their indigenous plants.

Sharing curriculum ideas and developmental processes is integral to the growth and sustainability of language and culture programs at tribal colleges. To ensure continued development, Little Big Horn College, through the Learning Lodge Institute, communicates new ideas and provides information through a website, quarterly newsletters, and attendance and presentations at regional and national conferences focused on language revitalization.

Development of Teaching Tools

Planning, preparing, publishing, and sharing teaching tools and texts should be encouraged across indigenous/tribal communities and institutions. Planning should include determining which subjects will be taught in the mother tongue and which ones might be taught in a bilingual manner. In addition, the curriculum should include material that teaches students how to participate and contribute to both their native communities and the larger (state, national, and global) communities of contemporary society. Pedagogy, which includes visual learning, metaphors and imagery, and observation and experiential learning as well as abstract verbal instruction, should also be an area of focus. From successful tribal college programs we have learned that activities that stress teamwork instead of individual competition engage students in ways that increase learning in both the cognitive and affective domains and build commitment to community. (For more information, see More, 1987; Reyhner, 1992; Swisher & Deyhle, 1989; Tafoya, 1982.)

An example of the effort to develop teaching tools is a program established at Little Priest Tribal College, where W. K. Kellogg funding has supported the integration of the Winnebago language and culture into the core curriculum of the reservation schools. Recently, language and culture scholars published the *Bibliography of Winnebago Language and Culture Materials*, which includes 26 written publications, eight videotapes, 10 audiotapes, and two interactive games. The project directors are now working to locate support to more fully develop these materials with the addition of an annotated bibliography. In additional, the funding supported the completion of the *HoChunk Curriculum Guide for K–6*. These materials include a list of learning competencies, teaching materials, examples of student work, and letters from parents. This curriculum guide is also used as foundational material for HoChunk language classes offered to non-Winnebago speaking adults at Little Priest Tribal College. Classes held at the elementary school and the tribal college have been supplemented with a 3-week summer language-immersion program for community members. A key to the success of this program is the understanding of language and culture scholars that families and extended families must be involved in this important learning process. To this end, they are piloting a Native American parenting education series that is grounded in HoChunk culture and traditions (and is partially funded through grants from U.S. Department of Education).

An initiative undertaken at Humboldt State University, in partnership with D-Q University, is another example of an effort to create needed and useful curriculum tools. In essence, the initiative sought to develop an American Indian civics program for K–12 schools, to develop programs to increase higher education faculty's awareness of Indian issues (specifically at Humboldt State University), and to integrate more Indian-specific knowledge into the learning and teaching practices of both institutions. Although the partnership between both institutions recalls turf issues and lack of trust, several curriculum tools have emerged that are worthy of mention. For example, the initiative involved new faculty at Humboldt State, who, in partnership with native students and professors, added more American Indian subject matter to their classes and developed new research areas including the history of land use in Indian country and the relationship between property rights and sovereignty, and incorporating Indian cultural constructs into economics. Additionally, Humboldt State and D-Q University faculty and students hosted an American Indian Civics Day for high school teachers and students in grades 11 and 12. This was coupled with a week-long, follow-up summer institute for K–12 teachers that focused on developing lesson plans on American Indian civics for their classes. Follow-up and publication of their work, integral components of sustainable curriculum development, are planned.[3]

Development of Evaluation Tools

Planning, preparing, publishing, and sharing evaluation and testing materials should be encouraged across indigenous/tribal communities and institutions. Also, these materials should be aligned with national standards. The purpose of evaluation, in this case, is not only to provide ongoing feedback for program improvement, but to also provide information to a broader community about the needs and strengths of language and culture programs. For example, tribal college scholars and consultants need to assess the effect of their program(s) on youth and community foundations. Such efforts would include both qualitative and quantitative measures that might illuminate the achievements of the program for the purposes of replication, to define educational and public policy, and to help philanthropic organizations understand how they might become involved. Although there are few examples of ongoing, sustained evaluation initiatives, due to the newness of many of the programs, it is imperative that data collection and analysis strategies be developed now. (For a more extensive discussion of this topic, see Paul Boyer's chap. 7, this volume).

Integral to this evaluation process would be assessments that highlight the effect of the program on children and youths, families and adults, tribal communities (cultural, social, and economic foundations), and educational institutions (pre-K to postsecondary). In addition, evaluation materials must address the ways in which the program has evidenced sustainability through effective partnerships, effects on policy, and other resource-generating activities. Given the importance of this effort, the challenge to create effective evaluation strategies requires immediate action by

---

[3]Face-to-face language instruction has been enhanced by current efforts at New Mexico State University to provide their first indigenous language course, in partnership with Southwestern Indian Polytechnic Institute, via distance learning.

budgeting resources and leadership for this effort and providing advanced preparation in evaluation strategies for project participants.

Learning Models Linked to Community Building (Economic Development)

> At Crownpoint Institute of Technology (New Mexico) we've been able to build new facilities, clinics for our animals, and new buildings to house our students. Community development is important, but we can never forget that it is tied to our students. Our board of directors insisted on tying what we do to four sacred mountains. So, knowledge must contribute to community, which is rooted in culture and language that sustains a nation. We have a cultural learning center. It is important! Our challenge for our nation it to unite old ways with new modern ways of living. Our nation's number one priority next to sustaining family is sustaining flock, water, land, and air. (Jay DeGroat, March, 2001)

What has emerged from a study of tribal college programs is the idea that adult and community learning must be closely linked to community-building and economic-development initiatives. The close interconnection between the learning institution and community vitality, among many features of the tribal college or university, makes this organization a unique and valuable partner on tribal lands. Many of the programs funded by the W. K. Kellogg Foundation have been undertaken to locate ways that genuinely involve families/extended families and the community in adult students' learning experiences. For example, educative programs have linked discipline-oriented learning experiences to action-oriented projects that address contemporary issues (e.g., economics, health and well-being, and social policy).

The Northern Plains Bison Education Network is a partnership between United Tribes Technical College (UTTC) and nine other tribal colleges; Cankdeska Cikana Community College, Fort Berthold, Little Priest, Lower Brule Community College, Oglala Lakota, Sinte Gleska, Si Tanka, Sisseton, and Sitting Bull. NAHEI funding and UTTC fiscal management have assisted with the development of culture-related bison curriculum and teaching tools (e.g., the *Bison Education Resource Guide* for students), supported community-based bison awareness programs and seminars (e.g., Lower Brule Community College Tatanka Studies, a short summer course), and aided in the establishment of a bison herd to be used for research to educate bison producers and to improve cooperative range use (degree programs are offered at many of the participating institutions). A bison herd not only supports the spiritual foundation of many tribes, but also provides a marketable commodity.

The role of tribal colleges and universities as agents of service to the communities they serve is essential to the lifeblood of native people. Through the expertise of faculty and staff, coupled with the institutions' power of convening, tribal colleges can (and often do) provide tribal governments with the information, resources, and programs needed to frame social programs, generate and share cultural knowledge, and define and implement economically solid initiatives. For example, Turtle Mountain Community College's Center for New Growth and Economic Development (Turtle Mountain Chippewa Tribe, Belcourt, North Dakota) provides much needed demographic data that support tribal planning, proposal development, and congressional testimony. The center also has worked to bring together policymakers, students, and tribal leaders to develop small businesses, and has developed a new program to prepare young people to take the lead in economic and social development programming.

An example of integrating language and culture to build community and economic empowerment is the Lower Brule Community College's (LBCC) Tatanka Studies Summer Institute. Seventy people, including international exchange students, ranchers, state agricultural employees, tribal wildlife management staff, and tribal college students and instructors, attended this summer program. It is important to note that LBCC collaborated with their state's tourism department and received supportive funding from South Dakota State University. A highlight of this seminar was the inclusion of a "buffalo kill ceremony" by a spiritual leader, which reminded participants of the sacred meaning and significance of the bison. This particular point is reflected in every bison project and has fueled current work to develop bison research that is respectful of the bison's relationship with the earth and its meaning to native communities.

What We Are Learning

The inclusion of sociocultural elements empowers native communities. Because the curriculum and pedagogy being developed at tribal colleges and universities are intended to balance the traditional and the contemporary through the spirit, intellect, emotion, and physical health of the learners, the importance of family and land has engaged and empowered native/tribal communities. For individual learners, the connections to traditional knowledge and growing fluency (literacy and orality) in both the mother tongue and English have been essential to their academic achievement and cultural self-esteem. Native teachers, many of whom are becoming bilingual, understand the fundamental value of the mother tongue and culture as a medium of learning and teaching. Hence, in many learning settings, the value of mutual reciprocity, a sociocultural principle, enhances giving and respect.

To advance the mother tongue as a contemporary and living way of knowing and being, mutual reciprocity is also being nurtured between the classroom and the community, and between native and nonnative institutions and communities. We are learning that prekindergarten and tribal college/native-controlled institutions must make a commitment to connect, collaborate, and include community dialogue within their own clan/tribe, across diverse native communities, and with nonnative, mainstream institutions. In addition, educators are developing diverse opportunities for learners to integrate the mother tongue and traditional cultural practices into activities that address real social, political, and cultural tensions. This has generated bridging activities that have fostered a collective community ethic that encourages civic responsibility. This engagement affirms the principles that sovereignty and empowerment matter and that commitment to the common good can encourage entrepreneurship and break the cycle of resignation and colonial psyche.

We have also learned that successful language and culture programs require genuine commitment from all stakeholders. For example, postsecondary institutions must commit resources to recruiting of and training native, bilingual certified teachers (see Darling-Hammond & Sclan, 1996; Hatton, 1988; and Pavel, Larimore, & VanAlstine, Chap. 10, this volume). A partnership between the College of Menominee and the University of Wisconsin-Green Bay is an example of a fiscal, professional, and disciplinary articulation agreement. Tribal colleges and tribal governments must articulate language and culture policies that support planning and development, design, research, outreach, and evaluation of educational programs grounded in native epistemology. Although many of the attitudinal barriers that once kept governing boards from defining effective policies have been overcome, the implementation and sustainability of needed programs continue to be challenged by fiscal constraints. Funding, therefore, must come from a partnership among private, federal, and tribal organizations. There appear to be a variety of funding sources, however, much of that is symbolic (see the lack of substantial funding of the Native American Languages Act) rather than actual at the operational level. Many of the exemplary programs described in this chapter, because they survive on a shoestring, have not reached their full potential and influence because of languishing funds still caught in murky waters.

In addition, successful language and culture programs in K–12, postsecondary, and adult and community education venues require the commitment and participation of elders, educational leaders, teachers, parents and families, and students. Building community support and participation, we have learned, can result in the use of native language in the daily lives and activities of the community. A comprehensive, holistic approach that partners with community members would be acceptable to native people, therefore, all language and culture programs must maintain their native integrity. Hence, teacher education and educational leadership (degree and nondegree) programs must be grounded in well-developed publications (learning tools) that are written in the mother tongue and that capture cultural history and values. This would lead to the commitment of native scholars to conduct ongoing research and inquiry explaining and clarifying native/indigenous language, culture, ways of knowing, and ways of teaching and learning.

NEXT STEPS FOR LANGUAGE AND CULTURE POLICY AND PRACTICE

The above-mentioned lessons learned are essential to current and future policy and practice. Indeed, policymakers should address developing strong planning, well-developed tools (materials), trained personnel (bilingual teachers, bilingual teacher's aides, bilingual school leaders and administrators and bilingual staff), ongoing assessments and evaluations for improvement, genuine inclusion of cultural scholars, and long-term funding of learning environments that value the mother tongue and culture. In many native communities, scholars and students alike ponder how to save and revitalize the mother tongue and culture *and* to increase academic success, intellectual connections, and understanding of the 21st century world. Given this challenge, what are the implications for tribal colleges?

1. Policies should be developed that require a tribal college/native-controlled institution to have an active and productive native/indigenous language and culture department (see Brigham Young University-Hawai'i, Diné, and Sinte Gleska University, to name a few). The work of these departments would be integrated across the college/university curriculum.

2. A policy should be established, requiring all students at tribal colleges/native-controlled institutions to take, at a minimum, conversational native language courses, and to participate in a community-based service project that supports their knowledge of native ways of knowing.

3. Policies should be instituted that are culturally appropriate and build institutional infrastructure that supports native language and culture scholars' and teachers' efforts to develop and articulate native epistemologies and pedagogies.

4. Policies should be established that link pre-K through postsecondary institutions in collaborative efforts to define, develop, implement, and evaluate ongoing professional development in mother-tongue learning and teaching, mother-tongue curriculum and instruction development, and assessment and evaluation of mother-tongue initiatives. Also, polices should be established to support the development of curriculum materials that meet national standards and expectations of a global community.

5. AIHEC should develop a policy requiring tribal colleges/native-controlled institutions to both individually and collectively define and support efforts that recruit native/indigenous educators and to integrate mother-tongue instruction in their postsecondary teaching experiences (formal and informal). (See Pavel, Larimore, & VanAlstine, this volume; also see model programs in Becket, 1998; Haberman & Post, 1998.)

6. Policies of practice should be developed that encourage intergenerational research, as well as development, implementation, and evaluation projects focused on mother-tongue and culture educational programs for K–12, postsecondary, and community settings in both native and nonnative institutions. This support would enhance the exploration of philosophies, processes, and outcomes of educational programs in which the mother tongue is the primary medium (and/or bilingual medium) of instruction and prepare for the native tongue to be used in a formal school setting.

7. Continued efforts must focus on financing the above policies through full federal funding from the NALA, increased funding for Johnson O'Malley and higher education scholarships through the BIA, increased grants from foundations, and increased support and infrastructure from tribal governments and tribal education departments.

8. On a more fundamental level, native and nonnative scholars should study issues of language lexicon, the evolution of language (e.g., introduction of new words), and cultural transference without the mother tongue.

9. Finally, given the growing information-technology capacity of many tribal colleges and universities, and the need for distance education, researchers should look closely at how technology is being used. That is to say, is learning going on? Is the learning culturally appropriate? Are issues of access and equity being addressed?

If the preceding discussion seems at all reasonable to the reader, there are certain aims that follow. First, native and nonnative communities must do everything possible to avert the loss of language and cultural wealth, thereby protecting global diversity. Second, because language embraces the spiritual, intellectual, historical, and cultural competencies and capacities of the people who use it, the syntax, lexicon, and cultural treasures embodied in language must be taught in safe places. And third, in safeguarding individual native languages and culture, we appreciate the diversity and worth of unique intellectual traditions and the roles they might play in contemporary human intellectual life.

REFERENCES

Baird, P. (2001, March). *Focus group discussion*. Santa Fe, NM.

Becket, D. R. (1998). Increasing the number of Latino and Navajo teachers in hard to staff schools. *Journal of Teacher Education, 49*(3), 196–205.

Benham, M., & Cooper, J. (2000). *Indigenous educational models for contemporary practice: In our mother's voice*. Mahwah, NJ: Lawrence Erlbaum Associates.

Boyer, P. (1993, Spring). Culture with literacy: Language and culture are inseparable, says linguist Bill Leap. *Tribal College Journal of American Indian Higher Education, 4*, 15–19.

Boyer, P. (1995). Tribal college of the future. *Tribal College Journal of American Indian Higher Education, 7*, 11.

Brod, R. L., & McQuiston, J. M. (1997). The American Indian linguistic minority: Social and cultural outcomes of monolingual education. *American Indian Culture and Research Journal, 21*(4), 125–159.

Butterfield, R. A. (1983). The development and use of culturally appropriate curriculum for American Indian students. *Peabody Journal of Education, 61*, 49–66.

Chester, D. T. (Ed.). (1997). Secretary Riley seeks support for plan. *Teacher Education Reports, 19*(15)4.

Crawford, J. (1995, Winter). Endangered Native American languages: What is to be done, and why? *The Bilingual Research Journal, 19*(1), 17–38.

Crawford, J. (1996). Seven hypotheses on language loss causes and cures. In G. Cantoni (Ed.), *Stabilizing Indian languages*. Flagstaff, AZ: Northern Arizona Press.

Darling-Hammond, L., & Sclan, E. M. (1996). Who teaches and why: Dilemmas of building a profession for twenty-first century schools. In J. Sikula, T. Buttery, & E. Guyton (Eds.), *Handbook on research on teacher education* (pp. 932–960). New York: Macmillan.

DeGroat, J. (2001, March). *Focus group discussion*. Santa Fe, NM.

Estrada, L. J., & Vasquez, M. (1981). Schooling and its social and psychological effects on minorities. In W. E. Sims & B. B. de Martinez (Eds.), *Perspectives in multicultural education* (pp. 53–73). New York: University Press of America.

Geertz, C. (1973). *The interpretation of cultures*. New York: Basic Books.

Geiogamah, H., & Darby, J. T. (Eds.). (1999). *Stories of our way: An anthology of American Indian plays*. Los Angeles: UCLA American Indian Studies Center.

Geiogamah, H., & Darby, J. T. (Eds.). (2000). *American Indian theatre in performance: A reader*. Los Angeles: UCLA American Indian Studies Center.

Gollnick, G. (2000). Creating a ceremony: "Nature's model from the Longhouse people." In M. Benham & J. Cooper (Eds.). *Indigenous educational models for contemporary practice: In our mother's voice* (pp. 101–111). Mahwah, New Jersey: Lawrence Erlbaum Associates.

Haberman, M., & Post, L. (1998). Teachers for multicultural schools: The power of selection. *Theory Into Practice, 7*(2), 96–104.

Hatton, B. R. (1988, December). *The education and culture program's minority education program.* Discussion paper presented to the Board of Trustees of the Ford Foundation, New York.

Hinkle, J. (2000, October). For Mille Lacs, language immersion may be the answer, *American Indian Report*, p. 14.

Houser, S. (1991). Building institutions across cultural boundaries. *Tribal College Journal of American Indian Higher Education, 2*, 11–17.

Jaimes, M. A. (1991). The stone age revisited: An indigenist view of primitivism, industrialization, and the labor process. *Wicazo Sa Review, 7*, 34–44.

La Plante, M. P., & Carlson, D. (1992). *Disability in the United States: Prevalence and causes* (Report No. 7). California University—San Francisco, Institute for Health and Aging. (ERIC Reproduction Service ED 400635)

More, A. J. (1987). Native Indian learning styles: A review for researchers and teachers. *Journal of American Indian Education, 27*(1), 17–29.

Native American Languages Act. Pub. L. No. 101-477 1152 (1990).

Ortiz, A. (1990). Seeking life: Definitions of religion and the sacred. In P. V. Beck & A. L. Walters (Eds.), *The sacred ways of knowledge, source of life.* (pp. 3–31). Tsaile, AZ: Navajo Community College.

Reyhner, J. (1992). *Teaching American Indian students.* Norman: University of Oklahoma Press.

Reyhner, J., & Eder, J. (1992). *A history of Indian education.* Billings: Eastern Montana College Press.

Rosier, P., & Holm, W. (1980). The Red Rock experience: A longitudinal study of a Navajo school program (Saad Naaki Bee Na'nitin). In *Bilingual education series: 8. Papers in applied linguistics.* (ERIC Document Reproduction Service No. ED 195 363)

Schorr, L. B. (1989). *Within our reach: Breaking the cycle of disadvantage.* New York: Anchor/Doubleday.

Sianjina, R. R., Cage, B., & Allen, V. A. (1996). African-Americans' participation in teaching education programs. *The Educational Forum, 61*(1), 30–33.

Swisher, K., & Deyhle, D. (1989). The styles of learning are different but the teaching is just the same: Suggestions for teachers of American Indian youth. *Journal of American Indian Education, 21*, 1–14.

Tafoya, T. (1982). Coyotes' eyes: Native cognition styles. *Journal of American Indian Education, 21*(2), 21–33.

Tozer, S., Violas, P. C., & Senese, G. B. (1998). *School and society: Historical and contemporary perspectives* (3rd ed.). New York: McGraw-Hill.

Troike, R. (1978). Bilingual education in the United States: The first decade. *International Review of Education, 24*(3), 401–405.

Trueba, H. T. (1988). Instructional effectiveness: English-only for speakers of other languages? *Education and Urban Society, 2*(4), 341–362.

Van Hamme, L. (1996, Winter). American Indian cultures and the classroom. *Journal of American Indian Education, 35*(2), 21–36.

Weatherford, J. (1988). *Indian givers: How the Indians of the Americas transformed the world.* New York: Fawcett Columbine.

White Hat, A. (2001, March). *Focus group discussion.* Santa Fe, NM.

Yazzie, T. J. (1999). Culturally appropriate curriculum: A research-based rationale. In K. G. Swisher & J. W. Tippeconnic, III (Eds.), *Next steps: Research and practice to advance Indian education.* Charleston, WV: ERIC Clearinghouse on Rural Education and Small Schools.

10

A Gift to All Children: Native Teacher Preparation

D. Michael Pavel
Washington State University
Colleen Larimore
NINHLE
Matthew Jason VanAlstine
Michigan State University

OUR NEED, OUR FUTURE

In 50 years, students of color will comprise the majority of K–12 students in American classrooms. Unfortunately, this nation's teaching workforce is not nearly so diverse. At present, 9 of 10 classroom teachers are white, and minorities make up just 15% of those enrolled in teacher training programs. Native Americans are one of the youngest and fastest growing segments of our population, and yet, native people comprise just 0.4% of those currently teaching and 1% of those enrolled in teacher training programs (Alliance for Equity in Higher Education, 2000). As a result, native students, and other students of color, are denied having valuable role models as part of their educational experiences. White students, too, are being deprived of learning from teachers of color who embody the increasingly diverse world in which they are growing up.

A widely accepted strategy to improve American Indian and Alaskan Native student learning outcomes is increasing the number of native and nonnative teachers who are properly trained to meet the needs of native students (Indian Nations at Risk Task Force Report, 1991; U.S. Department of Education, 1997). Knowledge of native language and culture can positively influence schools, students, and communities. A properly trained teacher can develop trusting relationships with students and make the difference between promoting negative stereotypes and portraying realistic and empowering views of native people.

Both statistical and observational research have suggested that the absence of adequate numbers of native teachers and the lack of specialized training for both native and nonnative teachers may place native students especially at risk for attrition. Ethnographic evidence cited later has shown that native students' culturally influenced learning behaviors, communication styles, and values are often misinterpreted in the classroom and clash with their teachers' dominant-culture perceptions of how a "normal" student learns and behaves. Research on native students' difficulties in dominant-culture classrooms has yielded three major findings about their learning behaviors and the conditions they typically encounter at school.

First, native students from many different tribal backgrounds learn best by processing visual information, such as by observing, then modeling the behavior of parents, elders, and older siblings. They have the most difficulty acquiring new skills taught only through verbal instruction. Unfortunately, verbal instruction is still the predominant mode of communication in public school classrooms.

Second, native children of many different tribes avoid publicly performing new skills and are unprepared or ill-at-ease when pushed into doing so without adequate opportunity for private practice. For native students, the steps involved in acquiring and demonstrating knowledge at home versus at school are reversed. At home, observation, private self-testing, and demonstration of a task for approval are essential steps in the learning process. In school, native children are expected to learn by publicly responding to direct questions from teachers, even if they are uncertain of the answers, and rarely have an opportunity to practice new skills privately before performing them publicly.

Third, native children from numerous tribal backgrounds are socialized to avoid competing with peers and are more likely to participate in classroom situations that emphasize cooperation rather than competition. The childrearing practices of many tribes impress upon children norms such as generosity, sharing, social interdependence, and cooperation. In comparisons of white and native students, whites were found to be more competitive and, even when cooperative behavior was rewarded, they still preferred to compete with classmates rather than cooperate.

Our experience is that native students are influenced by their cultures to be peer-cooperative, visual learners who prefer to acquire competence privately before performing new skills publicly. However, dominant-culture classrooms are most often teacher-dominated settings in which verbal instruction and peer competition are stressed. What can we do to address this incongruence? It is clear that assimilationist education policies aimed at changing native students' learning styles have failed. Given that the strength of cultural identity is actually beneficial to native students' academic success, the only reasonable course of action is to prepare teachers to be more responsive to the needs of native learners.

Native and nonnative teachers benefit from training that focuses on American Indian and Alaskan Native learners. At present, most mainstream universities provide little or no training pertaining to native learners. As a consequence, teachers being trained today do not necessarily know how to translate cultural sensitivity into teaching techniques that have been proven effective with native students, especially if those students come from an array of tribal cultures.

Teachers' instructional styles do have a significant influence on native students' classroom participation rates and academic success. Thus, teacher preparation programs should provide teachers with the knowledge and experience of how to incorporate native students' learning strengths into classroom instruction. Teachers must be taught to build on native students' existing learning repertoires in ways that do not compromise their cultural identities or spark their resistance.

EVOLVING LANDSCAPES

The increasing demand for and short supply of native teachers requires a concerted effort similar to addressing the need for more minority teachers nationwide. It is a complex and rewarding undertaking to develop teacher preparation programs that meet the diverse cultural and educational needs of indigenous students. This strategy, however, is not always effective when applied in the absence of a broader landscape of educational reform.

We need to go beyond simply increasing the number of native teachers and creating programs to meet the needs of teachers who will serve native students. These and other issues go beyond teacher commitment or training; to encompass frustrations inherent in language loss and resistance of school personnel and native community members also do not fully embrace the indigenous language and culture. Language and culture are not generally the center of curriculum in public schools, nor do all native parents see them as important to surviving in a modern society.

Many reasons exist for the lack of value ascribed to native language and culture. For example, classroom instruction in public schools does not stress the importance and value of native students actively developing and using their language and culture. Many teachers are inclined to rely on passive learning methods, which are not effective means of improving learning outcomes that parents would support. Instructional efforts are further hampered because there is a lack of locally developed quality materials for language/cultural learning, leading some parents to be resigned about dedicating time and resources to reviving a "lost" language and culture.

Our attention should be directed at the overall movement of reforming the educational system or engaging in the cultural negotiations necessary to better meet the needs of native students. Although native children may learn in cultural and language programs that are autonomous from the school system or simply stand-alone programs, it is unlikely they will achieve any degree of fluency from these efforts. The most effective and sustainable course of action appears to be developing teacher-training programs in the context of the overall educational reform in schools serving a high percentage of native/indigenous students.

In summary, it is important to develop programs that prepare teachers to improve the learning outcomes of American Indian and Alaskan Native youth. Students in teacher-training programs and teachers can gain invaluable insights through an examination of native language and cultural influences. Too often, however, having more and better trained teachers can be accepted as a panacea to address the educational needs of our children. We tend to forget the systemic structures that created unacceptable classroom environments for native students. Both native and nonnative teachers would benefit from educational reform that addresses issues throughout the school, community, and society.

MOVING FORWARD

Tribal Colleges and Universities (TCUs) are currently taking on the task of developing curriculum to train teachers for native learners. This occurs through individual institutional efforts and partnerships between existing 4-year teacher education programs and TCUs. In either case, the TCUs base their service delivery on a firm understanding of local control and equal access to education. Public and private institutions of higher education (IHEs) that choose to partner with TCUs have unique opportunities to build bridges of understanding and to work collaboratively on educational reform to pave the way for culturally responsive education across all levels.

Words serve as a key purveyor of cultural information for generations to come. Recognizing the critical role of language in cultural continuity, native governments have charged TCUs with the responsibility for renewing native language through curriculum development and implementation efforts. As specific examples, Turtle Mountain Community College in North Dakota has developed a written Chippewa/Cree dictionary, and Sinte Gleska University in South Dakota recently produced a textbook to accompany its Lakota language course work (Ambler & Crazy Bull, 1997). Fort Peck Community College immerses preschoolers in Dakota and Nakota instruction, while their parents are simultaneously taught to facilitate Dakota and Nakota language acquisition in the home environment (Campbell, 1998). This program blends language immersion with traditional spiritual practices, legends, games, art activities, music, and foods. In this manner, the language is integrated back into the traditional culture out of which it has grown.

Looking more broadly at cultural transmission, elders play a central role in shaping the cultural ethos of TCUs. As culture bearers, elders pass on traditional skills, knowledge, values, and beliefs through various forms of involvement in colleges. Some TCUs, such as Chief Dull Knife College in Montana, involve elders in forums and advisory committees. Others, such as Lac Courte Oreilles Ojibwa Community College in Wisconsin, provide a cultural foundation by involving students in talking circles with elders and integrating traditional knowledge into mainstream teacher training programs. Salish Kootenai College's Cultural Leadership Program in Montana brings students and elders together to pass on traditional knowledge and practices in natural sites (Finley, 1997).

Traditional culture takes center stage in both educational content and process at TCUs because native educational systems have always revolved around a caring attitude. Pavel (1997) found caring to be an essential feature in making higher education accessible to TCU students. He identified sincerity and honesty as primary attributes of caring interactions, with further recognition given to encouraging and comforting relationships. Because of the collective nature of tribal communities, caring extends beyond the individual student to his or her family, as well as to the larger community. Caring is also synonymous with a firm belief in the capacity of Indian students to learn. As a result, caring TCU faculty and staff involve themselves in taking action to integrate traditional native values and concepts into the educational process.

Moreover, through the ethic of caring, TCU faculty recognize that native students' cultural backgrounds embody strengths that can be used to enrich the learning experience. Native communities often emphasize cooperation and sharing in both knowledge acquisition and the demonstration of learning (Swisher, 1990). Members of native communities view life as a whole and emphasize the interconnections that exist among all things. At TCUs such as Little Big Horn College, these cultural concepts translate into cooperative and interdisciplinary curricular emphases that are viewed as assets for students grappling with the highly complex problems of today's rapidly changing world.

In summary, whether independently or in partnership with mainstream IHEs, TCUs are becoming important participants in the movement to develop teacher-training programs with a focus on meeting the needs of native students. The overall TCU movement into teacher training is still relatively young; nevertheless, there is increasing evidence that language and culture are being integrated into the curriculum, effective support programs are being developed, and students are graduating. There are challenges that resemble the obstacles that Indian educators often encounter (acceptance, addressing the diversity of native languages and culture, and so on). Approaches that are promoting systemic change rely on identifying and meeting community needs, using educational technology, and forming partnerships. TCUs have assumed a high level of responsibility to integrate language and culture into the educational system and make the effort to involve youth and elders in the same classroom environment. Pervasive throughout the TCUs' delivery of educational programs is the ethic of caring necessary to gain the trust and respect of native students.

CREATING A CIRCLE

The W. K. Kellogg Foundation has supported native teacher preparation through the Native American Higher Education Initiative (NAHEI) and recent sponsorship of two conferences. The conferences proved to be most informative, and insights gained from them are presented in a report developed by the American Indian College Fund entitled *Tribal Colleges: Training Teachers for Today & Tomorrow, A Call to Action.* The American Indian College Fund organized the conferences so that tribal college personnel representing 31 institutions could share information, foster partnerships, define best practices, and explore fiscal and policy-related concerns (American Indian College Fund, 2000). On the basis of the knowledge and experience, conference participants offered powerful examples of best practices in the areas of student-centered program design and instruction, tradition-based curriculum, promotion of language and culture, authentic assessment, practicum experiences, student support, and collaborations/partnerships.

For example, the foundation of student-centered program design and instruction in Sinte Gleska University's and Blackfeet Community College's teacher-training programs is a commitment to honor native students' previous experience and teaching to native students' learning styles. As exemplified by Haskell Indian Nations University, tradition-based education is about preparing teachers to teach children from a native perspective and further American Indian pedagogy while becoming knowledgeable about current research on teaching and learning. The promotion of native language and culture is central to the mission of TCUS. As evidenced by Chief Dull Knife College and Diné College, foundation courses in some teacher preparation programs focus on native language and culture. As a result, graduates are widely recognized as experts in promoting native language, culture, and history in the classroom.

In the area of authentic assessment, Turtle Mountain Community College is developing "matrices that specify everything that teacher preparation students are expected to learn" and apply in performance-based tasks and projects documented in portfolios (American Indian College Fund, 2000, p. 9). Both students and faculty benefit from knowing what is expected, identifying areas of need, and establishing benchmarks. Moreover, tribal colleges and universities are working closely with local schools so that students are given more extensive learning opportunities in their practicums to relate field experiences to classroom learning objectives.

TCUs are also providing extensive student support services to ensure retention, and Lac Courte Oreilles Ojibwa Community College and Fort Berthold Community College staff typify the outreach and empathy that resonate with students in the teacher training programs through mentoring, tutoring, facilitating access to financial aid resources, advising, assisting with preprofessional and professional tests, and addressing other issues that are present barriers to success. Barriers are far reaching and include inadequate transportation, child care, and housing; nevertheless, tribal college staff are making extraordinary efforts to address these and other barriers.

Collaborations and partnerships have been important strategies to support the development of native teacher preparation programs. As shown by programs at the College of the Menominee Nation, Northwest Indian College, and Blackfeet Community College, partnerships can occur between tribal colleges and universities and mainstream institutions. TCUs like Sinte Gleska University and Sitting Bull College are also furthering the rights of sovereignty and self-determination when developing intertribal college and university partnerships that lead to expanded degree offerings.

CREATING DOMAINS OF NATIVE TEACHER PREPARATION

If you want to teach your own people, you should learn from home, and Diné College to me, is home.
(Fonda Rae Beatty, Diné Teacher Education Program student)

Diné Teacher Education Program

On the Navajo Reservation, the Diné Teacher Education Program (DTEP) at Diné College in Tsaile, Arizona, was influenced by the Australian indigenous strategy of local communities and schools selecting candidates for teacher education programs who then return to their home schools/communities to teach. DTEP has been in existence for 12 years and has enjoyed considerable success. NAHEI funding is being leveraged with other foundation (e.g., Phillip Morris), federal (National Science Foundation and National Security Agency), and tribal resources. A memorandum of understanding has been renewed, ensuring that Arizona State University (ASU) and Diné College will continue a flexible and cooperative collaboration until the 2002 school year.

DTEP has been successful in matriculating and graduating Navajo students for K–8 teaching positions in schools primarily serving the Navajo Reservation. As in other TCUs, Diné College's native teacher preparation program remains the college's "marquee" program. By August, 1999, DTEP had graduated 19 students with bachelor's degrees (8 in Year 1, 11 in Year 2). All received job offers before or just after graduation, and 18 of the 19 were employed in schools on the Navajo reservation. Nine more graduates are expected for Year 3 and 13 students for Year 4. Most of the recent graduates had transferred to DTEP from other institutions because of the native teacher focus, and students who are just now entering the program came from Diné College. Navajo students who used to leave the reservation to get a teaching degree can stay on the reservation to receive their training now that the DTEP program is in place.

There are more coherent linkages between A.A. and B.A. elementary education programs, as well as between lower level and teacher education programs at other institutions in the area. This is combined with transfer check-sheets from Diné College's 2-year offerings into B.A. teacher education programs at the three major teacher education programs in the area, namely, Northern Arizona University, Fort Lewis College, and the University of New Mexico-Gallup. Ongoing program assessment is designed to collect interview and survey data to monitor the program's effectiveness in preparing Navajo students to teach bilingually and biculturally. These feed-back loops have become a permanent feature in the ongoing program development efforts. Counseling services have been expanded to address substance abuse, domestic violence, personal finance, and other personal needs of the students.

A student recruitment plan resulted in a threefold increase in the number of applicants; there were more than 105 inquiries and applicant contacts in 1998–1999, with 17 new students admitted into Cohort IV (13 began classes in fall 1999) and 16 admitted to Cohort V for fall 2000. DTEP faculty currently work as mentor teachers in local schools, encouraging teachers to pursue a M.Ed. degree offered at Diné College in the summer; this program is accredited by ASU and funded jointly by ASU and the Navajo Scholarship Office. The Navajo Department of Higher Education is a collaborating partner and pays for scholarships for teacher education students.

Support systems are being developed for graduates during the "induction" phase of their professional development to ensure that they remain in the field of teaching and continue to perfect ways of improving learning among Diné children. Diné College and DTEP staff are also creating linkages with other initiatives involving the New Mexico Education Department, and the Early Childhood Education Program funded by the W. K. Kellogg Foundation to develop a program check-sheet, course syllabi, and funding schemes for an A.A. degree in early childhood education.

Cultural integrity is ensured through involvement of the Diné Educational Philosophy Committee, which provides advice about cultural practices, philosophy, and so on, in the educational coursework. Cultural aspects are implicit in the entire program design, ranging from coursework and curriculum development to events like an orientation ceremony for new students. Because some of the new students are not familiar with traditional practices, this is further reinforcement for them in cultural ways and "ways of knowing." Staff members originally assumed that "culture would come with the language" but now realize that more time is needed to incorporate Navajo history and culture into the DTEP.

OKSALE Native Teacher Preparation Program

The Native Teacher Preparation Program at the Northwest Indian College (NWIC) campus on the Lummi Indian Reservation in Washington State is named OKSALE (meaning teacher). OKSALE, in partnership with Washington State University (WSU), is moving in several directions toward certifying and licensing native teachers in Washington. The first graduating cohort, on May 2000, included six students with B.A. degrees in elementary education. Eight students are enrolled in the program for the 2000–2001 academic year; 12 more students are expected to be enrolled by spring 2001. Recruiting and retaining students are priorities. The impact that OKSALE has made in just 3 years indicates a solid foundation for the future.

The delivery of courses has changed significantly and reflects the telecommunication system using the K-20 network. NWIC has one licensed K-20 technician (certified by the state education office) who facilitates the classes. In addition to the two students at Hood Canal School District who are being served by distance technology, NWIC will connect to at least two more sites at local public school districts for winter semester 2001 and serve four to five students at each site. In addition, offerings will expand from five to 10 courses. About half of those classes will be offered via distance technology and half will be taught on site.

The Hood Canal School District has a site coordinator (principal) and a course facilitator, as well as interactive television classes in which all students can communicate and interact as the lesson is taking place. The site coordinator handles scheduling and administration at the site; the course facilitator acts as a teaching assistant and serves as lead teacher should a technological failure occur. This format will be used as each site is added. There are regularly scheduled curriculum committee meetings to oversee and advise on ongoing revision of current syllabi to incorporate identified cultural curricular strands and instructional methods.

The 4-year accreditation process has gained momentum, and OKSALE staff have initiated a dialogue with Western Washington University (WWU) to enter into a partnership with NWIC to offer secondary courses. Facilitating an early childhood degree along with a middle school degree was favored by WWU. OKSALE staff are redefining the (digital) virtual library service as one of the 12 tribal community colleges identified by the American Indian Higher Education Consortium (AIHEC) that receive support for virtual-library implementation. OKSALE staff is eager to begin a dialogue with an outside researcher in regard to applying and complying with the state standards to achieve 4-year accreditation, and they hope to develop this process extensively in the new year.

Funding for the OKSALE Native Teacher Preparation Program has been received from the following sources; W. K. Kellogg Foundation, Co-Teach (a grant that subcontracts with NWIC), the U.S. Department of Education, PSU/PT3 (technology for faculty development) Rural Systemic Initiative/National Science Foundation. Further funding from the W. K. Kellogg

Foundation and other organizations is desired in order to fund an accreditation person, as well an additional faculty with doctorate degrees to develop a program that is qualified to meet accrediting requirements.

Turtle Mountain Teacher Education Program

Dr. Virginia Allery, Program Director of the teacher education program at Turtle Mountain Community College (TMCC), Belcourt, North Dakota, shared that the program, initiated August, 2000, serves the Turtle Mountain Band of Chippewa. The program reflects holistic and integrative methodologies, fluid disciplinary boundaries, integrative technologies, and culturally adapted courses grounded in the ancient, holistic spirit of the native culture. The philosophical underpinnings provide an in-depth understanding of the thinking behind each area. For example, in the area of integrative methodologies, learning was operationally defined as essentially a relational experience. That is to say, micro and macro concepts are best understood when viewed in relation to cultural, social, philosophical, and spiritual contexts, and when teaching and learning are seen as integral to the academic and geopolitical community. Given the relational nature of teaching and learning, methodologies emphasize cultural and social relevancy, continuity, and the culmination of the "marriage" of theory and practice. For example, all theoretical approaches are grounded in practical applications, new information is linked to prior knowledge, and principles are emphasized in lieu of individual techniques and strategies.

Fluid Disciplinary Boundaries. As curricula become increasingly connected and integrated, boundary lines will become harder to draw. For example, scholarship in language-based courses will incorporate children's literature, reading, and language arts into one course, borrowing from the humanities, philosophy, and the social sciences. Mathematics and the sciences will be related as much as possible to the arts and music. Community service learning experiences will be related to human relations and multicultural issues. Focusing courses on complex problems and topics and exploring the relationship between science and society essentially transforms the curriculum from linear and isolated skills to integrated domains and themes. These interdisciplinary fields will serve as enclaves for new research and curricular innovations.

Integrated Technologies. Consistent with the philosophical grounding in connection and relationships, the logical extension to integration of technology into the curriculum is clearly beneficial. All students will be expected to learn the various software applications that will enhance their teaching. The curriculum will integrate technology across all the courses, requiring teachers and students to model this integration in their presentations and assignments. Recently, TMCC received a federally funded grant (PT3) focused on technology training for future teachers. Participants in the grant-funded activities learned how to plan lessons by integrating technology into all areas of the curriculum. National technology standards were also applied.

Culturally Grounded.   Intersecting the cultural and the contemporary may be "dangerous" for the TMCC Teacher Education Program. Questions of the meaning, parameters, dynamics, and interpretations of traditions and culture will arise when applied to contemporary problems and contexts. Nonetheless, the program is undertaking this challenge in order to get out of the "boxes" that are not working for our students. TMCC is convinced that the answer for us as native people lies in the exploration of our indigenous roots. Clearly these roots are resonating within the deeper reaches of our psyche and are pointing to the ancient teachings of relationship (*mitakuye oyasin*, which when translated means "all my relations") that reflect the connections of self to the other and self to nature and the earth. The implications, particularly for the teaching of science, are exciting and may open up vistas to understanding what it means to "investigate" a truth.

Program Description.   When the teacher candidates have completed the program, they will graduate with a bachelor of science in elementary education (K–8). They will be licensed and certified according to North Dakota state requirements. The candidates will enter the elementary education program in their junior year of college, with the assumption that they have completed their general education requirements and have taken prerequisite courses for their major. Before beginning their major, they will be encouraged to take electives in social studies, mathematics, and science. They will also be required to take the course entitled "Introduction to Teaching and Learning."

From the outset, there were up to 176 possible candidates, so this large number had to be reduced to accommodate a cohort model of a maximum of 30 students. The admissions process was lengthened considerably to ensure a fair and equitable procedure for admittance. Criteria were clearly identified, and applicants proceeded through a four-step process that included (a) an initial review of their transcripts to determine whether they had completed all of the general education requirements, (b) a spontaneous writing sample,

(c) a brief biographical sketch and a self-report inventory to survey their interest in mathematics, science, and culture, all of which culminated with (d) a personal interview conducted by the selection committee.

The Curriculum.   The various semesters are divided into thematic strands. The first strand focuses on the foundations of teaching and learning. Courses emphasize educational issues from a native perspective in contemporary and historical contexts, service learning to help students bond with the larger community, and courses that ground them in general theories of human relations and multicultural education. The second strand bridges theory and practice. Emphasis is on cognitive, psycholinguistic, and anthropological principles, with practical curricular and community applications. These interdisciplinary "threads" are clearly evident in the literacy, storytelling and drama, curriculum development, and writing courses. The third strand focuses on methods of teaching and learning. Mathematics, science, health, art, music, and social studies courses are concentrated on practical applications as direct preparation for the next semester of student teaching. The fourth and final strand includes a 14-week student teaching experience and seminars to help student teachers integrate their field experiences with the various courses they took the previous terms.

Leech Lake Tribal College Teacher Training Project

The expressed mission of Leech Lake Tribal College (LLTC) in Cass Lake, Minnesota, is to create and maintain an atmosphere in which the traditional and contemporary values of the Anishinaabeg are honored and practiced. An institutionwide goal is to increase the number of native students who enroll in and complete a baccalaureate program. Through LLTC's partnership with Sinte Gleska University, a highly successful 4-year teacher-training project has emerged, which is indicative of institutional pride and a model of collaboration between tribal colleges. Currently, 35 students at LLTC are preparing to become teachers.

These students were attracted to the teacher-training project because of institutional commitment and staff's willingness to deliver curricula using a mix of traditional classroom courses, interactive television, flexible scheduling, internship opportunities, and Internet classes at partnering schools (e.g., Sinte Gleska University, Bemidji State University, and TMCC). The 4-year curriculum in elementary education was implemented at LLTC through a cooperative agreement with Sinte Gleska University in South Dakota.

According to the LLTC web page (www.lltc.org),

> those wishing to continue their studies beyond the Associate of Arts degree
> may enroll in the Bachelor of Science Degree in Elementary Education of-
> fered by Sinte Gleska University on campus at Leech Lake Tribal College.
> This degree program is fully accredited and allows students to apply for cer-
> tification as elementary school teachers in the state of Minnesota.

Students must have completed an A.A. degree in one of the majors available at LLTC, or, if they are transferring in with an A.A. degree, students
need to meet the Anishinaabe studies requirements for an LLTC A.A. degree before they are admitted.

Graduates qualify for certification to teach in elementary schools upon
completing a program that consists of (a) required courses in general education, (b) required courses in Anishinaabe studies, (c) content and methods
courses specific to elementary education, (d) courses specific to an area of
concentration, and (e) a number of professional education courses and student teaching. Although a minimum of 2 years of coursework is required after completion of the A.A. degree, "most students will find that 3 additional
years beyond the A.A. degree are required. Although the curriculum is designed to meet certification requirements in South Dakota, through Sinte
Gleska University, the program also meets certification requirements in
Minnesota."

The teacher-training project's enrollment of 35 students is approximately 15% of the total enrollment at LLTC. The first graduates of the program received their teaching degrees in spring 2001, and it is noteworthy
that the students completed fully accredited courses. LLTC personnel, students, and community members are all proud of the fact that the
teacher-training project has become one of the most exciting and successful
programs at LLTC. It is easy to share their sentiments, given that the project
is delivering on the institutional promise to meet the critical needs of Leech
Lake Reservation for fully credentialed elementary school teachers.

STUDENT VOICES

Much of what we have had to say thus far about native teacher preparation is
sociocultural in nature. There is the social condition that demands native
representation in the classroom that will properly guide our future. The
evolving landscapes are replete with well-established programs at TCUs
across the country. The W. K. Kellogg Foundation has served as a capable
steward in facilitating an environment of institutional capacity building and

organizational solidarity. Domains of native teacher preparation have emerged to become institutional and community sources of pride and stability. Still, this question needs to be addressed: What do students say about the training they are receiving in TCU native teacher preparation programs?

We surveyed a sample at NWIC OKSALE students to inquire about their experiences in the program. The open-ended nonquantitative query was simple and was intended to be nonintrusive. Students were asked: How has the native teacher preparation program influenced your life? How has or will the program influence the lives of native children? The responses were inspiring and are included here for readers' enjoyment.

> I work in a community program now serving youth and the OKSALE program greatly expanded my knowledge base as far as community-school programs and school reform. It has provided me with insights as to the aspects of teaching and learning (constructive model) that I can utilize in the youth program I am now coordinating, improving the experience for the learners (youth). It has also given me directions to continue working for social change in native communities through education and empowerment. I could not have done this without the scholarship and flexibility OKSALE has offered me. I have applied my class learning to my current work with Native youth and the leadership curriculum we are creating for a community program. It has also given me ideas for new programs, including community-school programs serving Native youth. I think they are better served by providing a culturally-based teacher preparation program. Mahalo! —Tami Chock

> I am very thankful for the OKSALE program. The dream of becoming a teacher is being obtained through this program. Traveling 100 miles daily is just a small sacrifice to attend OKSALE. I chose this program over the Western Washington Education because of the quality and support that the staff has given me. Without the personal touch of each and every member of OKSALE staff, I would not be where I am today and I plan to be in the future. I plan to serve in my own community of LaConner, Washington. I feel this program is providing me with the proper skills to serve and enhance the Swinomish children's education. Being a role model is an awesome responsibility. Through this program I feel comfortable to fill this role for the Swinomish children. I have worked as a paraprofessional for LaConner and have seen the effect that a tribal member, in the schools, can make. I hope to make a positive effect, as a teacher, on the Swinomish children. —Loran James

> The OKSALE Native Teacher Preparation Program has inspired me to become a more effective teacher for not only Native American young people, but also all students. I've been given the opportunity to prove to myself that I can be a productive teacher. I also have an increased awareness and belief

that I can perform and accomplish the necessary tasks of a successful teacher. In addition, I am more inspired because the OKSALE staff has faith in me as a future teacher—they have been supportive, encouraging, and accommodating. This demeanor has influenced me to have faith in the OKSALE program and in my future as an educator. When children see that other Native Americans can succeed in the education profession it gives them hope that they can succeed just as well. I have not had the opportunity to apply much of what I've learned since I began the program. However, I've shared with young people the need for Native American teachers and that having this kind of program within their own community is something to be optimistic about as it will give any of its members an opportunity to pursue the necessary teacher credentials and, in turn, make a positive difference in the lives of many youth. As a role model, it is important to succeed at education before I (or anyone) can promote it. —Randy Vendiola

I have been inspired to be a teacher at the local tribal school with confidence and enthusiasm. I have volunteered with OKSALE students at the local tribal school and other students that are members of the American Indian Business Leaders in the 5th grade class. I saw the awe and light in the children's eyes when three Indian men and three Indian women walked in all dressed in business attire and taught them about beginning and running a business in the class. It was a success and the kids saw native teachers in action. —Heather Jefferson

Without the financial assistance and scholarship, I would not be able to go to school or have this opportunity. It has enabled me to reduce my workload and devote more time towards my career choice of becoming a Native American teacher. It allows for Native Americans to meet their tribal school goals to hiring Native American teachers. Having a native teacher standing up in front of the students in class will be inspiring to the students and to the community. Put pride back into the community and students. Encourage other natives to pursue teaching as a profession when they see one who has accomplished receiving their degree in teaching. —Loretta Johansson

OKSALE has been great. The classes are wonderful and intimate. It makes you realize that as a teacher the smaller the classes are, the more individual attention you get. You also get to know *who* your teachers and classmates are. The teachers are also willing to help when available. The OKSALE program has made me aware of the Native American culture. I enjoyed learning about the culture and traditions and the education movement. It helps me to become aware and to keep up with the research so that the students are always getting the full potential of learning that they deserve. —Kathy Getzin

The OKSALE Native Teacher Program has made it possible for me to become a teacher. Without the availability of OKSALE, I doubt that I would have pursued this professional path. The OKSALE program is preparing me, I believe, like no other program to effectively teach the diverse populations in America's classroom. The OKSALE program will greatly benefit the children in this community by providing them with caring, understanding, and culturally grounded teachers. —Larisa Koenig

The OKSALE Program has made it possible for me to pursue my goals in education. In addition, it has allowed for Lummi education to fulfill one of its major goals to recruit and retain Native American teachers. It has increased my awareness and desire to support our tribal school teachers in raising test scores as they are required and often go unsupported. I only worked part-time in an after school program at Lummi Tribal School and was able to connect with students but lacked the ability to assist them with mathematical problems. When I become a certified instructor, I will be equipped and able to help more children with homework and to understand. My advantage is I'm confident I will be able to connect with them. They prefer to be taught by a person of their own culture. —Alesha Rodiquez

It has given me the opportunity to pursue a teaching career (a dream). Financially, I would have been unable to continue my desire to teach. It has moved a huge mountain for me. I feel that Native teachers, as role models, will provide the Native child a chance to be proud of themselves and to learn their own heritage comes from caring and knowledgeable relatives. Native teachers can give the child, and the school, a stable environment and commitment because most Native teachers want to be at home in their environment and to teach their children. —Joette Thayer

I know that I wanted to pursue a profession that will allow me to work with kids, and I know I wanted that profession to be within my tribe. The only problem was I had no funding to further my education. Therefore, OKSALE has given me the ability to further my education and pursue my dream. I think that the OKSALE teachers will be one step ahead of other teachers because they will have a better understanding and knowledge to meet the needs and address children of different cultures. —Caniece Romar

Without the OKSALE Program, I don't think I would have been able to pursue my teaching career. For a number of financial reasons, it is necessary that I work to contribute to the support of my family. The OKSALE Program accommodates my schedule. I had nearly given up on my dream to be a teacher when I heard about this program. It has given me hope in more ways that I can tell. The information I am learning is incredible! I wish every prospective

teacher could see education from this viewpoint. The Native community has lost its "invisibility" to me. I am learning important information about meeting the educational needs of Native children as well as all other children.
—Patti Moreno

These student voices are a reminder that native teacher preparation programs expand the knowledge base that positively promotes social change throughout Indian country. Students are making sacrifices and investments to participate in a program that will fulfill their lifelong dream of becoming a teacher. In return, students are receiving the personal care and support that is characteristic of a TCU. As a gift, all children in the circle receive instruction from successful role models who are highly trained in their professional field.

CONCLUSION: ESTABLISHING THE CONTEXT OF CONNECTIVITY

The foundation of native teacher preparation programs is establishing connectivity. Connectivity in the education of American Indian and Alaskan Native people means feeling that you are part of the educational process. For teachers and professors, this means understanding the language and cultural issues of native communities and being able to incorporate these insights into classroom instruction. For the community, it means accepting teachers and postsecondary education representatives openly and inviting them to be part of the formal and informal learning in the native community that extends beyond the school grounds.

Achieving connectivity will require that every teacher and professor (native and nonnative) suspend their biases, stereotypes, and perceptions of Indian children and communities that create environments of inequality. Achieving connectivity also will require that teachers and postsecondary representatives be welcomed into all aspects of community members' lives. Such an invitation is important so that every K–12 teacher and professor is enlightened about important aspects of how language and culture influence learning in native communities.

Connectivity means K–12 and postsecondary institutions establishing relationships with the native community, and information technology facilitates this process. Imagine that we live in a community where teachers and parents feel comfortable communicating freely and openly with one another, locally and globally. For educational personnel, this means being able to converse with native parents about their children's learning development or being able to talk with professors about ways to promote American

Indian and Alaska Native learning outcomes in the classroom and community. For native parents, open communication presents the opportunity to be involved in the formal instruction of their children and to talk with other parents and educational professionals about educational issues.

In whatever form it takes, connectivity is about finding a way to talk about ourselves as spiritual people and allowing us to talk about things with each other so that we share our worldview in a way that is accepted and respected by K–12 and postsecondary representatives. Connectivity is both our greatest challenge and our greatest opportunity to make a difference in the education of American Indian and Alaskan Native students. We believe it is possible to reach the time in our lives when every K–12 teacher, higher education professor, native parent, native student, and native community member is able to say, "I feel connected to the educational system and do whatever I can to breathe life into the school and community environment of American Indian and Alaskan Native people."

ACKNOWLEDGMENTS

The authors thank Ms. Vivian Delgado for her invaluable assistance in the writing of this chapter.

REFERENCES

Alliance for Equity in Higher Education. (2000). *Educating the majority: The role of minority-serving colleges and universities in confronting America's teacher crisis*. Washington, DC: The Institute for Higher Education Policy.

Ambler, M., & Crazy Bull, C. (1997). Survey: Tribal colleges deeply involved in research. *Tribal College, 9*(1), 12–15.

American Indian College Fund, (2000). *Annual report*. Denver, CO: Author.

Campbell, M. H. (1998). Fort Peck combines language immersion with Montessori methods. *Tribal College, 9*(4), 15.

Finley, V. (1997). Designing a cultural leadership program. *Tribal College, 9*(2), 19–22.

Indian Nations at Risk Task Force. (1991). *Indian Nations at Risk: An educational strategy for action*. Washington, DC: U.S. Department of Education.

Pavel, M. (1997). Who pays to educate tribal college students? Victory in Wisconsin important precedent. *Tribal College, 9*(3), 52–54.

Pavel, D. M., & Curtin, T. R. (1997). *Characteristics of American Indian and Alaska Native education: Results from the 1993–94 and 1990–91 schools and staffing survey*. (NCES 97-451), Washington DC: U.S. Department of Education, National Center for Education Statistics.

Swisher, K. (1990). Cooperative learning and the education of American Indian/Alaskan native students: A review of the literature and suggestions for implication. *Journal of American Indian Education, 29*(2), 36–43.

IV

Extending the Reach
of Tribal Colleges and Universities

11

Student Access, Retention, and Success: Models of Inclusion and Support

Anna M. Ortiz
Michigan State University
Iris HeavyRunner
Fort Peck Community College

INTRODUCTION

Betty began attending classes after she was divorced. She lived about 30 miles from the college campus. Betty excelled and made the honor roll every semester she attended. During the fall semester, her car broke down and she could not afford to fix it. She also became ill and missed two weeks of class. Her ex-husband refused to give her any financial support, and she was nearly evicted from her home because she had no money to pay the rent. Betty came to the counselor and said she intended to withdraw from college. The counselor suggested that she not withdraw until the counselor had spoken to the instructors. Later, Betty came to the counselor to report that the instructors had gone to their church congregations and asked for donations to help her buy a car. They were able to raise enough money so Betty could buy a used car. As she told her story to the counselor, Betty was so overcome by their concern that she couldn't stop crying. Thanks to two caring instructors, Betty continued to do well in her classes and graduated in 2001.

(Personal communication, April 20, 2000)

Tribal colleges and universities (TCUs) have helped students like Betty overcome personal and family problems while attending those institutions. Many tribal college students begin classes with good intentions and high expectations. Unfortunately, for more than half who enroll, these expectations of completing college and finding a better life are not realized. Students bring with them the baggage of many years of failure—failed marriages and relationships, periods of unemployment and welfare dependency, and, for some, histories of drug and alcohol addiction (Bowker, 1992; Ewen, 1997; O'Brien, 1992). Enrolling in college represents a new beginning, but to succeed, the students need to learn strategies to overcome the failures of the past.

The story of Native Americans in higher education is filled with successes and challenges. As with other ethnic minority groups, Native Americans' participation in higher education is a complex picture. Although the proportion who participate in higher education is slightly higher than their representation in the nation's population, thus indicating parity[1] (1% versus .09%, respectively), their numbers remain small. Of the more than 14.2 million students in our nation's colleges and universities, only 145,300 are American Indian (all statistics in this section are drawn from the *Chronicle of Higher Education*, 2001). African American and Hispanic students participate below parity, but far greater numbers of these students attend college than do Native Americans (see Table 11.1). Because the presence of a significant number of coethnics on campus leads to greater individual success in terms of retention and satisfaction with college, the fine distinctions between parity and achievement of critical mass are important (Tinto, 1997).

A close look at patterns of participation of Native American students reveals areas of additional concern as well as evidence of success. For instance, in academic year 1997–1998, Native Americans received only .6% of the bachelor's degrees, .5% of the master's degrees, and .4% of the doctoral degrees awarded in the United States (see Table 11.2). A study of the educational progression of freshmen admitted in 1989–1990 indicates that only 15.8% of Native American students who began their college careers received their bachelor's degree by 1994 and only 11.9% received their associate's degree (*Chronicle of Higher Education*, 2001). These numbers are lower than those cited by Brandt (1992) who found a dropout rate of 50.9% among Navajo students. However, there are strong signs of improvement. For instance, the number of Native Americans enrolling in higher educa-

---

[1]When participation in an educational institution matches the proportion of that ethnic or racial group in the population, that group is judged to have reached parity in terms of participation.

Table 11.1

Participation in Two- and Four-Year Institutions by Ethnic Group

Ethnic Group	Two-Year Institution	Four-Year Institution	Total Population	Total Student Population
Native American	72,100 (49.6)	73,400 (50.4)	(0.9)	145,300 (1.0)
Asian American	355,800 (39)	553,900 (61)	(3.6)	909,700 (6.0)
African American	687,700 (41)	962,000 (59)	(12.3)	1,640,700 (11.5)
Hispanic	735,100 (55.8)	581,400 (44.2)	(12.5)	1,316,600 (9.2)
White	3,670,400 (35.8)	6,592,200 (64.2)	(75.1)	10,262,500 (71.9)
Total	5,512,100 (38.6) (38.7)	8,762,700 (61.4)		14,274,800

Note. Foreign students were not included in the analysis. Percentage of ethnic group distribution in percentages.

Table 11.2

Degrees Conferred in 1997–1998 by Ethnic Group

Ethnic Group	Associate Degree	Bachelor's Degree	Master's Degree	Doctorate Degree	Professional Degree
American Indian	6,200 (1.0)	7,894 (0.6)	2,049 (0.5)	187 (0.4)	561 (0.7)
Asian American	25,047 (4.4)	71,592 (6.0)	21,088 (4.9)	2,334 (5.0)	7,712 (9.8)
African American	55,008 (9.8)	98,132 (8.2)	30,097 (7.0)	2,066 (4.4)	5,483 (6.9)
Hispanic	45,627 (8.2)	65,937 (5.6)	16,215 (3.8)	1,270 (2.7)	3,547 (4.5)
White	411,336 (73.6)	900,317 (76.0)	307,587 (71.5)	28,747 (62.5)	59,273 (75.4)

Note. Percentages of total degree category in parentheses.

217

tion has been rising each year since 1976. In fact, current rates of participation are twice as high in 1976. In addition, in the past several years, Native Americans' patterns of attendance in sectors of higher education have shifted from majority enrollment in 2-year colleges to majority enrollment in 4-year colleges and universities (50.4%). This shift is significant because there is ample evidence that attaining a bachelor's degree confers fringe benefits that exceed those gained by earning an associate's degree (Astin, 1985). This shift may also signify tribal colleges' success in having student transfer to 4-year higher education institutions.

Part of the enrollment picture includes the vast number of Native American students who choose to begin their college careers at a local TCU. This choice is appropriate for students who wish to or need to remain close to home, who value culturally relevant higher education, and who find the low cost of TCUs attractive (Wright, 1989). Enrollment patterns in the 33 tribal colleges that have been established over the past three decades have also evidenced shift and growth. In 1982, 2,100 American Indians were enrolled in tribal colleges. By 1991, tribal colleges were serving almost *seven times* that many students, with an enrollment of 13,800 full- and part-time students, representing 14% of the American Indians enrolled in higher education [American Indian Higher Education Consortium (AIHEC), 1999]. By 1995–1996, enrollment over the 12-month academic period reached 24,363 undergraduates and 260 graduate students (AIHEC, 1999). Enrollment continues to climb rapidly, and many TCUs are struggling to keep up with the growing demand (Boyer, 1997a).

Another piece of the picture includes the participation of women and older students in higher education, which has changed quite dramatically over the past 20 years, and this pattern is also evident in TCUs. For instance, in fall 1996, 56% of the undergraduates at all public institutions were women, as compared to 64% at tribal colleges (U.S. Department of Education, 1990–1997).[2] In fact, from the beginning of the tribal college movement in 1968, most tribal college students have been older and most have been women. The typical tribal college student is often described as a single mother in her early 30s [American Indian College Fund (AICF), 2000]. Tribal college officials explain that this population is the least served by higher education, yet it is the most eager to receive a degree. American Indian women with children, especially, are often determined to get off welfare and provide for their families, but they are unable or unwilling to leave

---

[2]These figures vary by institution; 76% of the students at Sisseton Wahpeton Community College were women as compared to 46% at Haskell Indian Nations University (U.S. Department of Education, 1990–1997).

home and attend schools in distant cities. For them, tribal colleges are the only option (Boyer, 1989). The fact is that, even with the recent surge of interest in persistence, we still know relatively little about the specific attributes of attrition among older women. Yet, common experience tells us that the experience of older students and of females differs, at least in part, from that of younger male college students (Tinto, 1997).

With near exponential growth over the past 20 years, TCUs serve over a third of all native students in 2-year colleges. As is illustrated elsewhere in this book and in this chapter, this growth has occurred in environments with significant challenges. Whereas the institutions confront problems with financing, governance, and tribal relations, the Native American student faces problems of equal complexity. Experiences in college often include difficulties of how to juggle academic, family, and community responsibilities as well as academic challenges that their precollege experiences have not prepared them for. These challenges, in addition to issues about cultural continuity, are explored in this chapter. The chapter concludes with examples of model programs that have been developed to specifically address the concerns of the Native American student.

HALF THE BATTLE: GETTING TO COLLEGE

Tribal communities, in which most of the tribal colleges are located, face staggering unemployment rates, ranging from 45% to 90% (AIHEC, 1999; Boyer, 1997b; Karger & Stoesz, 1998; Stein, 1992). In addition to economic hurdles, tribal college students and their families face many social obstacles. For example, the suicide rate for American Indians is more than twice that of other racial/ethnic minority groups, the death rate from alcohol-related causes is very high, and the already large number of single-parent households continues to increase (O'Brien, 1992). Students' K–12 experiences often reflect the effects of poverty and family difficulties. As with other patterns of educational achievement, success in college reflects students' high school experiences and socialization in the home community.

Students often find the cultural disconnect between school and community to be an obstacle to their academic success. Reyhner, Lee, and Gabbard (1993) found that it was not environmental or cognitive deficits that caused poor performance in high school, but rather cultural discontinuity between home and school. They found that high schools did little to make the curriculum or teaching styles culturally relevant to students. However, Ambler (1998) questioned the soundness of cultural infusion at the expense of basic education stating, "In their attempt to emphasize culture, programs may not devote enough attention to science, resulting in students who are ghettoized and competent to enter only their local tribal employment market" (p. 8). Instead, she advocated the creation of curricula that reflect the experiences of Native American students, where they can see themselves in literature read in English courses and where native interpretations help students learn science.

Disagreements about the curriculum and its effects are compounded by the treatment Native Americans often receive from their nonnative teachers. In addition to a feeling that such teachers may not care about or understand native students (Shields, 1999), they often have lower expectations for these students, which tends to reinforce belief in a cultural deficit model. Teachers often make judgments about students' home, family, and resources that affect how they work with these students. Shields found this pattern in her study of native high school students and their teachers. Teachers believed that students generally came from one-parent families, had few modern conveniences in the home, had families that were unsupportive of educational goals, and came from communities that did not nurture Navajo culture.

However, Shields (1999) did not characterize their homes in this way. More than half of the students reported that their homes had electricity and running water, and two thirds lived in two-parent homes. More than 80% said that their primary identification was Navajo, and nearly as many reported that they could speak Navajo fluently. Further, the students' home environment seemed to promote education. The average number of books in the home was 50, and reading materials were purchased on a regular basis.[3] Nearly all students said that their parents would not let them quit school. Students in Shields' study also reported that they were involved in their high school through both academics and extracurricular activities. Other studies have confirmed these findings. Brandt (1992) found that Navajo families did encourage and support education and were regularly involved in school activities. Ewen's (1997) study supported the above-mentioned findings. Students in that study also primarily identified themselves with their Indian nation and did not experience a negative impact on their education from living on a reservation.

It is important to remember that the kinds of family systems native youth experience in their communities do vary. Although the evidence cited earlier demonstrates that students often persist and achieve in concert with

---

[3]The number of books in the house and regular purchase of reading materials are common variables in studies of the effect of the home environment on educational persistence and literacy.

their native identity and despite negative images or stereotypes that educators may hold, there are also times when family systems and cycles of poverty do interfere with students' educational pursuits. At times, family responsibilities disrupt school attendance, primarily because the student's earnings are needed to sustain the family (Dehyle, 1992).

Bowker (1992) found that some students attributed their lack of success in high school to the traditional orientation of their families. They thought they were not encouraged to succeed in school due to expectations that they assume traditional roles in the family and community. Ewen's (1997) study confirmed these findings as students reported that they dropped out primarily due to problems at home or a lack of encouragement from their families to excel. However, Bowker also noted that just as many students from traditional backgrounds did succeed. There is evidence that students' families, whether traditional or nontraditional, are critical to their academic success in college (Lin, 1990; Wenzlaff & Biewer, 1996).

Critics also have cited the communities that many Native American high school students live in as being related to academic underachievement. However, researchers have found that the problem is more complex than socioeconomic factors and also includes the lack of the presence of mentors and models who let students know that education is a valued path to success that can be achieved while still maintaining and nurturing one's native identity. When students see educated community members employed in low-paying jobs in the community, they are less likely to see the value of educational success (Dehyle, 1992; Reyhner et al., 1993). Shields' (1999) findings were related, but notably different. In her study, students could not explain how educational attainment related to success in life, but they believed that they could achieve their goals through education.

Researchers have also speculated that students often view academic success in a negative way, as leading to a future identity as part of the dominant culture in contrast to their Indian identity. This kind of resistance to the dominant culture plays an important, and complex role in how Native American youth interpret their academic experience and commitment to success. The students in Dehyle's (1992) study said they rejected the path to college because they saw that choice as "non-Indian." Students who did achieve felt separated from their Indian peers. A student who was in college-prep mathematics said, "I was the only Indian! So I moved back to basic math. I knew it all 'cause I had it before, but it was all Indian and I felt better. I was the top in that class" (p. 37). Other students like that one commonly report that they are bored in remedial courses. Boredom in class and a dislike of school are often precursors to a host of behavioral difficulties. Indeed, behavioral difficulties stemming from an active dislike of the school experience were the cause of attrition for one third of the students in Dehyle's study.

In the literature on precollege experiences of native youth, there is ample evidence of success despite difficulty. Although Dehyle (1992) found that students might drop out due to attitudes toward school, she did not find evidence of attrition due to academic problems, marriage, or pregnancy. Similarly, Bowker (1992) found that despite living in poverty, prevalence of teen pregnancy, various kinds of abuse, and alcoholism, more than half the women in his study "survived the environment, graduate from high school (and often college), and became very productive citizens within their tribal group, and for some, leaders in their tribes and in their states and nation" (p. 14). Certainly, these are the stories of success that also characterize native experience in higher education.

COLLEGE EXPERIENCES

Experiences of Native American students in college vary by the type of institution they attend and by their family circumstances. Many of the same factors that contribute to success in high school also contribute to success in college. Likewise, barriers that make achieving an education difficult in high school have similar effects in college. And in college, as in high school, native students achieve great success even in the face of seemingly insurmountable odds. However, the fact remains that Native American students have the lowest educational attainment of all ethnic/racial groups and that their participation in higher education is skewed toward 2-year colleges (*Chronicle of Higher Education*, 2001). Of course, the prevalence of Native American students in 2-year institutions is explained by their participation in TCUs, which are predominantly 2-year colleges. Many of the differences in native students' college experiences are associated with whether they attend TCUs or predominantly white universities. Whereas many native students experience a highly supportive environment (the tribal college), others encounter one that is often hostile to their presence (the predominantly white institution).

Factors Affecting Success in College

The connection between family members' experience and history in higher education cannot be overstated. Because Native American students often remain with their families or live in close proximity to them, family members continue to play an important role in students' academic progress. The phenomenon of the first-generation college student is often used as an explanation for the poor performance of native students in higher education (Boyer, 1997a).

Conversely, when students have close relatives and role models who have had successful experiences in college, they are more likely to be successful themselves (Wenzlaff & Biewer, 1996). Support from same-gender family members has been found to play a critical role in academic success. In Bowker's (1992) study of successful college graduates, he found that:

> one factor which seemed to stand out above all others in the lives of girls who succeeded … was the support of their families and particularly that of their mothers and grandmothers. In the case of those who graduated from college, there was often tremendous family support which extended beyond the immediate family. (p. 16)

Furthermore, the nature of the family, for example whether it is modern or traditional, has an influence on the student attending college. Students from modern families (delineated by the mother's education level), were more likely to get support and encouragement in college and felt less of a disconnect between home and college (Lin, 1990). However, students from traditional families were more likely to exhibit behaviors that led to success in college, such as being task and achievement oriented, earning higher grade point averages, and spending more time doing homework (Lin, 1990). These findings are good example of the complex interactions between family and education for native students. Other researchers (Falk & Aitken, 1984; Pavel & Padilla, 1993) confirmed the link between retention and academic success and family support and educational attainment. In fact, college retention was facilitated by family support (Falk & Aitken, 1984).

Although family support is important, family obligations often make it difficult for native students to succeed in college. Tate and Schwartz (1993) discovered that two thirds of the students they studied had family obligations that were serious enough to interfere with school. These problems centered on being nontraditional students with child care, transportation, alcoholism, drug abuse, domestic violence, and employment concerns (Boyer, 1997b). When native students attend predominantly white universities, these family concerns are often dramatically different from those of their white peers (Taylor, 2001). For instance, in Wenzlaff and Biewer's (1996) study, one woman said, "If anything happened to a family member, I would leave in a second to be at home with them" (p. 41). This student thought her white peers would react differently in such a situation.

Academic preparation also plays a significant role in the college success of native students. Although Falk and Aitken (1984) reported that family support was most important in retention, they noted that academic preparation, in the form of study skills, mathematics skills, and career information, reached a close second. Poor academic preparation often offsets Scholastic Aptitude Test (SAT) scores for Native American students, who score higher on this standard test than do African Americans and Latino/as (Reddy, 1993). Remediation becomes a significant barrier for students because they need to spend time and tuition dollars on remedial courses before they can advance to do college level work (Boyer, 1997a). However, students' educational aspirations can counteract the effects of poor academic preparation and might be considered an element of academic preparation. In fact, researchers have found that having high educational aspirations is an important ingredient for success (Brown & Robinson-Kurpius, 1997; Pavel & Padilla, 1993).

Tribal College Experiences

TCUs offer opportunities for Native American students to participate in higher education in ways that support their identity as native people. TCUs recognize the unique challenges in attending college given complex factors such as economics and family dynamics, hence these institutions offer culturally relevant learning that serves to promote the individual and the group. Students at tribal colleges experience a better "institutional fit" that often compensates for the usual 2-year college effects that inhibit transfer and student development (Machamer, 1998). This fit is achieved through integration of Indian thought into the entire curriculum, thus making subjects more accessible and relevant to students (Boyer, 1989). Many TCUs also offer cultural sensitivity training for non-Indian service providers. For students who have spent little time away from the family or the reservation, these measures help to make college less of a disorienting experience.

Students report high satisfaction with tribal colleges even though these institutions are more poorly resourced than traditional 2- and 4-year colleges. Many tribal colleges have student service programs that offer native students additional support that they might not experience in a predominantly white institution. Tutors and academic support and assistance programs offered at tribal colleges give students individual attention, taking into account varied levels of college preparation and the time constraints students may have from fulfilling multiple life roles (e.g., parent and student; Machamer, 1998). Because poor academic preparation is a key factor in attrition once students transfer to 4-year institutions (Falk & Aitken, 1984), these support programs are critical in helping native students meet their higher education goals. Tribal colleges also give students an opportunity to take remedial courses in a supportive environment that is less expensive than a 4-year institution. Courses in basic writing and mathematics skills, and Native American studies are highly valued by students (Wright, 1989).

Faculty members at tribal colleges play key roles in students' success (see Tippeconnic & McKinney, chap. 12). Students at these colleges experience high levels of support from faculty, which helps prevent academic isolation and, ultimately, enhances retention (Buckley, 1997). Boyer (1997b) reported that students often awarded "heroic" status to their professors, whom they perceived as being completely dedicated to their success. When students transferred to predominantly white 4-year institutions, their expectations of faculty were elevated due to the close relationships they thought they had with their tribal college faculty. However, students also felt that tribal college faculty should have higher academic expectations of students (Boyer, 1997b). Support needed to be balanced with appropriate challenges so that students could succeed in a predominantly white environment.

Although tribal colleges provide culturally relevant curricula and supportive institutional climates for Native American students, they experience many of the same afflictions that affect these students' success in higher education. Students face difficulties with poverty, financing higher education, alcohol and drug abuse, language differences, and family dysfunction (Dodd, Garcia, Meccage, & Nelson, 1995). Similarly, the institutions suffer from insufficient academic and financial resources (see also Stein, Shanley, & Sanchez, chap. 4). Students may find that the tribal college in their community has limited offerings of majors and programs, and therefore they leave the institution (Boyer, 1997a; Wright, 1989).

The tribal communities and governance structures that create and support TCUs may, at times, interfere with the institutions' ability to function smoothly. Political conflicts and resource-distribution disagreements within the tribal community often affect the leaders of the tribal college (see Stein chap. 2; Shanley chap. 3; Stein, Shanley, & Sanchez chap. 4, this volume). The tribal council may serve as the college's board of trustees, thus exerting influence on the academic program and personnel decisions that influence the education students receive. Students commonly know of these conflicts and experience their effects. Machamer (1998) found that conflicts between staff, administrators, faculty, and boards of trustees also took their toll on students' satisfaction with their college. Because resources in tribal communities can be scarce, many tribal colleges also have poorly maintained facilities and lack of space to conduct college business (Boyer, 1997a).

Experiences at Predominantly White Institutions

Ideally, tribal colleges help students develop the self-esteem and academic skills they need to succeed at predominantly white institutions when they transfer to earn a baccalaureate degree. Native Americans must go to these campuses fully prepared because they face considerable obstacles in predominantly white institutions. No longer are student services all located in one office; rather, they are dispersed throughout the campus. Wenzlaff and Biewer (1996) recommend that students connect early with people who can help them negotiate the larger, more complex environment. Students in Taylor's (2001) study spoke of at least one person at the university who encouraged them and motivated them to succeed. They acknowledged that a connection with more than one person is also important as students need to develop strong bonds with native peers and faculty. This is critical when students leave home and the tribal community to attend college. Data indicate that native students are incredibly resilient. Lin, LaCounte, and Eder (1988) found that, although Native American students achieved lower grade point averages and felt more hostility and isolation than their white peers, they were more positive about their college experience and had educational aspirations similar to those of their white peers.

At predominantly white colleges, academic and social integration are strong predictors of retention and degree completion (Tinto, 1997). The same was confirmed for native students in a study by Pavel and Padilla (1993), who found that academic integration and students' intentions to complete their degrees were among the most important variables that directly and indirectly affect postsecondary outcomes. Academic integration is important because precollege academic factors such as high school rank, SAT scores, and grade point averages do not predict college success for native students. High-achieving students were found to be just as likely to have difficulty as their less prepared native peers (Benjamin, Chambers, & Rieterman, 1993). Academic integration is a function not only of success in courses, but also of relationships with faculty and staff. Students reported that having professors who were caring and willing to find answers helped them succeed in college (Dodd et al., 1995). Staff and/or faculty at TCUs provide native students who are the first in their families to attend college with academic advice and guidance that others may receive from family members who have college experience (Taylor, 2001).

Social integration also plays a significant role in the success of native students. Friendships in general (Dodd et al., 1995) and those formed through student organizations and activities enhance student retention (Wenzlaff & Biewer, 1996). Students in Taylor's (2001) study speculated that having native cultural centers on campus, places that symbolize the center of the community, would promote student retention. Cultural centers are key because it is important for students to feel that they are a part of the institutional culture and experiences. Institutional and student culture and values need to be congruent for social integration to be successful. Tinto (1997) posited that when students are in close alignment with the culture of the institution, their social integration is more complete. When students' values differ significantly from those of the mainstream institution, the incongruence can lead to a sense of isolation and early attrition. Taylor (2001) found that native students believed that their values were incongruent with those of the mainstream institution. They felt the university had capitalist values, was Christian in nature, had a competitive ethos, was materialistic, and had a Western orientation. They also thought the university had limited definitions of family and family obligations, making it difficult for native students to manage their family obligations and succeed academically.

Tinto (1997) also argued that if there is a critical mass of students at the institution, students can form strong subcultures that, although marginal, play important roles in social integration and retention. Native students find their subculture through staff and support services directed at the native student community and through native student organizations on campus. The notion of critical mass is important because there must be enough native students at a particular campus to form a supportive group. Native students also experience discrimination, racism, and other "microagressions" that alienate them from the college environment. Despite some evidence that there are no differences in retention rates for students who experience discrimination (Brown & Robinson-Kurpius, 1997), the problem is persistent enough for students to feel isolated on campus without the presence of a native student community on campus.

Predominantly white institutions do offer support services that benefit many native students. Larger institutions may have offices specifically designated for native student support services and cultural programs, but this model is rare in typical 4-year institutions. Most often, support programs for all "minority" students are streamlined in a common office, with cultural-program implementation being delegated to the native student organization on campus. Efforts made by administrators of predominantly white institutions often are not highly valued by Native American students. In Taylor's (2001) interview study of native students at a mainstream institution, students neglected to mention many institutional initiatives (special support services, native student organizations, summer programs, and Native American studies programs) designed to support native and other minority students as sources of support for retention. Neither did they mention that the institution had given the native student organization $70,000 to fund their annual pow wow. Students explained that one of the reasons support programs and administrators were seen as unsupportive was that staff members from those offices seldom came to events and had little contact with native students. When administrators learned of this dissatisfaction, they became frustrated because they believed the funding itself was sufficient to meet student needs.

Faculty in predominantly white institutions also pose challenges to Native American students. Because academic integration is important for student success in higher education, faculty play a crucial role in the lives of native students (Bowker, 1992; Dehyle, 1992; Tate & Schwartz, 1993). Faculty determine the pedagogy that will be used in the classroom. Some evidence has indicated that native and white students learn differently. Wilson (1997) found that native students tended to prefer an active-experimentation orientation to learning, in which they learn by engaging in projects and small-group discussions. This contradicts the preferred style of white students (abstract conceptualization) and the dominant form of teaching in the university—lecturing. Nearly half of the nation's faculty reported that they used extensive lecturing in their courses (Sax, Astin, Arredondo, & Korn, 1996). In contrast, only a third of the faculty used cooperative learning methods and only 20% used experiential learning (Sax et al., 1996). The content of courses is also important. Faculty play an instrumental role in making sure that Native Americans are depicted in the material used in class. They have the ability to provide some of the assets of the tribal college experience through integrating tribal culture and values into the course (Boyer, 1997a; Taylor, 2001).

Faculty who are accessible, approachable, and available motivate students to succeed (Wilson, 1997). In Boyer's (1997b) study, many students expected their professors at 4-year institutions to be similar to the faculty at their tribal college, where students perceived faculty as being more than dedicated to students. Conversely, Tate and Schwartz (1993) found that poor faculty contact was a barrier to retention. Further, students thought that faculty at mainstream institutions did not understand their educational needs or family responsibilities.

EFFECTIVE MODELS AND PROGRAMS

The Native American Higher Education Initiative (NAHEI) programs and models demonstrate exceptional examples of increasing native students' access to and retention in higher education. Collaborations between TCUs and mainstream institutions of higher education (IHEs) include programs in which resources are shared, course content and scheduling are realigned to fit articulation agreements, and student support services are connected and streamlined. These initiatives have been developed over the course of 5 or more years, bolstered with funding from the W. K. Kellogg Foundation in 1996. One of the key objectives of the NAHEI project was to develop and enhance student support programs, in addition to several other objectives focusing on the institutions and their associated communities. In this section, several of these projects are highlighted as examples of programs that have been successful in attracting students to higher education and retaining them once they are enrolled. These initiatives answer the call in the literature presented earlier in this chapter. They show that education that is connected to culture, services that are responsive to diverse family and community relationships, and programs designed to build the efficacy of native communities can be instrumental in enhancing student progress and success.

A Focus on Students and Their Families: Family Education Model

The Family Education Model (FEM) is an integrated system designed to improve retention rates among students at TCUs. The FEM, based on principles of education and social work, was developed and implemented at four tribal colleges in Montana (Blackfeet Community College, Salish/Kootenai College, Stone Child College, and Fort Peck Community College). The model shifts the paradigm from a focus on drop-outs to a family-centered approach, building on student and family strengths. "The strengths based perspective is an approach honoring the innate wisdom of the human spirit, the inherent capacity for transformation of even the most humbled and abused" (Saleeby, 1996, p. 3). In the FEM, the focus is on seeing students not at-risk, but at-promise. From their inception, tribal colleges have been at the forefront of providing student support services that view students in the context of their extended kinship structures and traditional cultural values.

The FEM offers strategies to help tribal college students develop a sense of connection with the college. Students' families are involved in cultural activities such as social dancing, feasting, storytelling, traditional dressmaking, gardening, and cooking. In this way, the entire family feels a part of the college experience, instead of resenting the time the student spends on his or her studies. These activities continue throughout the student's involvement in the college (e.g., orientation, registration, midterm, and graduation). Establishing and maintaining a sense of "family" both at home and at college is a critical factor in the retention of American Indian students (Dodd et al., 1995; Mainor, 2001; Rousey & Longie, 2001; Shanley, 1999; Wenzlaff & Biewer, 1996).

As another strategy, faculty initiate the Search and Rescue Team, a form of intrusive monitoring, when students appear to be at-risk for leaving college. For example, the team receives a referral from faculty and sends a postcard asking the student to contact student support services. When one student, Sara (not her real name), received such a postcard and contacted the counselor, she said she was ready to withdraw. The counselor asked her to explain why she felt she could not continue in college. Sara said she had a 6-month-old baby with a cold and the day-care center would not take her. Because Sara had no one who could care for her baby, she stayed home with her. Sara also told the counselor that she had been walking from her apartment to the day-care center downtown and then walking more than a mile to the classroom building. As the weather turned colder, she did not like taking the baby out.

After team members were told about Sara's situation, they went to work. The assigned team member contacted Sara's instructors, who provided her home-study assignments so that she could make up the work she had missed. The financial-aid officer helped Sara obtain a $300 supplemental grant so she could purchase a used car. Sara's name did not appear on the referral list thereafter, and she completed the semester with a 2.3 grade point average. The frequency and perceived worth of interaction with faculty, staff, and other students, is one of the strongest predictors not only of student persistence, but also of student development (Tinto, 1997).

A third strategy of the model, family life skills, covers such topics as resource management, decision-making skills, communication skills, conflict resolution, parenting skills, anger management, star quilt making, traditional food preparation, and the study of native plants. Students are encouraged to attend the seminars with their spouses and children. Gilda Ferguson, director of Family Focus in Chicago's North Lawndale neighborhood, believes that if parents are nurtured, they in turn can nurture their children (Schorr, 1997). Likewise, if the families of tribal college students are nurtured, they in turn will nurture these students.

Linkages Between TCUs and IHEs:
Leech Lake Tribal College and Bemidji State University

Leech Lake Tribal College (LLTC) and Bemidji State University (BSU) developed strategies to help LLTC students transfer to BSU. Specifically, having a NAHEI-funded native mediator/counselor resulted in a 50% decrease in early withdrawals, a 38% increase in LLTC student transfers, a 200% increase in enrollment of LLTC students at BSU, and a 300% increase in the number of Indian students earning 4-year degrees in the 1998–1999 academic year. (For more information on linkages see Nichols & Monette, chap. 6, this volume.)

Focus on Student Affairs Professionals: The National Institute
for Native Leadership in Higher Education (NINHLE)

The National Institute for Native Leadership in Higher Education (NINHLE), founded in 1993, is a national nonprofit organization affiliated with the University of New Mexico. Members of the strategic alliance include 125 educational professionals from more than 95 public and private universities, TCUs, and national education organizations across the United States and Canada. Through the Training Fellowship Program, those responsible for designing and implementing effective retention programs share their expertise with others who will then attempt to replicate this success in their own institutions and organizations. In their evaluations, participants consistently give the training fellowship program top marks, not only for skills training and networking, but also for personal empowerment and spiritual renewal. The annual meeting brings together native students from mainstream postsecondary institutions throughout the country for an intensive leadership development program. Participants are asked to approach the gathering as they would a ceremony—in a good way, with minds and bodies unclouded by alcohol or other drugs and with hearts and spirits open to giving, receiving, and sharing.

As native people, we know that humor is often the best medicine, so each Institute starts with icebreaker games, and the first evening is devoted to playing NINLHE's own game show, Indians in Jeopardy. Each day begins with prayer and reflection by elders-in-residence who also lead activities such as sweat lodge ceremonies, talking circles, and a sunrise ceremony. Participants take time each day for personal reflection and physical exercise by making use of the walking trails and sports facilities at the meeting site. In all these ways, the training is designed to help participants make connections to each other and reclaim a balance among the physical, intellectual, emotional, and spiritual aspects of themselves.

Rather than work directly with students, as several other organizations already do, NINLHE works to bolster the skills and staying power of those professionals responsible for improving Native American recruitment, retention, and graduation rates. By strengthening these key individuals, NINLHE can, by extension, improve the educational experience of thousands of native college students. At the institutional level, NINLHE works to improve retention rates among native students and student affairs professionals by changing higher education institutions into more supportive learning and working environments for Native Americans.

A Culturally Relevant Academic Programs: Crownpoint Institute of Technology (CIT)

The literature has indicated that learning is enhanced when students can connect content and theory to real life experiences. The Crownpoint Institute of Technology's (CIT) Alternative Livestock and Veterinary Science Program is an example of this theory-to-practice relationship. The program, which involves raising elk and llamas, provides genetic-research opportunities in embryo transfer, artificial insemination, and other reproductive technologies. The project has pursued a small business and entrepreneurship program marketing elk velvet antler products as health supplements rather than raising the elk for the marketing of meat products. As a means of increasing student retention, the project offers cultural-awareness activities for students. These activities include workshops and presentations by Diné elders, who use tribal history and language to teach about traditional medicines and animal health practices.

Providing Access Through Distance Education: Salish Kootenai College (SKC)

As a leading institution in distance education, Salish Kootenai College (SKC) developed the Expanded Access to Guided Learning Environments (EAGLE) Project in which two upper division baccalaureate degree programs were developed, one in environmental science and the other in tribal human services. By fall 2000, SKC faculty had designed 22 of 52 upper level courses required for the new baccalaureate degree programs. The degrees are offered to 27 TCUs offering only associate of arts degrees. In anticipation of receiving approval from its accrediting body to offer degrees through online education, SKC tested and implemented a system for online student admissions and registration. In November, 2000, SKC hosted the first International Indigenous Peoples Distance Education Conference. The objectives of the conference were to embrace learning from ancient wisdom, share experiences, understand how education in cyberspace can preserve tribal culture, and develop a networking forum with indigenous professionals from around the globe. (For more information on the project, see O'Donnell, chap. 13, this volume.)

Partnerships to Build a Virtual University: The North Dakota Intertribal College Partnership

The North Dakota Intertribal College Partnership is a consortium of six tribal colleges serving American Indian students and communities in North and South Dakota. The purpose of this statewide collaboration is to develop a virtual college (i.e., a way to serve students in several colleges by sharing courses using distance education technology) to increase access for native students to higher education. By August, 2000, 11 interactive video network (IVN) courses had been provided to 233 students; these courses generated 23 hours of credit. Twenty-six Internet courses were being offered on the North Dakota Association of Tribal Colleges (NDATC) Website. The courses range from the arts and sciences, to macro and microeconomics, to speech classes. Some courses provide unique viewpoints that are rarely available in mainstream institutions of higher education (e.g., Holocaust From a Native American Perspective).

A Native-based Teacher Education Program: OKSALE

The lack of Native American teachers in native communities is a significant issue in the academic progress of students in K–12 systems. Native American teachers' ability to connect with the experiences of native children and to teach in a way that honors native culture and language is key to academic success. In an effort to "grow our own," Northwest Indian College (NWIC) and Washington State University (WSU), through an NAHEI- funded partnership, implemented the baccalaureate-level OKSALE Native Teacher Education Program, which reaches out to native K–12 students in native communities and tribes within the entire state. The partnership secured a $10 million 5-year grant from the U.S. Department of Education, which provides subcontracts to its partner TCU and public and tribal schools in the state that serve native students. Through teacher training as well as technical training and assistance, the subcontracts focus on improving the ways in which the educational needs of native students are met. Enhancing this

NAHEI-initiated partnership is the inclusion of tribal governments in the form of a tribal advisory board to WSU, comprising of tribal chairpersons from participating tribal governments. (For more information on this project; see Pavel, Larimore, & VanAlstine, chap. 10, this volume.)

Developing K–12 Educational Leaders: The Oyate Consortium

Professional development of teachers is also enhanced by opportunities to participate in graduate education. When graduate education is provided within the framework of native education, teachers can be trained to be more effective with native youth. The Oyate Consortium (Oglala Lakota College, Si Tanka College, Sitting Bull College, Sinte Gleska University, and Sisseton Wahpeton Community College) in collaboration with the University of South Dakota established the *Akicita Oyuha Waste* (warriors making things work well) master's degree program with an emphasis on educational administration for K–12 school principals. Program personnel have worked with the University of South Dakota to gain state board of education approval for the degree. Forty graduate students are enrolled in the master's degree program. In the year 2000, the first student graduated with a master's of arts degree. Currently, graduate courses are being offered at Oglala Lakota College, Si Tanka College, and Sitting Bull College. This is the only tribal college graduate program nationwide that leads to state certification as a principal.

RECOMMENDATIONS

The story of Native Americans' success in TCUs and in higher education in general has difficulties, but, in general, improvement has been consistent and meaningful in recent years. TCUs have been particularly adept at providing education that meets the needs of students who are seeking vocational training, high school equivalency, academic preparation for higher education, and transfer to four-year institutions. They have done all this with limited resources, little supportive centralization, and largely without state or federal support. Several recommendations are made here in the hope of strengthening the educational experiences of students at TCUs.

Recommendation #1: That a Student Database System be Designed That is Both Evaluative and Educational in Nature

TCUs would benefit from a consistent, high-quality, and collaborative system of tracking students' aspirations and progress. Having a national database for all 33 TCUs would help to reflect more accurately the impact of these institutions on student success and on the tribal communities in which they reside. At a minimum, the database could house enrollment statistics, academic outcomes such as grade point average, program-completion information, credit-taking patterns, and transfer rates. A more sophisticated database could also record student characteristics that have been shown to affect retention, participation in support programs designed to enhance persistence, and program completion. If collected annually, information on these variables can be linked to show what experiences and characteristics contribute to departure, as well as where students are interfacing with the institution in meaningful ways. The student database system can assist TCUs and mainstream IHEs track and report progress in student retention in terms of recruitment, placement, advising, financial aid, and tutoring. In addition to providing important feedback to the institution about the progress of its students and the effectiveness of its programs, a collective database for the TCU sector of higher education can also help in securing philanthropic and government funds for additional programs and resources.

Recommendation #2: Institutional Staff (i.e., Retention Officer, Student Support Services, Counselor, Financial Aid Officer, Faculty, Distance Education Coordinator) Should Design Systems-Oriented Interventions to Reduce the Number of Withdrawals

Systems-oriented interventions focus on the reciprocal interactions between college and family and assist individual students see how they contribute to their own persistence. Tribal college staff with this orientation draw heavily on cultural/interaction theory, assisting students learn to express their needs and feelings in nonthreatening ways and to listen attentively; such staff model for students effective problem-solving skills (Hepworth, Rooney, & Larsen, 1997). Systems-oriented student support services acknowledge that students must be successful in several areas of life in order to effectively navigate and succeed in higher education. The examples cited in this chapter characterize a systems approach to student support. The programs attend to the learner's academic needs, to the learner's responsibilities (such as families), to the learner's culture, and to the learner's tribal community. When these systems are synchronous, the learner stands a better opportunity for success. As a part of such systems, retention efforts that are grounded in the concepts of cultural resilience (e.g., feasts, humor, elders, spirituality), family kinship, and community can help students achieve their educational goals.

Recommendation #3: Native Students Should be Helped to Negotiate the Policy Maze of Higher Education

First-generation college students often rely on high school and college administrators and advisors to help them understand the myriad policies that govern participation in higher education. Tribal college student service staff can help students understand financial aid policies and how their attendance patterns may affect their eligibility for aid. For instance, students who simply leave college, rather than officially withdrawing, risk severe consequences in terms of financial aid if they decide to return to college in the future. This point is critical because more than 90% of TCU students receive financial aid.

Attendance and course-taking patterns also impact other policies. Unexpected absences due to family emergencies or planned absences due to tribal ceremonies may negatively affect student's grades. Students should be encouraged to work closely with professors so that they will not be penalized for these absences. Advisors can also help students to understand how the grade point average can affect financial aid eligibility and the ability to continue at a particular institution. The importance of making good academic progress needs to be stressed. Advisors and faculty at TCUs should be informed in articulation or transfer agreements with 4-year institutions. In this way, they can guide students in selecting courses that will meet their overall degree requirements. Finally, advisors should consistently help students to understand time to degree policies. Whereas undergraduate students are seldom affected by these policies, they are strictly enforced for graduate students. Advisors and faculty working with undergraduate students planning to attend graduate school should make sure that these policies are understood.

Recommendation #4: Native Youth Should be Encouraged to Attend TCUs as a Way to Prepare for Transferring to Mainstream Institutions of Higher Education

Not all students who attend TCUs aspire to attain a baccalaureate degree. Those who do are increasingly able to complete the degree at a TCU or through distance-education partnerships with mainstream institutions of higher education. However, many students who aspire to attain a baccalaureate intend to do so at a predominantly white 4-year institution. Students who are underprepared academically for study at these institutions should be encouraged to attend tribal colleges to prepare for transfer. Tribal colleges are better designed to provide a supportive environment for remedial education. Students can take remedial courses at a lower cost than at a 4-year institution, often without the stigma associated with taking these courses at a mainstream institution. Students can also take advantage of the support services and culturally relevant course content and pedagogy characteristic of tribal college educational experiences.

Recommendation #5: Native Students Should be Helped to Choose an Appropriate College

Many tribal college students find that their educational and career aspirations can be met at the tribal college, but others might want to pursue undergraduate or graduate education at a predominantly white institution. K–12 school and college advisers, and community leaders can help native students choose the institutions that have the greatest potential to help them meet their goals. Ample research has demonstrated the importance of a critical mass of native students in enhancing retention. Native students should be encouraged to attend institutions where there are significant numbers of native students in attendance. Students should ask about the vitality of native student organizations and their activities. Campuses with solid support programs designed specifically for native students should especially be encouraged. Because many "satellites" of support have been found to be important for retention, students should consider campuses where there are visible and involved native faculty and staff, and where there are evident linkages to nearby native communities.

Recommendation #6: TCUs Should Continue to Establish and Enhance High-Quality Student Support Services

Much of the research on student satisfaction has indicated that tribal college students are most influenced by faculty and staff. Excellent and caring staff leading effective advising and support programs make a significant difference at institutions that are poor in terms of physical and financial resources, yet rich in human resources. The rescue teams at Fort Peck are an ideal example of how staff and faculty can network to create a safety net for students. These networks can be expanded through the use of peer mentor programs and regular visits from students who have "made it," either in their chosen occupations, tribal leadership, or mainstream institutions of higher education. An extensive team of support individuals can help students overcome the challenges they face as they attempt to fulfill their educational goals while managing childrearing and care issues, transportation difficulties, and the residuals of substance abuse.

FINAL REFLECTIONS

Great strides have been made in tribal college education and in the persistence of native students in higher education. TCU and mainstream student affairs professionals can continue to work to decrease the occurrence of student attrition in higher education by creating supportive learning environments in which native students can attain their educational goals, thereby improving their own lives and those of their families. These efforts require the collaboration that has been shown in AIHEC, NAHEI, and the numerous partnerships among native communities, tribal colleges, and mainstream institutions of higher education. Just as collaboration among these sectors and organizations of higher education is necessary, we must also be mindful that students have their own networks of collaborations, which include family responsibilities, financial commitments, and personal goals. Helping students meet all of these challenges while staying focused on their prize is the noble goal we hope to fulfill.

REFERENCES

Ambler, M. (1998, Fall). Land-based colleges offer science students a sense of place. *Tribal College Journal of American Indian Higher Education, 10*(1), 6–8.

American Indian College Fund. (2000). *Annual report.* Denver, CO: Mansfield, Brewer & Cadue.

American Indian Higher Education Consortium and the Institute for Higher Education Policy. (1999). *Tribal colleges: An introduction.* Washington DC: Author.

Astin, A. W. (1985). *Achieving educational excellence.* San Francisco: Jossey-Bass.

Benjamin, D., Chambers, S., & Rieterman, G. (1993). A focus on American Indian college persistence. *Journal of American Indian Education, 29*(3), 25–40.

Bowker, A. (1992, May). The American Indian female dropout. *Journal of American Indian Education, 31*(3), 3–20.

Boyer, P. (1989, Summer). Higher education and Native American society. *Tribal College of American Indian Higher Education, 1*(1), 10–18.

Boyer, P. (1997a). *Native American colleges: Progress and prospects.* Princeton, NJ: Jossey-Bass.

Boyer, P. (1997b). First survey of tribal college students reveals attitudes. *Tribal College Journal of American Indian Higher Education, 11*(2), 36–41.

Brandt, E. A. (1992). The Navajo area student dropout study: Findings and implications. *Journal of American Indian Education, 31*(2), 48–63.

Brown, L. L., & Robinson-Kurpius, S. E. (1997). Psychosocial factors influencing academic persistence of American Indian college students. *Journal of College Student Development, 38*(1), 3–12.

Buckley, A. (1997). *Threads of nations: American Indian graduate and professional students.* (ERIC Document Reproduction Services No. ED 444771).

Chronicle of Higher Education. (2001). http://chronicle.com.free/almanac/2001/index.htm

Dehyle, D. (1992, January). Constructing failure and maintaining cultural identity: Navajo and Ute school leavers. *Journal of American Indian Education, 31*(2), 24–47.

Dodd, J. M., Garcia, F., Meccage, C., & Nelson, J.R. (1995). American Indian retention. *NASPA Journal, 33*(1), 72–78.

Ewen, A. (1997, Winter). Generation X in Indian country. *Native American, 14*(4), 24–29.

Falk, D. R., & Aitken, L. P. (1984). Promoting retention among American Indian college students. *Journal of American Indian Education, 23*(2), 24–31.

Hepworth, D. H., Rooney, R. H., & Larsen, J. (1997). *Direct social work practice: Theory and skills* (5th ed.). Pacific Grove, CA: Brooks/Cole Publishing Company.

Karger, H., & Stoesz, D. (1998). *American social welfare policy: A pluralist approach* (2nd ed.). New York: Longman.

Lin, R. (1990, May). Perception of family background and personal characteristics among Indian college students. *Journal of American Indian Education, 29*(3), 19–28.

Lin, R., LaCounte, D., & Eder, J. (1988, May). A study of Native American students in a predominantly White college. *Journal of American Indian Education, 27*(3), 8–15.

Machamer, A. M. (1998). Survey reflects student development at D-Q University. *Tribal College Journal of American Indian Higher Education, 10*(2), 38–43.

Mainor, P. (2001). Family matters: Fort Peck Community College tests holistic approach to student success. *Tribal College Journal of American Indian Higher Education, 12*(4), 10–13.

O'Brien, E. M. (1992). American Indians in higher education. *Research Briefs, 3*(3). Washington, DC: American Council on Education.

Pavel, D. M., & Padilla, R. V. (1993). American Indian and Alaska native postsecondary departure: An example of assessing a mainstream model using national longitudinal data. *Journal of American Indian Education, 32*(2), 1–23

Reddy, M. A. (Ed.). (1993). *Statistical record of native North Americans.* Washington, DC: Gale Research.

Reyhner, J., Lee, H., & Gabbard, D. (1993, Spring). A specialized knowledge base for teaching American Indian and Alaska Native students. *Tribal College Journal of American Indian Higher Education, 4*(4), 26–32.

Rousey, A. & Longie, E. (2001). The tribal college as family support system. *American Behavioral Scientist, 44*(9), 1492–1504.

Saleeby, D. (Ed.). (1996). *The strengths perspective on social work practice.* New York: MacMillan.

Sax, L. J., Astin, A. W., Arredondo, M., & Korn, W. S. (1996). *The American college teacher: National norms for the 1995–96 HERI faculty survey.* Los Angeles: University of California, Los Angeles, Higher Education Research Institute.

Schorr, E. (1997). *Common purpose: Strengthening families and neighborhoods to rebuild America.* New York: Anchor Books.

Shanley, J. (1999). Traditional Assiniboine family values: Let us bring back something beautiful. *Tribal College Journal of American Indian Higher Education, 11*(1), 12–17.

Shields, C. M. (1999). Learning from students about representation, identity, and community. *Educational Administration Quarterly, 35*(1), 106–129.

Stein, W. (1992). *Tribally controlled colleges: Making good medicine.* New York: Peter Lang.

Tate, D. S., & Schwartz, C. L. (1993, Fall). Increasing the retention of American Indian students in professional programs in higher education. *Journal of American Indian Education, 33*(1), 21–31.

Taylor, J. S. (2001, April). *Through a critical lens: Native American alienation from higher education.* Paper presented at the Annual Meeting of the American Educational Research Association, Seattle, WA.

Tinto, V. (1997). *Leaving college: Rethinking the causes and cures of student attrition* (2nd ed.). Chicago: University of Chicago Press

U.S. Department of Education, National Center for Educational Statistics. (1990–1997).

Wenzlaff, T. L. & Biewer, A. (1996). Native American students define factors for success. *Tribal College Journal, 12*(4), 40–44.

Wilson, P. (1997). Key factors in the performance and achievement of minority students at the University of Alaska, Fairbanks. *American Indian Quarterly, 21*(3), 535–544.

Wright, B. (1989). Tribally controlled community colleges: An assessment of student satisfaction. *Community/Junior College Quarterly, 13*, 119–128.

12

Native Faculty:
Scholarship and Development

John W. Tippeconnic, III
Pennsylvania State University
Smokey McKinney
Haskell Indian Nations University

INTRODUCTION

American Indian and Alaskan Native faculty (native faculty) often have both a rewarding and a challenging experience at tribal colleges and universities (TCUs). Most likely, the philosophy of the tribal college is congruent with the philosophy of the native faculty member—both based on a tribal perspective grounded in native culture. The result is a more rewarding experience for faculty members that supports their personal commitment to teach and work with native students and other community members to help improve their education and job skills.

The role of native faculty at TCUs can also be difficult and demanding, mainly because there are not enough of them to meet the demand and they have a desire to do more with limited resources. As noted later in this chapter, native faculty must perform a number of roles. Clayton and Born (1998) found that most faculty at tribal colleges teach overloads, often in excess of "20 credits per term" (p. 4). Hence, it becomes difficult to find the time for other activities, especially research, scholarship, and faculty development activities in such environments.

The role of native faculty at mainstream institutions is different from that at TCUs. Native faculty may still come from a tribal perspective and be committed to native students and programs, but the institution's philosophy and expectations are different. Often there is a lack of congruence between what the native faculty member wants to do and what the institution expects. As we note later, the difference may be so great that the tenure and promotion of some native faculty are jeopardized.

The purpose of this chapter is to discuss the role of native faculty, with special attention given to faculty at TCUs. We first discuss the role of faculty in general, and then focus on native faculty at mainstream universities and TCUs. We identify major issues that native faculty face; discuss scholarship and research, faculty development, and some suggestions that show promise; present a vision, and identify some challenges for the future.

THE ROLE OF FACULTY

The role of a member of the professorate or faculty depends on many factors. Two major factors are the type of appointment and the type of college or university at which one works. In a general sense, faculty roles and responsibilities fall into the three main areas of teaching, research and scholarly productivity, and service to the institution, the public, and the profession. The degree to which teaching, research, and service are emphasized and expected of faculty depends on the college or university.

There are different types of colleges and universities. The National Center for Educational Statistics (NCES, 1998), in reporting their higher education data, identified colleges and universities by level, either 2 or 4 year, and by control, either private or public. Most tribal colleges and universities are 2 year, but increasing numbers are developing 4-year programs. Also, tribal colleges are controlled locally and are not considered public institutions.

Using a Carnegie classification system, Clark (1987) identified different types of higher education institutions as (a) doctorate-granting institutions, (b) comprehensive universities and colleges, (c) liberal arts colleges, (d) 2-year institutions, and (e) specialized institutions. Approximately one third of the more than 3,000 higher education institutions are 2-year institutions. The five types are not clearly distinctive from one another; rather, institutions can go from one type to another as they develop. Tribal colleges are usually 2-year institutions or community colleges, although several offer 4-year degrees and two even offer a master's degree. All institutions emphasize teaching, research, and service; it is just that some tend to focus on one area more than others. For example, doctorate granting institutions tend to focus on research especially if they are research I or II universities. Two-year institutions tend to focus more on teaching. The role of faculty would then be related to the institutional emphasis.

The type of faculty appointment is a second key factor in the role they perform. Faculty can be hired full-time or part-time. Part-time hires are usually for a specific time and purpose, like teaching a course or assisting with a research or service project. At times, faculty may be classified as adjunct faculty or faculty affiliates. These are usually nontenure track positions. Full-time faculty are expected to teach, conduct research, and provide service depending on the type of institution. Faculty are expected to be successful and advance through a promotion and tenure system that progresses from assistant professor, to associate professor to full professor.

Faculty are also expected to be part of the university governance and decision-making systems. Faculty participation on committees, such as search committees, diversity committees, curriculum committees, faculty senates, promotion and tenure committees, budget committees, student admission committees is an important part of their service to the college or university.

The Role of Faculty at Tribal Colleges and Universities

The role of faculty at TCUs depends on the institutions' purposes. In general, tribal colleges are 2-year, community-based institutions, although a number have developed 4-year and graduate degree programs. TCUs have unique circumstances and are "part of a movement for fundamental social change within reservations" (P. Boyer, 1997, p. 57). TCUs are considered essential to the future of Native American nations as they (a) establish learning environments that support students who have come to view failure as the norm, (b) celebrate and help sustain Native American traditions, (c) provide essential services that enrich surrounding communities, (d) become centers for research and scholarship (P. Boyer, 1997). Further, TCUs are unique in the sense that their cultural identities are reflected in virtually every aspect of college life [American Indian Higher Education Consortium (AIHEC), 1999]. Each tribal college has a philosophical statement that includes its own tribal background and each has developed academic programs that incorporate that tribal background (Stein, 1992).

It is in this context that TCU faculty work. Rifkin (2000) indicated that commitment to teaching is the hallmark of faculty in community colleges. He further stated that the "community college professorate teaches an increasingly wide range and growing number of students across an array of collegiate, occupational, remedial, and distance learning programs" (p. 1). This is certainly true of TCU faculty, as teaching is considered their primary responsibility. Providing service to the community and the institution is a secondary role, and research and scholarly productivity are increasing in importance.

NATIVE FACULTY

American Indian or native faculty at TCUs are expected not only to teach, provide service, and conduct research activities, but also to provide leadership in sustaining and integrating native cultures and languages as they perform their duties. These responsibilities are also expected of many native faculty at mainstream institutions. This is not an easy task, given the complexities and diversity associated with tribal languages and cultures, native students, curriculum content, and institutional goals. Native faculty are expected to be better teachers, service providers, researchers, and mentors, and to support students more, because of their knowledge and experience in working with native people, and because of their personal commitment to improve the condition of native people in this country.

Native Faculty: Demographics and Characteristics

The total number of native faculty at colleges and universities is increasing. Approximately 30% of the faculty at TCUs are native, whereas at mainstream institutions, natives make up less than 1% of the faculty (AIHEC, 1999). The NCES (1998) reported that tribal colleges employed about 7%of the 3,407 native faculty in all of higher education. The NCES (1998) also indicated that the institutions with the highest percentages of native faculty were tribal colleges: Turtle Mountain Community College (69%), the Institute of American Indian Arts (66%), Fort Belknap College (56%), and Haskell Indian Nations University (54%). The NCES also found that 44% (71 of 161) of the native faculty were employed part-time, whereas 27% (166 of 620) were employed full-time.

Clayton and Born (1998), reporting on a recent Bush Foundation faculty development project, estimated that there were 1,058 faculty at TCUs, and that their salaries typically ranged from $15,000 to $30,000. They surveyed nearly one third, or 290, of those faculty and found data similar to NCES; 34% of TCU faculty were American Indian, and 56% of the native faculty were affiliated with the host tribe of the tribal college. Clayton and Born also found that 67% of the respondents were full-time faculty members, of whom "185 have at least a bachelor's degree, 147 have a master's degree, and 34 have doctoral degrees" (p. 2).

ISSUES FACING NATIVE FACULTY

At Tribal Colleges and Universities

The recruitment and retention of native faculty remains a problem at TCUs, as it does at mainstream institutions. Turnover rates, poor pay, and geographic isolation of tribal colleges are also concerns (AIHEC, 1999; P. Boyer, 1997). Tribal colleges, unable to provide salaries and benefits that are competitive with those at other institutions of higher education, have had their "tribal members with graduate degrees ... lured away to better paying positions off the reservation" (P. Boyer, 1997, p. 33). Many TCUs work at mentoring and nurturing their own students and community members, but lack the resources needed to maintain and nurture such long-term endeavors.

In addition, at tribal colleges and universities, faculty are required to wear many hats. Clayton and Born (1998) reported that 87% of tribal college faculty have some administrative duties. As is true of many community-based colleges, faculty at TCUs have greater teaching loads. Clayton and Born (1998) found that faculty at TCUs "often have responsibility for 6–10 courses a year, so they are severely overworked" (p. 5). Faculty also spend a great deal of time advising students and working in the communities that surround their college campuses. Increased administrative, teaching, student advising and mentoring, and community-involvement roles impose limitations on the time tribal college faculty can contribute to research and writing.

Research and scholarship activities often are not visible in the TCU environment. Although research and scholarship are recognized as being important to both discipline development and to the faculty members' own intellectual growth, often too many more urgent matters demand faculty's attention and time. As a result, TCU faculty members who are engaged in research and scholarship activities often work harder and contribute their own time to the effort. P. Boyer (1997) also noted that the TCUs "reserve a special place for tribal members as instructors of culture, language, and traditional philosophy courses" and that "tribal elders also serve as formal and informal advisors to the college(s), especially on cultural issues" (p. 33).

Despite issues facing faculty at tribal colleges, P. Boyer (1997) reported that students at these institutions were convinced they were receiving an education superior to what they would receive at many mainstream institutions. TCU students, many of whom also attended nontribal colleges, believed their instructors were knowledgeable, accessible, and enthusiastic;

that they enjoyed teaching; and that they encouraged their students to participate actively in classroom discussions.

At Mainstream Colleges and Universities

Sotello-Turner and Myers (2000) summarized some of the major issues facing faculty of color, including native faculty, at colleges and universities. First, they acknowledged that there are few native faculty, and thus the amount of literature that is available on their experiences in higher education is limited. Failure to include native faculty in national studies and data-gathering efforts is an important issue that must be addressed if we are to fully understand and resolve the issues these faculty face. Small sample sizes are a major problem facing researchers who do study natives at colleges and universities (NCES, 1998).

Sotello-Turner and Myers (2000) found that faculty of color identified racial and ethnic bias as the most troubling and difficult challenge at colleges and universities. Other issues that these faculty identified were "feelings of isolation, lack of information about tenure and promotion, unsupportive work environments, gender bias, language/accent bias barriers, lack of mentorship, and lack of support from superiors" (p. 87). Faculty of color also believed they confronted challenges not experienced by white faculty. The researchers identified seven major concerns that were "troubling and burdensome" (p. 87); (a) being denied tenure or promotion due to race or ethnicity, (b) being expected to work harder than whites, (c) having color or ethnicity given more attention than credentials, (d) being treated as a token, (e) lacking support for or validation of research on minority issues, (f) being expected to handle minority affairs, and (g) having too few minorities on campus.

These concerns are prevalent issues for native faculty. Native faculty are the least likely to be tenured of any minority group (NCES, 1998). Further, many native faculty think they have to work harder to be recognized and accepted as scholars by their white colleagues. Too often native faculty are seen as token minorities, which results in their appointment to faculty committees that deal with affirmative action and minority concerns. Native faculty are often viewed as the "Indian experts" on all matters related to native issues; this places a tremendous amount of responsibility on native faculty. Often, this relieves nonnative or white faculty from getting involved and assuming responsibility for learning accurate information about natives that they can use in their scholarly activities.

Teaching can be a "mixed bag" for native faculty. It can be an enjoyable experience if students are open to native ways of knowing or if the students are natives. This is especially true if native faculty are teaching in an Indian studies program or in some other native academic program. However, teaching can be frustrating and difficult, especially if the majority of the students show little interest in the course content or exhibit racist attitudes toward faculty of color. It is also frustrating if student evaluations, used for promotion and tenure, reflect how students feel about faculty of color rather than assessing faculty's teaching ability.

The recruitment, retention, and graduation of native students is a major issue at many colleges and universities and is, in many ways, directly related to native faculty. Native faculty often serve as role models and are instrumental in working with students to ensure their retention and academic success. One strategy for recruiting and retaining more native students is to recruit, retain, and promote more native faculty. It is difficult to separate native faculty from native students in most situations.

Sotello-Turner and Myers (2000) further reported that identity is a major concern among American Indian faculty. It is difficult for native faculty to "maintain ties to their own Indian community while at the same time being part of an often culturally incompatible academic community" (p. 98). Because of their ties to tribal communities, native faculty often provide assistance or service to meet tribal needs, even though that service might not be valued or recognized by the college or university, especially in the promotion and tenure process.

There are many more issues that native faculty at TCUs and mainstream colleges and universities have to be concerned about and negotiate to be successful. On occasion, native faculty get together to discuss these issues. For example, the Association of American Indian and Alaska Native Professors meets annually, and native education faculty confer at the annual meeting of the American Education Research Association. These gatherings of native faculty are helpful in developing networks, sharing scholarly work, and building support systems across institutions.

Scholarship and Research

Scholarship and research are established parts of the mindset at mainstream institutions and are supported by and expected of their faculty. Although scholarship and research is not as well-established practices at TCUs, native faculty at those institutions have great potential to become national leaders in native scholarship and research. Teaching is a high priority at TCUs, but scholarship and research are increasingly being emphasized by faculty, administrators, and others associated with the colleges.

P. Boyer (1998) noted that tribal colleges are becoming centers for scholarship and research by working collaboratively with other colleges and universities, research institutes, and government agencies. The capacity to support scholarship and research is being realized as TCUs develop libraries, tribal archives, and technological support to access information and data sources. The collection of tribal histories and tribal historical documents, with a focus on tribal languages and aspects of tribal cultures, is essential to the maintenance and growth of tribal communities. The connection of these tribal and cultural collections to the TCUs uniquely positions them to play a primary role in Indian research and scholarship. The capacity to share and disseminate research and scholarship among the TCUs and with the national research community is being developed through the *Tribal College Journal of American Indian Higher Education*, AIHEC meetings, and tribal, state, and national meetings and conferences.

TCUs are developing research agendas and research protocols, and conducting more research—including conceptualizing and analyzing information and data from native perspectives. They are providing leadership in challenging the Western scientific approach to research and developing models that are based on indigenous knowledge and native ways of knowing. This is significant as TCU faculty join other native scholars in developing research methodologies that can result in ownership of the research process, authentic knowledge, and findings that are relevant to local needs. This has the potential to enhance the research process for indigenous people of the world, as well as to transform traditional academic research and reporting practices.

Faculty Development

Colleges and universities are made up of people, including faculty. A good faculty will result in excellent teaching, productive research and scholarly work, and meaningful service to the institution and the community. A good faculty will attract good students, funds, public support, and local and national recognition (Rosovsky, 1990). The growth and development of good faculty are important aspects of all colleges and universities.

How does a college or university obtain good faculty? There are basically two ways. New faculty can be hired and the skills and knowledge of new and existing faculty can be further developed through meaningful activities. Thus, faculty development is concerned with hiring new faculty and offering opportunities to new and existing faculty to improve their abilities to teach, conduct research, and provide service.

We have already noted that there is a need to hire more native faculty in colleges and universities, including TCUs. The W. K. Kellogg Foundation (1997) recognized this need in stating that a purpose of its Native American Higher Education Initiative (NAHEI) was to "improve the success rates of Native Americans in mainstream education and increase the pipeline of potential Native American faculty for Native-controlled and mainstream institutions" (p. 3).

The recruitment and hiring of native faculty can be difficult. However, one thing is certain: Institutions must make concerted efforts to hire native faculty. It is not enough to have a strategic or diversity plan that indicates more native faculty will be hired. It is not enough to advertise in *The Chronicle of Higher Education* and expect results. The potential pool of native faculty is small, so the focus must be on those places where faculty are being prepared or where they currently work. Native American studies programs are good sources of native faculty. Advertisements should be placed in publications that natives read, for example, *Tribal College Journal of American Indian Higher Education*, the *Indian Country Today* newspaper, or specific tribal newspapers. Informal networks of native faculty and gatherings like the Native Professor's Association that purposefully target Indian students for development into the professorate, are also important considerations. The Nativeprofs list-serve at the University of Wisconsin at Milwaukee and other Internet sites also are becoming effective ways to disseminate information about faculty openings.

Development of existing faculty continues to be a need at TCUs. One lesson learned from the W. K. Kellogg Foundation's NAHEI is that TCUs have not placed a great deal of emphasis on increasing the pool of new native faculty. Rather, the emphasis has been on developing existing faculty and strengthening the role that faculty play at their institutions. It is not that TCUs do not recognize the need for new native faculty—they do and would welcome more native faculty. It is just that priority has been placed on providing opportunities to develop the faculty they currently employ. Therefore, although development of current faculty must remain a high priority, TCUs must not neglect recruitment and placement of new native faculty.

In 1989 (E. Boyer) and again in 1997 (P. Boyer), the Carnegie Foundation for the Advancement of Teaching recommended that comprehensive faculty development programs be established at tribal colleges. These reports identified several barriers for faculty at tribal colleges, including isolated college locations, limited opportunities to interact with colleagues, limited budgets, young developing institutions, heavy teaching loads, work in the native and nonnative cultures, and students who are not fully prepared academically for college. Finding the time to conduct faculty development activities is a challenge in itself.

TCU faculty surveyed by Clayton and Born (1998) reported high interest in their professional development. Eighty-one percent of the faculty surveyed said they would pursue additional college training if it were accessible. Of that group, 34% were interested in obtaining a master's degree, 8% an EdD, 34% a PhD, and 24% other (unspecified) advanced degrees. Faculty development priority areas for these faculty were teaching methodologies, proposal writing, program assessment, curriculum development, and learning styles. Clayton and Born suggested that the best means or modes of delivering faculty development were workshops or summer programs, low-residency graduate degree programs, distance (Internet, Instructional TV, or correspondence) programs, use of graduate student interns from other institutions, faculty exchanges, annual tribal college networking conferences, and access to elders as advisors and mentors. These different ways of delivering faculty development activities took on added significance when faculty were committed to remaining on site at their TCU locations.

Many TCUs are taking advantage of opportunities to use federal and foundation funds to develop their faculty. In 2000, the Bush Foundation funded faculty development at the following TCUs; Bay Mills Community College, Diné College, Chief Dull Knife College, Fort Berthold Community College, Lac Courte Oreilles Ojibwa Community College, Northwest Indian College, and Sinta Gleska University (http://www.bushfoundation.org). This influx of outside funding allowed TCUs to provide faculty development programs that were previously difficult to achieve. Haskell Indian Nations University, supported by a Title III grant from the U.S. Department of Education, is currently developing faculty in four ways, by providing (a) five faculty with one-year sabbaticals to finish their doctorates, (b) release time from classes to develop new coursework, (c) travel funds for faculty who make scholarly presentations at national conferences, and (d) a year of support for a six-faculty member cohort to develop a research, training, and service agenda for the university.

SUGGESTIONS THAT SHOW PROMISE

No one solution works for all colleges and universities. TCUs are diverse, and each has different factors that influence its needs and approaches to faculty development. Even within colleges, the needs of faculty differ, depending on such factors as a faculty member's life experience, formal education, academic discipline, employment status, and responsibilities; the institutional mission; and whether faculty are native or nonnative.

One key factor that works has to do with leadership. Leadership is needed at the administrative and faculty levels to demonstrate commitment to and support of faculty development, and to make it a priority. The active support of the college president, deans, and faculty leaders is absolutely essential. Leaders can also identify and allocate resources, especially money, time, and space, to ensure that faculty development has a strong institutional presence and becomes institutionalized in the policies, procedures, and day-to-day operations of the college. Without leadership, faculty development tends to get lost in the complexity of the tribal college experience and either loses out to other priorities, becomes one-shot efforts that have minimal impact, or even ceases to exist.

Funding that provides support for faculty development is also critical. Support provided to TCUs by the Bush Foundation, the W. K. Kellogg Foundation, and federal agencies is a prime example of how money makes a difference. As noted, the Bush Foundation continually supports faculty development at TCUs, including the recent survey conducted by Clayton and Born. The W. K. Kellogg Foundation's NAHEI made faculty development a goal and provided funds so that TCUs can support faculty activities. Without this financial support, it would have been difficult for the colleges to support their faculties.

Faculty development cannot be addressed in isolation from other areas of the college where faculty are involved. P. Boyer (1997) suggested that there was a need for a comprehensive approach to faculty development at tribal colleges, one that would take into account the faculty functions of teaching, research, and service and relate them to areas of institutional development. The benefit of this approach is that it empowers faculty while strengthening institutional academic programs. For example, Fond du Lac Tribal and Community College focused on institutional accreditation and student assessment in its faculty development program. The college collaborated with four other TCUs and held sessions that brought faculty together to interact with each other and with officials from the North Central Accreditation Association. The result was a better understanding of accreditation and the institutionalization of accountability, student assessment, and cultural content in courses. At Leech Lake Tribal College, faculty development activities focused on the curriculum. Faculty were brought together for the first time to evaluate courses and attend workshops away from campus. In the end, a faculty governance system at the college is taking shape.

Technology is also playing an important role in both faculty and student development at both TCUs and mainstream institutions. Any student who graduates these days needs to know how to use computers and the World

Wide Web; the same is therefore true of the student's instructors. Several TCUs have moved ahead both in supporting existing instruction with technology and in offering courses at a distance. Faculty receive training and experience in these environments that improve their teaching and enhance their careers. Distance technology also overcomes (at least in part) the geographical barriers that have long separated native faculty, making possible the sharing of texts in collaborative scholarship, quick and reliable communication, and even face-to-face discussions and interactions. Technology increases the potential for partnering among TCUs, and between TCUs and mainstream institutions, and distance education tools can be used not just to talk about faculty development, but to deliver it as well. New opportunities need to be created and sustained in which faculty can exchange information and experiences, related to the desired scholarship and research. Technology offers some exciting new alternatives that need exploring.

Mentoring has proven to be a successful way to develop and keep faculty. Mentoring can be defined as a relationship between experienced and knowledgeable individuals and less experienced individuals, especially between junior or new faculty and senior faculty. Senior faculty with institutional knowledge and content knowledge, familiarity with native culture and language, and political savvy can help junior or new faculty succeed at colleges and universities. It is common for TCUs to employ tribal elders to teach as well as mentor others in tribal languages and cultures. At Leech Lake Tribal College, for instance, each faculty member has a mentoring relationship with a tribal elder.

Sotello-Turner and Myers (2000) indicated that faculty of color, including American Indian faculty, reported that mentoring programs "help new minority faculty become acclimatized to academia and the campus culture as a whole" and that they suggested "establishing mentor relationships as a strategy" (p. 160). American Indian faculty indicated it was important to have a "structured mentoring relationship" rather than something informal and that mentoring established social networks that helped faculty realize they were not all alone on campus.

At one mainstream institution, The Pennsylvania State University, a senior minority faculty mentor position was established in the Office of the Provost to work with junior faculty of color to help ensure their success. Workshops on promotion and tenure, professional writing, teaching, proposal writing, and other faculty activities were held for junior faculty. In addition, receptions and other social events were planned to bring faculty together at locations other than their offices. Faculty valued these social activities at safe places where they could discuss common concerns and develop professional relationships. The senior minority faculty mentor also met individually with faculty members to provide them with direction and guidance, administered a budget that allocated funds to junior faculty to travel to and attend professional meetings, and conducted exit interviews with faculty who were leaving the university. Another function of the senior mentoring faculty was to oversee a summer scholars program that brought junior faculty of color from other institutions to the Penn State campus during the summer to teach or conduct research with senior faculty. The junior faculty were recruited from minority-serving institutions, mainly historically black colleges and universities. One intention of the program was to recruit and hire faculty of color at Penn State. The senior faculty mentor program gave development for faculty of color a strong presence on campus and provided an outlet through which to express their concerns. The only limitation was that the senior minority faculty mentor was not full-time. Thus, it was suggested that a faculty development program of this nature employ a senior faculty member who could devote full time to mentoring junior faculty.

Mentoring was a key feature in the production of this book. In the W. K. Kellogg Foundation's NAHEI, emerging scholars from both TCUs and mainstream institutions were paired with established scholars and shared in cluster writing workshops to produce successive drafts of the chapters in this volume. The realities of juggling time, negotiating collaborative draft exchanges, and developing mutual admiration were factors contributing to this learning and mentoring experience.

Finally, much can be said for simply creating opportunities for native faculty, whether they work at TCUs or mainstream institutions, to get together and share stories and ideas with each other. The Association of American Indian and Alaska Native Professors is an excellent example of such a forum for discussion and dialogue, but it currently has more participants from mainstream institutions than from TCUs. A strong agenda is not necessary or even desirable for such gatherings, but the resulting dialogue is encouraging to participants, resources are shared, collaborations are formed, and materials are developed that help sustain the faculty at various institutions and their respective programs.

As noted, faculty development should not be a one-shot activity. A variety of activities and opportunities should be planned and implemented over a long period of time. P. Boyer (1997) suggested activities like faculty exchanges with non-Indian colleges and universities, summer research programs, faculty release time for research, and programs that increase the number of native faculty. As stated earlier, holding on-campus workshops, providing funds to attend conferences, and finding the time and resources to bring faculty together to collaborate, build networks, and discuss common concerns are other valuable activities.

VISION

As we look toward the future, the vision that many people share is to significantly increase the number of native faculty who are successful at TCUs and at mainstream colleges and universities. That is, native faculty will be hired, developed, retained, promoted, and valued. New native faculty will join existing native faculty to form a collective national faculty that is knowledgeable about their academic subject area, teaching strategies, research methods, and how to provide meaningful service to their institutions and communities. Native faculty will be knowledgeable about and provide leadership in integrating tribal languages and cultures into effective teaching, research, and service. As a result, indigenous knowledge and native ways of knowing will be respected and used to improve the social, economic, political, and educational conditions of native and nonnative people.

This vision is based on the successful implementation of a comprehensive faculty development effort that keeps faculty renewed and excited about working at TCUs and mainstream institutions with native students. As more native faculty succeed, more native students also will be successful and graduate from higher education institutions.

Although the number of native faculty is increasing, we are not where we want to be in hiring and retaining native faculty at TCUs and mainstream institutions. The vision of having more native faculty and greater student success has not been realized. It is clear that more needs to be done to increase the number of new native faculty and to retain and promote those who are currently faculty members. Institutional leadership, commitment, and allocation of resources are essential if this vision is to be realized. The future of the tribal college movement is bright, but attaining the best future possible will require a concerted effort to increase the scholarship and development of native faculty.

REFERENCES

American Indian Higher Education Consortium. (1999). *Tribal colleges, An introduction.* Alexandria, VA: Author.
Boyer, E. (1989). *Tribal colleges: Shaping the future of Native America.* Princeton, NJ: Princeton University Press.

Boyer, P. (1997). *Native American colleges: Progress and prospects.* Princeton, NJ: Princeton University Press.

Boyer, P. (1998). Many colleges, one vision: A history of the American Indian Higher Education Consortium. *Tribal College, 9*(4), 16–22.

Bush Foundation. (2001, August). *Bush Foundation Grants $28 million at November board meeting; $54 million in 2000* [online]. Available: http://www.bushfoundation.org/news/11172000.htm

Clark, B. R. (1987). *The academic life. The Carnegie Foundation.* Princeton, NJ: Princeton University Press.

Clayton, D., & Born, D. (1998). *Report to the Bush Foundation on tribal college faculty development needs.* Duluth: University of Minnesota.

National Center for Educational Statistics, U.S. Department of Education. (1998). *American Indians and Alaska Natives in postsecondary education.* Washington, DC: U.S. Government Printing Office. (Pub. No. 98291)

Rifkin, T. (2000). *Public community college faculty* (New Expeditions Issues Papers, No. 4). Washington, DC: American Association of Community Colleges.

Rosovsky, H. (1990). *The university: An owner's manual.* New York: Norton.

Sotello-Turner, C., & Myers, S. L. (2000). *Faculty of color in academe: Bittersweet success.* Needham Heights, MA: Allyn & Bacon.

Stein, W. J. (1992). *Tribally controlled colleges: Making good medicine.* New York: Lang.

W. K. Kellogg Foundation. (1997). *Native American Higher Education Initiative, "Capturing the dream," The implementation.* Battle Creek, MI: Author

13

Information Technology and Tribal Colleges and Universities: Moving Into the 21st Century

Michael O'Donnell
Michelle Mitchell
Al Anderson
Lori Lambert (Colomeda)
David Burland
Kim Barber
Salish Kootenai College

INTRODUCTION

While the rest of the nation enjoys the economic and educational benefits of information technology (IT), Indian tribes lack the physical and human resources to use IT to improve the lives of Indian people. The tragic irony is that Indian tribes continue to endure the very problems that IT can help to overcome; economic stagnation, geographic isolation, inadequate health services, and lack of higher education opportunities. The President's Information Technology Advisory Committee (National Coordination Office for Information Technology Research and Development, 1998) emphasized the importance of IT to the future of America:

Information technology (IT) will be one of the key factors driving progress in the 21st Century. It is quite literally transforming the way we live, learn,

257

work, and play. Advances in computing and communications technology will create a new infrastructure for business, scientific research and social interaction. That infrastructure will provide us with new tools for communicating throughout the world, and for acquiring knowledge and insight from information. Information technology will help us to understand our effect on the natural environment, and how to protect it. It will provide a vehicle for economic growth. Information technology can make the workplace more rewarding, improve the quality of health care, and make government itself more responsive and accessible to the needs of its citizens. (p. 1)

Indian tribes want to be included as active partners in the new economy and the information age. But partnership suggests equality, fairness, and equal access, three qualities that were absent in tribal–U.S. government relations in the past.

A TRIBAL VIEW OF THE HISTORY
OF INFORMATION TECHNOLOGIES
IN THE UNITED STATES

Throughout American history, native people have been denied the opportunity to use IT for a better life, thereby limiting their access to information that might help them participate more knowledgeably in a broader community. For example, the first newspaper in the Colonies, *The Boston News-Letter*, began in 1704, whereas the first tribal newspaper, *The Cherokee Phoenix*, was first published in 1828, and 10 years later, was closed when the Georgia Guard destroyed its printing press. WWJ, the first national commercial radio station, first broadcast on August 20, 1920, whereas the first tribal radio station—WYU—started in Red Spring, North Carolina, in 1970 (Keith, 1995).[1] The National Broadcasting Company began television broadcasts in 1939, and the first Native American television station, KYUK, opened in Bethel, Alaska, in 1970.[2]

Indian reservations and Alaskan Native villages were also among the last areas in the nation to receive electric power and telephone service. Despite the growth of commercial radio and television and the experience of reservation-based radio and television stations, the percentage of Indians employed in the communications industry is less than half that of Indian people in the general population (.5% versus 1%). And even the strongest

---

[1]Today, 52 tribal radio stations serve their respective native communities.
[2]Half a dozen low-power tribal television stations are broadcasting today on reservations in Montana, New Mexico, and Arizona.

tribal radio and television stations cite low budgets, poor equipment, and lack of technical expertise as factors that threaten their existence. Indian tribes cannot wait 124 years (newspaper), 50 years (radio), or 31 years (television) to fully participate in digital IT. The delays in tribal ownership of newspapers, radio, and television have made Indian people the victims of lies and stereotypes. Given the delay in Indians' access to previous IT and the paucity of Indian employees in the communications industry, many Indian leaders fear that the past is prologue for Indian tribes in the information age (see Brown, 1996; Keith, 1995; F. Tyro, personal communication, January 9, 2001).

THE DIGITAL ECONOMY

Much of the nation's recent economic progress can be traced to the influence of IT. Neal Lane (1999), Assistant to the President for Science and Technology, described the strength of IT today: "The digital economy—defined by the changing characteristics of information, computing, and communications—Is now the preeminent driver of economic growth and social change" (p. xx). Since 1992, IT businesses have contributed one third of the total growth in U.S. production, and created millions of new jobs. IT innovations have been crucial to improving national and regional business, finance, defense, health care, and transportation systems. Higher education, local governments, small businesses, and public school districts have increased efficiency and lowered costs using IT equipment and software. Hundreds of colleges and universities have adapted IT to distance education and offered courses and degrees to thousands of students throughout the United States.

In 2000, the Information Technology Association of America reported an IT workforce of 10 million with 1.6 million new job openings, half of which went unfilled for lack of skilled applicants. The shortage of IT workers has raised salaries throughout the industry (Information Technology Association of America, 2000). Unfortunately, Indian tribes have largely missed out on the economic windfall of the new economy. By 2006, half of the total U.S. workforce will be employed in IT-related industries, and the demand for IT professionals will continue to grow.

THE DIGITAL DIVIDE IN INDIAN COUNTRY

Indian tribes face two major problems in using IT; (a) lack of infrastructure, and (b) lack of Indian computer professionals. Recent data support this assertion. *Falling Through The Net: A Survey of the "Have Nots" in Rural*

and Urban America (U.S. Department of Commerce, 1995) reported that
(a) of all races, Native Americans in rural areas possessed the fewest telephones, computers, and modems, and (b) for those taking online courses,
Native Americans in rural areas who owned a computer and modem were
the most likely of all races to take online courses. *Falling Through the Net II:
New Data on the Digital Divide* (U.S. Department of Commerce, 1998) indicated that: (a) Rural households earning $5,000 to $10,000 own the
fewest personal computers (7.9%) and have the least online access
(2.3%); (b) of all races, American Indians are most likely to use the
Internet at K–12 schools in rural areas and public libraries in urban areas;
and (c) since Digital Divide I, minorities are losing ground with regard to
computers and modems in the home. A third survey in the series, *Falling
Through the Net: Defining the Digital Divide* (U.S. Department of Commerce, 2000) stated that: (a) Rural American Indian households have the
fewest telephones, computers, modems, and have the least Internet access; and (b) the gap between the information "haves" and "have nots" is
growing over time. Minorities are losing ground in terms of computers and
Internet access.

For the past 3 years, Salish Kootenai College (SKC) collected data from
551 Indian tribes in the United States on the status of tribal computer technology and the need for college courses and degree programs of study delivered via the Internet. Although the study is not complete, preliminary data
suggest that Indian tribes lack adequate computer equipment, have poor
access to the Internet, and want distance-education degree programs of
study (SKC, 2001). Data on the status of tribal computer technology include the following: (a) Only 146 of 551 tribes reported that the tribe
owned a computer; (b) only 121 of 551 tribes reported that the tribe had a
computer lab; and (c) only 91 of 551 tribes reported that the tribe had
Internet access.

Preliminary data on tribal needs for higher education show an interest in
asynchronous (Internet) bachelor's and associate degree programs of study.
Data on tribal needs for college courses and degree programs of study delivered via the Internet include the following: (a) of 551 tribes, 281 selected
bachelor's degree programs of study in environmental science, tribal human
services, nursing, education, and business; and (b) of 551 tribes, 249 selected associate degree programs of study in 17 areas including health science, health records technology, chemical dependency counseling, office
education, fisheries, forestry, computer science, tribal government, nursing,
early childhood education, dental assisting, paralegal, engineering, food
services, accounting, math, and English.

Indian communities have few IT professionals. Tribal institutions struggle to hire qualified computer personnel but are unable to pay market salaries and fringe benefits. Indian schools, health clinics, hospitals, businesses, and tribal departments rely on part-time consultants and computer technicians to maintain personal computers (PCs) and solve problems. In 1995, the National Science Foundation (NSF, 1996) reported that of the 839,600 employed computer scientists and engineers, only 1,200 were American Indians. Half of the 1.6 million new IT jobs in 2000 went unfilled for lack of qualified applicants. Further, half of all future IT jobs will be in two areas; technical support and network administration (Information Technology Association of America, 2000; U.S. Department of Commerce, 1997).

It is unlikely that the number of Indian computer professionals will increase in the near future. The American Council on Education (1998) reported that, in 1996, only 341 of 77,975 bachelor's degree graduates in engineering technologies were Indian. Only 51 of 22,663 master's degrees in engineering technologies were conferred on Indian students. And only 14 Indians were among the 6,305 people who received doctoral degrees in that field. The same year, the U.S. Department of Education listed only 91 American Indians among 24,098 bachelor's degree recipients in computer and information science. Even worse, only 25 of the 10,151 master's degree graduates in computer and information science were Indian. And, only 2 of 867 doctoral degrees in that field were conferred on Indian students, an improvement over 0 out of 884 the previous year (U.S. Department of Education, 1998, 2000).

The best way to produce Indian IT professionals is to strengthen tribal college resources. Currently, 24 of the 33 tribal colleges and universities (TCUs) offer an associate degree in computer science or a related field. Of all the tribal colleges, only Sinte Gleska University, which serves the Rosebud Indian Reservation in South Dakota, offers a bachelor's degree in computer science. All 33 American Indian Higher Education Consortium (AIHEC) colleges have computer labs and Internet access. In 1998, the dropout rate for Indian students at all U.S. colleges and universities was 64%. The same year, the dropout rate for Indian students at tribal colleges was 15%. Because tribal colleges are less expensive and more convenient for Indian students to attend and more effective in retaining and graduating Indian students than are mainstream institutions, it makes economic sense to strengthen tribal colleges' IT resources so as to increase the number of Indian IT professionals. Strengthening IT resources would help the tribal colleges offer more IT bachelor's degrees, add graduate degree programs of study, purchase state-of-the-art equipment for computer labs, and supplement tribal college faculty salaries to attract qualified IT instructors.

To this end, AIHEC and AIHEC-member TCUs are planning and implementing aggressive IT efforts, in particular the Advanced Networking with Minority Serving Institutions (AN-MSI) initiative. The NSF funds the project, which is operated through EDUCAUSE, a national organization noted for its leadership in educational technology as serving TCUs, historically black colleges and universities, and Hispanic-serving institutions. The program works toward improving executive administrators' awareness of the uses of technology, high-performance computing, Internet connectivity, remote technical support, and network architecture. In addition to these major areas of focus, the project is intended to assist TCUs with technology assessments and strategic planning for infrastructure and technology use. Four TCUs, Fort Peck Community College, Fort Berthold Community College, Turtle Mountain Community College, and Sitting Bull College, are involved in testing wireless connectivity.

In addition, with financial support and technical assistance from the W. K. Kellogg Foundation and in collaboration with the University of Michigan, 30 virtual libraries are running on 30 TCU campuses. The virtual library began as a project at Bay Mills Community College in Brimley, Michigan, when it secured the services of an IBM executive on loan to the college for one year. The purpose of that project was to develop a virtual library for the college. The utility of this effort was immediately evident, and when funding became available, AIHEC made disseminating this work a high priority. In just over a year, virtual library sites were available to 20 TCUs. Initially, these pages were "stand alone" in that each college had a copy of the pages. Now, however, a major effort that was part of this project has resulted in a database that contains all of the links that were on the original version but has the additional advantage of being easy to update and more readily administered. The utility of the project has already been demonstrated by heavy usage on the part of students at early adopting schools and accrediting teams' acceptance of the idea of a virtual library as part of information services.

An example of productive, fiscal-support linkages between TCUs and government agencies is partnership between TCUs and the NSF to increase skills in the fields of science and mathematics. In spring 2001, the NSF established a new program entitled the Tribal College and Universities Program (TCUP). This program is a result of collaborative efforts in which

AIHEC worked to obtain funding for a program that provided TCUs with funding for improvement in science and mathematics teaching.

THE W. K. KELLOGG FOUNDATION'S NATIVE AMERICAN HIGHER EDUCATION INITIATIVE

In a bold effort to help Indian college students, the W. K. Kellogg Foundation agreed to fund a variety of projects at America's tribal colleges. Nine of the projects were designed to improve campus IT; of that number, five projects strengthened tribal colleges' IT infrastructure. Cankdeska Cikana Community College completed its college website and local area network, and developed an online course. Lac Courte Oreilles Ojibwa Community College helped other tribal colleges use IT to access resources at mainstream universities. Little Big Horn College added new software to improve its management information system. Salish Kootenai College conducted a distance-education needs assessment of Indian tribes in the United States. And Southwestern Indian Polytechnic Institute improved student access to agricultural technology programs (see W. K. Kellogg Foundation, 2000).

Four academic, collaborative, and thematic model projects used IT to create and share courses and degree programs of study. Lac Courte Oreilles Ojibwa Community College developed an on-campus and Internet-based distance education degree program. Leech Lake Tribal College improved its ability to receive distance education courses and deliver them to five remote villages. The North Dakota Association of Tribal Colleges used the Internet to share associate degree courses, develop bachelor's degree courses, and bring graduate courses to five reservations in North Dakota. Salish Kootenai College created three Internet-based degree programs of study; Bachelor of Arts in tribal human services, Bachelor of Science in environmental science, and Associate of Arts in general studies. Both bachelor's degrees were designed as degree-completion programs (junior and senior year) for delivery to Indian associate degree graduates at tribal colleges. By January, 2001, SKC created 76 asynchronous courses and scheduled another 26 courses for construction. The college delivered 48 of the courses to 10 Indian reservations and to indigenous people in Canada, Finland, and Australia. Full implementation of the program began in fall 2001 (see W. K. Kellogg Foundation, 2000).

The W. K. Kellogg Foundation provided significant support for improving IT at tribal colleges. No other institution, public or private, allowed tribal colleges the freedom to define their IT needs and provided the funding to implement the solutions. It seems practical and appropriate here to examine one tribal college's experience with IT.

CASE STUDY: THE HISTORY OF INFORMATION TECHNOLOGY AT SALISH KOOTENAI COLLEGE

Overview

Despite limited funds, Salish Kootenai College (SKC) has tried to keep up with advances in IT. When the college opened in 1976, IT was limited to typewriters and correctional fluid. As IT entered the mainstream in the 1980s, SKC installed a few basic multiuser computers for administrative functions. Within a few years, the college purchased a minicomputer and installed a management information system (MIS). A few key faculty and staff also received Apple and Macintosh computers. In 1994, the college decided to switch to IBM PCs because of the growing variety of software and lower hardware costs. Since that time, SKC has endeavored to provide students, faculty, staff, and administrators with the best IT available at the lowest cost. Successful competitive grants and aggressive bargaining with vendors have supplemented the annual equipment budgets, which allowed the college to purchase modern computer hardware and software.

IT has improved teaching, learning, and administrative functions at SKC. Computers have been the foundation of educational certificates and degrees such as the office education vocational certificate and the computer science associate degree. They have allowed students to explore educational material in unique ways (computer-aided instruction). Students have also used computers to produce letters, term papers, maps, budgets, drawings, and resumes. SKC now offers two asynchronous bachelor's degree programs of study in environmental science and tribal human services using Lotus Notes Learning Space as the instructional platform and the Internet/World Wide Web as the delivery system. As of 2001, more than 500 Indian students from 10 states and 2 Canadian provinces have enrolled in SKC distance education courses.

The college's MIS relies on IT to coordinate important administrative functions such as admissions, registration, financial aid, business, and planning. The positive effect of the MIS is obvious. In the first decade of MIS operation, student enrollment more than doubled, but the student services and business departments have added only two new staff members. The increased volume, speed, and accuracy of MIS data helped administrators to make wise decisions and to anticipate needed changes.

Computers

The first institutional computers (Morrow and Leading Edge) provided basic word processing and accounting functions. Several years later, SKC purchased a few Apple computers, which not only offered basic computer functions such as word processing and accounting, but also had educational software that supplemented classroom instruction. The Apple Macintosh became the institutional choice and served the college well until Windows 95 was released. Although faculty and administrators liked the features of Macintosh computers, it became clear that the future of software development favored the PC. About that time, SKC purchased a Prime minicomputer, which ran the Datatel Colleague college software system. This software provided functions for student services such as registration, financial aid, and advising. This software also provided business office functions such as accounts receivable, accounts payable, purchasing, and budgeting. System users utilized a terminal program (the text only screen) to access the software. This worked fine for the Macintoshes. Access was provided by serial connections into the miniframe. SKC also had a number of "dumb" terminals that were used to access the Prime minicomputer.

Over time, SKC purchased newer Macintosh models and a few Intel-based PCs. After Windows 95 came out, SKC decided to obtain more PCs. In the mid-1990s, SKC moved its Datatel Colleague software from the Prime minicomputer to an IBM RS6000, which is about the size of a regular PC but is much faster and has more storage. The change also allowed SKC to make the move from terminals and serial connections to TCP/IP-based telnet sessions to access the administrative software. During this time, SKC acquired more new PCs (instead of Macintoshes) for use in computer labs. Eventually, price increases and vendor priorities forced SKC to change its administrative system from the Datatel Colleague software to CMDS's TEAMS Elite software. This change forced all of the administrative software users to switch from Macintoshes to Windows NT PCs. The college spent more than 10 months teaching employees to use the new administrative software and to operate the new Windows NT PCs. The rapid switch in MIS systems left the Information Technology Department with more than a few political scars. For several years now, SKC has standardized functions on Windows NT Intel based PCs and recently added Window 2000-Intel based PCs. Macintosh computers are still used on campus, particularly for art and graphics work.

SKC used Novell network file servers with several AppleShare file servers to support campus computer functions. With the change to CMDS

TEAMS Elite software, SKC introduced Windows NT servers that provided file services and network authentication. Very recently, SKC has made another move to Windows 2000 servers. In fact, right after these words appeared on paper, we turned off the Novell servers and the older Windows NT servers. The AppleShare servers were decommissioned several years ago. The current Windows 2000 servers use Active Directory to provide network services to both PCs and Macintoshes. SKC also has several Linux servers, providing Web and mail gateways services. SKC hosts its own e-mail using a Centricity FirstClass Macintosh server with Internet mail. SKC has been running this system for many years with various software and hardware upgrades. The college started out with Internet e-mail using Quickmail software running on a Macintosh SE that connected via modem to the University of Montana to collect e-mail.

Networking

At first, SKC had only a rudimentary network system. Buildings were connected with copper lines, but fiber optic lines were eventually installed. When the fiber was installed, a small fiber optic hub was utilized. Several GatorBox gateways were used to allow the Macintoshes, which were using LocalTalk on the copper lines, to access the fiber optic network. With the fiber also came a 386 PC server running Novell 3.1, which was used to provide AppleTalk Routing to the network. The GatorBoxes also provided Routing on the network. Initially, SKC ran AppleTalk as a network protocol. When the Novell server was added to the network, IPX was also added as a network protocol. With the addition of TCP/IP, the college had three different network protocols sharing one network. The next network evolution was the purchase of an Alantec Powerhub 7000 switching/router. This was a large enterprise network device that offered FDDI, Fast Ethernet, and multiple routing protocols. This reliable switch served SKC well, but has reached the end of its useful life. SKC recently purchased new Foundry Network's BigIron 4000 Gigabit Ethernet switch, which will provide a state-of-the-art Gigabit Ethernet backbone and allow for future expansion.

The Information Technology Department installs and maintains all of the fiber optic and copper lines on campus. These lines are installed in conduits that run to most of the buildings. SKC also has a campus-wide wireless network, and two new outlying buildings use wireless technology as their campus network connection. The college currently has two Internet T-1 connections, one via Centurytel and one via the Bureau of Indian Affairs.

Telephone System

In 1985, SKC installed a telephone PBX system, which the college owned, operated, and maintained. This gave SKC the flexibility to adapt the telephone system to changing institutional needs without incurring large costs. It also allowed for moving employee telephones as they changed offices. SKC also decided to operate and maintain voice mail systems for the same reasons. As the college has grown in enrollment and employees, newer voice mail systems have replaced obsolete ones.

SKC was originally served by a local telephone company (RTC), but when a T-1 Internet connection became available from another local telephone company, the college requested the new service. After a frank exchange of ideas at several meetings of SKC, the telephone companies, and state officials, SKC became the first institution in Montana to receive telephone service from two companies (RTC and Centurytel). The college also added supplementary service from Blackfoot Telecommunications for video teleconferencing via their ATM network.

Curriculum

Since 1982, SKC has used IT as a certificate and degree program of study and to supplement course content. Both the office education vocational certificate and the associate of science degree in computer science continue to be popular choices for SKC students. Computer software applications (statistics, simulations, and computer-assisted instruction) have been used to supplement instruction in science, mathematics, nursing, and writing. For example, the registered nursing degree program of study uses a number of software packages, which guide students through mock medical scenarios and provide information on the effects of various drugs. The library replaced the card catalog with a computerized version of the book and periodical collection. Students have access to the collection locally and at a distance through the Internet. The library also subscribes to several content-based research databases, which support instruction in mathematics, science, and the humanities.

In 1998, the college decided to create asynchronous courses and degree programs of study for delivery to Indian reservations not served by existing tribal colleges. After a yearlong evaluation process, SKC faculty and administrators chose Lotus Notes Learning Space as the instructional platform. Since that time, the college has developed two bachelor's degree completion programs of study (environmental science and tribal human services), and the freshman year of an associate degree in general studies. Another 76 asynchronous courses were created by January 2001, and 26 more asynchronous courses were finished by August 2001. The sophomore year of the associate degree in General Studies will be completed by August 2002. More than 500 Indian students from 10 states and 2 Canadian provinces enrolled in SKC distance-education courses. The complete bachelor's degree programs of study were offered for the first time during fall term, 2001.

Challenges

The primary challenges for campus IT have been adequate funding, employee retention, ongoing technical training, and distance education. Funding is always a challenge for TCUs. For more than 20 years, the U.S. Congress has provided TCUs with less than half the annual average dollars per full-time Indian student recommended by the U.S. Department of Education. SKC has been fortunate in obtaining competitive public and private grants to help pay the costs of IT. However, the constantly changing nature of technology, that is, the need to stay current, puts a tremendous financial burden on the college. Good decision making by the Information Technology Department has helped to contain costs. But human ingenuity and success in grant writing cannot be relied on to sustain IT into the future. Adequate and reliable funding through private foundations or through the Tribally Controlled Community College Assistance Act is the only reasonable option.

Employee retention is another critical challenge. It is difficult to hire qualified and experienced computer technicians. Few Indians are employed in the IT industry and fewer still are enrolled in bachelor's degree programs in computer science. The geographic isolation of most Indian reservations and the low salaries offered by tribal colleges are difficult obstacles to overcome when recruiting IT professionals. SKC believes that the best solution would be for tribal colleges to produce IT systems managers and technicians. SKC is developing an asynchronous bachelor's degree in tribal computer systems management to prepare Indians for careers in operating tribal computer systems. The degree program will be delivered through the Internet and be available to any Indian student with a computer, a modem, and telephone service. SKC has been fortunate to acquire and retain Indian IT professionals. The key to the college's success appears to be that tribal members want to live on the Flathead Indian Reservation, despite low salaries.

Ongoing technical training is necessary to understand rapid changes in IT. The college has little choice but to spend whatever is necessary to keep IT personnel up to date on technology issues. New and updated hardware and software require ongoing training. Annual training sessions involve travel and last from 1 to 6 weeks. The college must provide funds for training, or the IT system will eventually fail.

The final challenge also offers the most opportunity for success. There are 575 federally and state-recognized Indian tribes and 92 urban Indian centers in the United States. (See Table 13.1, Fig. 13.1 and Fig. 13.2.) And, as of this writing, 33 TCUs exist to serve them. Although most Indian reservations may be too small to sustain tribal colleges, the use of IT in distance education holds great promise to deliver accredited degrees and certificates to Indian populations not served by tribal colleges. SKC believes that asynchronous (Internet) distance education is a cost-effective and instructionally sound means of delivering college courses and degree programs of study to geographically isolated Indian populations in the United States.

The W. K. Kellogg Foundation and the Alfred P. Sloan Foundation provided funds to create SKC's asynchronous distance-education program. Although it is not easy to move classroom courses to an online environment, students, faculty, and administrators are working together to achieve this goal. The SKC distance-education model has been cited for excellence by an on-site visitation team of the Northwest Association of Schools and Colleges, the Alfred P. Sloan Foundation, and the Center for the Study of Theology and Science, the W. K. Kellogg Foundation, the U.S. Department of Agriculture, and the U.S. Department of Health and Human Services. Because the college receives funding through the Tribally Controlled College or University Assistance Act on the basis of Indian enrollment, it is possible to support distance education through increased Indian enrollment.

Benefits

SKC has benefited from the use of technology in many ways. Technology has facilitated the production and storage of documents such as grants, curriculum, coursework, policies and procedures, and the college catalog. Internet access has opened up many different avenues for the college. SKC has a distance-education program that relies on the Internet for course delivery. Also, general Internet access for students and faculty has enhanced education in numerous ways. The Information Technology Department relies heavily on the Internet for support of the college's technology. E-mail plays an important role in maintaining communications among faculty, staff, students, and outside people. Because of the technology, SKC can provide enhanced education with computer-based training in campus labs.

Through its incorporation into the curriculum, IT has also benefited SKC students in many ways, as mentioned in the preceding section. Students are much more likely to be life-long learners, especially if they have computers at home. That is the nature of IT. To stay current in the IT field, personnel must keep learning. This applies not only to students but to faculty, staff, and administrators as well.

Lessons Learned

Most of the lessons that SKC has learned from implementing and using technology involve people; training, policies, employment, consensus, communication, cooperation, and trust. It is very important that personnel have adequate notification of changes to their work environment, such as switching types of computers, for example, from Macintosh to Windows. When the college made the switch between computer types, people did not receive adequate notice or training, or at least that was their perception. Also, new software needs to be heavily advertised.

People need to be made aware of the impending change. Even a minor change needs to be communicated to people, especially if that change will disrupt their work environment in any way. Also, clear policies need to be in place, covering most of the issues that a user will face.

What this all comes down to is that projects involving technology need to be planned. On smaller projects, that may mean holding meetings to develop goals and timelines, which are written down and distributed to all involved. On larger projects (in addition to the goals and timelines), personnel needed, impacts, and resources needed are researched. Again, all of this is written down and distributed to the personnel involved. A responsible person needs to be identified for personnel to contact with questions or concerns.

Another lesson that SKC has learned is that the Information Technology Department has to be in constant communication with various other campus departments to share needs, requests, suggestions, and problems and solutions. A responsive online help desk system also supplements face-to-face communication. IT serves people. IT is not an end in itself, but a process that involves people in decision making.

SKC has also learned to be a good technology shopper. There is a lot more to purchasing technology than just price. With the rapid pace of change, IT personnel must stay on top of current trends. Key issues include considering the limitations and advantages of various hardware and software, and choosing reliable and flexible vendors. Each purchase requires research as to which product will best fit into the current architecture and which will work with the current systems and software. IT personnel must then re-search the vendor that has the best price and return policies, and that appears to be the most flexible in resolving problems. Purchasing IT is an art as well as a science.

Perhaps the most important lesson that SKC has learned is that technology is not perfect. Most people expect that computer technology will function without problems. The Information Technology Department at SKC reminds the campus community at every annual orientation meeting that problems will occur, and that working cooperatively will provide the fastest and most effective solutions. Although future IT problems can be mitigated by knowledge, training, data backups, redundant systems, and uninterrupted power sources, breakdowns will still occur. Cooperation and communication between people are still the best answers.

SKC will continue to work hard to secure the best IT available. The networks will become more efficient and add more bandwidth. Servers and workstations will continue to get faster with more storage space. Perhaps SKC can play a role in the evolution of IT as it moves toward becoming ubiquitous in the tribal world. SKC's role will be to teach IT to geographically isolated Indian people who have little access to the knowledge, experience, and services available in mainstream communities. SKC will do this by offering distance-education programs, expanding campus IT resources, educating tribal computer system managers, and working to find funds to support IT in Indian country.

THE FUTURE

Whether the information age began with the invention of the computer in 1946 or with the creation of the commercial Internet in 1993, Indian tribes lag far behind other Americans in using IT. Two reports published by the U.S. Department of Commerce (1998, 2000) identified Indians as the least represented racial group in the information nation. Although recent promises from the federal government to include Indian tribes in the IT revolution are encouraging, Indian tribes have learned to distrust government promises. Partnerships, therefore, between Indian institutions—like TCUs—and private-sector organizations—like foundations and corporations—offer the best hope for Indian tribes to share in the bright hope of the information age.

The knowledge and experience of American Indians have contributed much to modern life throughout the world; to agriculture (potatoes, tomatoes, corn, peanuts, chili peppers, beans, chocolate, and 47 varieties of berries); to medicine (quinine, emetics, laxatives, anesthetics, ointments, salves, and astringents); and to democracy (Benjamin Franklin successfully argued for including many of the political processes of the Iroquois League into the Constitution of the United States; Weatherford, 1988). Surely it is a mistake to deny Indian tribes, who have contributed so much to our nation and our world, the resources to apply their unique beliefs, views, and ideas to the information age.

REFERENCES

American Council on Education, Office of Minorities in Higher Education. (1998). *Minorities in higher education.* Washington, DC: Author.

Brown, D. R. (1996). *Electronic media and indigenous peoples: A voice of our own.* Ames: Iowa State University.

Information Technology Association of America. (2000). *Bridging the gap: Information technology skills for a new millennium.* Arlington, VA: Author.

Keith, M. C. (1995). *Signals in the air: Native broadcasting in America.* Westport, CT: Praeger.

Lane, N. (1999). *Speech to the first conference to explore the impact of the digital economy.* Washington, DC: U.S. Department of Commerce.

National Coordination Office for Information Technology Research and Development. 1998). *Interim report: President's information technology advisory committee.* Washington, DC: Author.

National Science Foundation. (1996). *Women and minorities in science and engineering.* Washington, DC: Author.

Salish Kootenai College. (2001). *Survey of tribal information technology and higher educational needs.* Pablo, MT: Author.

U.S. Department of Commerce, National Telecommunications and Information Administration. (1995). *Falling through the net: A survey of the "Have Nots" in rural and urban America.* Washington, DC: Author.

U.S. Department of Commerce, National Telecommunications and Information Administration. (1998). *Falling through the Net II: New data on the digital divide.* Washington, DC: Author.

U.S. Department of Commerce, Economics and Statistics Administration. (1999). *The emerging digital economy II.* Washington, DC: Author.

U.S. Department of Commerce, National Telecommunications and Information Administration. (2000). *Falling through the net: Defining the digital divide.* Washington, DC: Author.

U.S. Department of Commerce, Office of Technology Policy. (1997). *America's new deficit: The shortage of information technology workers.* Washington, DC: Author.

U.S. Department of Education, Office of Educational Research and Improvement. (2000). *Educational Statistics.* Washington, DC: Author.

Weatherford, J. (1988). *Indian Givers: How the Indians of the Americas transformed the world.* New York: Fawcett Columbine.

W. K. Kellogg Foundation. (2000). *Native American Higher Education Initiative Project evaluation reports.* Battle Creek, MI: Author.

Appendix: American Indian Demographics and Maps

Data in Table 1 show that American Indian/Alaskan Natives are younger, poorer, less employed, and less educated than the total U.S. population. American Indians are members of more than 1,000 tribes living in 37 states, on 317 reservations, and 237 Alaska Native villages. The complete 2000 Census Data on American Indians and Alaskan Natives will be available in 2003.

In a 2000 speech on the Navajo Indian Reservation, President Clinton provided more recent statistics: (a) Half the total Native American workforce is unemployed, (b) nearly one third of Native Americans live in poverty compared to 13% of the total U.S. population, (c) 38% of Indian children aged 6 to 11 live below the poverty level, more than twice the 18% rate for the total U.S. population, and (d) on America's largest reservation, 37% of Navajo households are without electricity and 70% are without telephone service, and more than half the community is without work (Clinton, W. J., 2000, April 18. *Remarks to the people of the Navajo Nation.* Shiprock, New Mexico.)

The maps that follow illustrate the variety, dispersion, and geographic isolation of Indian tribes in the United States.

TABLE 13.1

A Comparison of American Indian/Alaskan Native and Total Population Demographics.*

	American Indian/Alaskan Native	Total U.S. Population
Age (median)	24.2 years	32.9 years
Median household income	$ 21,750	$ 35,225
Unemployment rate	16.2%	6.4%
% Below poverty level	31.6%	13.1%
High school graduates	53.8%**	75.2%
Bachelor's degree	9.3%	20.3%
Graduate or professional degree	3.2%	7.2%

*Data from U.S. Department of Commerce, Economics and Statistics Administration, Bureau of the Census, "We the First American," Washington, DC, 1993.
**American Indians and Alaskan Natives living on reservations and trust lands.

Non-Recognized Indian Tribes of the U.S.

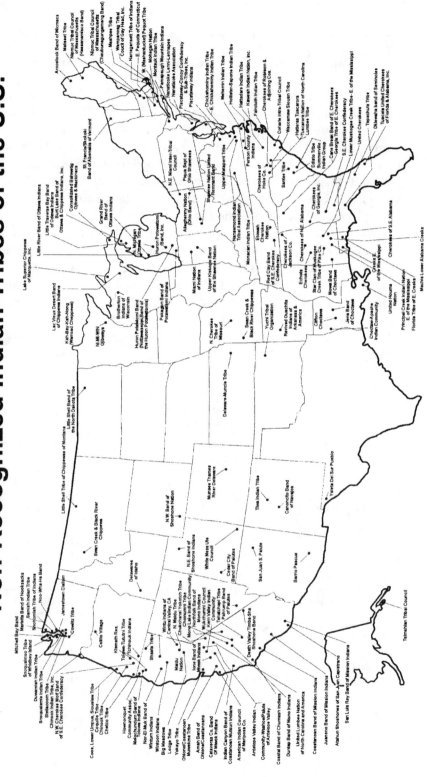

State and Federally Recognized Indian Reservations

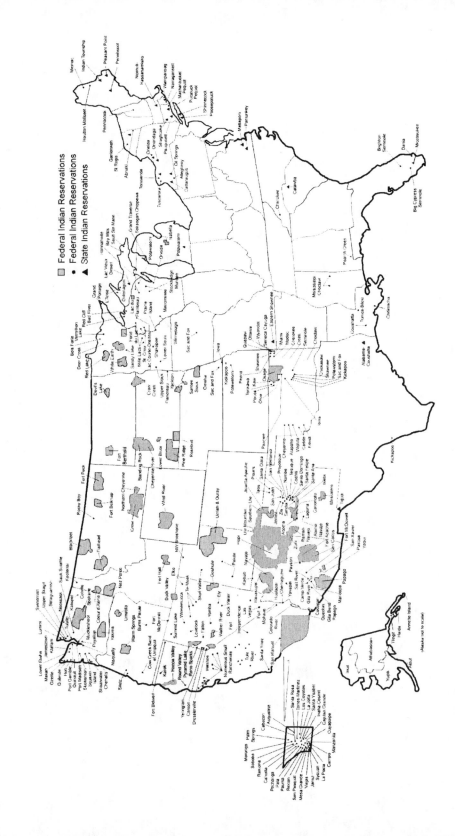

Federal Indian Reservations
Federal Indian Reservations
State Indian Reservations

(Alaska not to scale)

About the Authors

Maenette K. P. Ah Nee-Benham is Associate Professor of Educational Administration in the College of Education at Michigan State University. A Native Hawaiian scholar and teacher, her inquiry centers on the nature of engaged educational leadership particularly in native/indigenous communities, the wisdom of knowing and praxis of social justice envisioned and enacted by ethnic minority women and men school leaders, and the effects of educational policy on native/indigenous people. She teaches graduate-level course work in school leadership, school change, organizational theory, research methods, and school–family–community relations. Maenette has taught grades K/1, 3/4, and 7 through 12, and was both an elementary school administrator and a central office curriculum director. She is the lead author of numerous articles on these topics, and has published several books that include: *Culture and Educational Policy in Hawai'i: The Silencing of Native Voices* (Lawrence Erlbaum Associates), *Let My Spirit Soar! The Narratives of Diverse Women in School Leadership* (Corwin Press), and *Indigenous Educational Models for Contemporary Practice: In Our Mother's Voice* (Lawrence Erlbaum Associates).

Dr. Wayne J. Stein is Associate Professor of Higher Education and Director of the Center for Native American Studies at Montana State University in Bozeman, Montana. He works closely with the tribal communities, tribal governments, and the seven tribal colleges of Montana on a wide variety of topics and programs. His teaching responsibilities in the College of Education focus on topics in higher education at the graduate level that have particular relevance to minorities, especially Native Americans. He also teaches undergraduate courses in Native American Studies. Dr. Stein formerly served as President of Standing Rock College and as Vice-President for Academic Affairs at Ft. Berthold Community College, both tribally controlled colleges in North Dakota. Dr. Stein's tribal affiliation is Turtle Mountain Chippewa.

Dr. Henrietta Mann is a full-blood Cheyenne enrolled with the Cheyenne-Arapaho Tribes of Oklahoma. She is the Endowed Chair in Native American Studies at Montana State University, Bozeman. She taught at the University of Montana, Missoula for 28 years where she was a Professor of Native American Studies. She also has taught at the University of California, Berkeley, Harvard University, and Haskell Indian Nations University located in Lawrence, Kansas. Dr. Mann has served as the Director of the Office of Indian Education Programs and Deputy to the Assistant Secretary for [the Bureau of] Indian Affairs; she also was the National Coordinator of the American Indian Religious Freedom Act Coalition for the Association of American Indian Affairs. In 1991, *Rolling Stone* Magazine named her one of the 10 leading professors in the nation. She has been an interviewee and consultant for several television and movie productions and has lectured throughout the United States and in Mexico, Canada, Germany, Italy, and New Zealand.

Dr. Jack Barden was one of the founders and the first of three initial staff of the Standing Rock Community College in 1973, now known as Sitting Bull College. He worked with the American Indian Higher Education Consortium (AIHEC) since its inception in 1973, helping to develop higher education programs in Native communities across the nation and in Canada. Most recently, he helped the tribal colleges develop the infrastructure for information technology, including the AIHEC Virtual Library. Jack and his wife, Jean Katus, made their home in Fort Yates, North Dakota, on the Standing Rock Sioux Reservation, where he was fondly called "The Oldest Hippie on Standing Rock." A non-Indian of Irish descent, Jack received his Indian name (Wapaha Waste-Good Warbonnet) at a sun dance at the Sitting Bull campsite. He practiced tribal values and regularly attended traditional spiritual ceremonies. He frequently shared his cross-cultural knowledge with the readers of the Tribal College Journal.

Paul Boyer has committed much of his professional career to the advancement of postsecondary education for American Indian communities.

He conceived the *Tribal College Journal of American Indian Higher Education* as a means for tribal college presidents, staff, faculty, administrators, researchers, policy makers, and students to discuss their needs, successes, and evolving missions. Mr. Boyer has written a seminal piece on tribal colleges entitled *Native American Colleges Progress and Prospects* (1997) and is currently working on the second Merriam Report.

Dr. Gerald E. Gipp was appointed Executive Director for the American Indian Higher Education Consortium (AIHEC) in January 2001. Prior to joining AIHEC he served 6 years as a Program Director in the Division of Educational System Reform, Directorate for Education and Human Resources, National Science Foundation, Arlington, Virginia. Dr. Gipp is an enrolled member of the Standing Rock Sioux Tribe (Hunkpapa Lakota) from Fort Yates, North Dakota, where he graduated from the Standing Rock Community School. He is a graduate of Ellendale State Teachers College, North Dakota and earned a PhD in Educational Administration from the Pennsylvania State University. Dr. Gipp has an extensive background in the field of American Indian Education and Federal policy development and has enjoyed a diverse career. He has served as: Executive Director for the Intra-Departmental Council on Native American Affairs, U.S. Department of Health and Human Services. He was the first American Indian appointed as the Deputy Assistant Secretary for the Office of Indian Education, in the newly created U.S. Department of Education. He was the first American Indian to serve as President of Haskell Indian Nations University (formerly Haskell Indian Junior College) and remained there for nearly 9 years. He was a faculty member of the Educational Administration and Cultural Foundations of Educational Graduate School at the Pennsylvania State University, and was the first American Indian to serve as the Director for the American Indian Leadership Program.

Early in his career, Dr. Gipp was a school administrator, teacher, and athletic coach at the K–12 level in public schools in North Dakota, the Busby School on the Northern Cheyenne Reservation in Montana, and the Cheyenne-Eagle Butte school system on the Cheyenne River Reservation in South Dakota. The National Indian Education Association honored Dr. Gipp in 1984 as "Indian Educator of the Year." In 1995, he received the "Outstanding Leadership and Service Award" from the Pennsylvania State University, College of Education and the College of Education Alumni Society.

Iris HeavyRunner is a member of the Blackfeet Tribe in Montana. She is currently a Bush Leadership Fellow completing her dissertation in Social Work at the University of Minnesota. She has also been awarded a W. K.

Kellogg Foundation Fellowship and a Department of Education Faculty Development Fellowship. Ms. HeavyRunner has served in numerous professional positions at the University of Montana as a cultural program developer and a project developer with their Office of Minority Affairs. She has also done extensive community-based worked in health, welfare, family, and human services programs. Awarded for her commitment to public service, Ms. HeavyRunner has most recently worked to develop the Family Education Model at Fort Peck Community College. She is currently conducting her doctoral study on tribal college student persistence at Fort Peck Community College in Poplar, Montana.

Dr. Valorie Johnson is employed in her "dream job" as a program director in the area of youth and education at the W. K. Kellogg Foundation in Battle Creek, Michigan. In this role, she manages and monitors active projects, including the "Capturing the Dream" Native American Higher Education Initiative, and reviews and assesses new proposals. Previously, Dr. Johnson was director of Native American Affairs for the State of Michigan's Department of Social Services (DSS) in Lansing. She coordinated the activities of 20 outreach staff throughout the state, and led the development of a range of programs and services that served Native American children, families, and communities. Dr. Johnson began her career as a human relations executive with the National Education Association in Washington, D.C. She earned her PhD in educational administration from Michigan State University, MEd in educational psychology, and BS in Human Development from the University of Hawaii. As a consultant, Dr. Johnson has advised human service and educational institutions across the United States including the U.S. Health and Human Services department, Washington, D.C. She also served as a guidance counselor at the Institute of American Indian Arts in Santa Fe, New Mexico, and the Kamehameha Schools in Honolulu, Hawaii. From 1989 to 1992, Dr. Johnson was a Fellow in Group 10 of the Kellogg National Fellowship Program. She formerly served on the Board of Regents for Bay Mills Community College and now serves on the Board of Americans for Indian Opportunity.

Dr. Colleen K. Larimore is a 1985 graduate of Dartmouth College. She received a master's degree from Harvard's Graduate School of Education in 1990 and a doctoral degree in sociology from the University of California at Berkeley in 2000. Dr. Larimore has held several positions in higher education, including assistant director of admissions and acting director of minority admissions at Dartmouth College, director of Dartmouth's Native American Program, and director of minority graduate student affairs at Stanford University. She is currently the executive director of the National Institute for Native Leadership in Higher Education (NINLHE), a nonprofit organization dedicated to increasing Native American college student success rates and to strengthening the job skills and staying power of those education professionals who serve them. Dr. Larimore is the youngest of her family's four college graduates, and is of mixed Comanche and Japanese descent. Along with Andrew Garrod, she is co-editor of the book *First Person, First Peoples: Native American College Graduates Tell Their Life Stories*. Drs. Larimore and Garrod are currently working on a second edited volume on the life experiences of Asian-American college students and graduates.

Dr. Smokey McKinney has lived in Florida, New York, the Philippines, and Kansas, where he spent junior high through college. He received a Bachelor of Music Education from Baker University, a Biblical Studies degree from Harding University, an MA in Rhetoric and Composition and a PhD in Rhetoric and Professional Communication from Iowa State University. He has been at Haskell Indian Nations University since 2000, wearing multiple hats of Extension program director, American Indian Studies instructor and director, and most recently, head of the new Institute of Distance Education at Haskell. An enrolled member of the Prairie Band Potawatomi Nation, Smokey has maintained a website on the tribe's language and culture, and has also published several essays, including "Kansas Came Late," in *Flyway*, which was named among the top 100 notable essays of 1998 by Best American Essays.

Dr. Gerald "Carty" Monette is a member of the Turtle Mountain Band of Chippewa. He has been with Turtle Mountain Community College since 1973. In 1978, Dr. Monette was named President of the college. Under his leadership the college has developed from a young, fledgling institution to a nationally accredited institution of higher education with more then 650 Chippewa postsecondary students and approximately the same number of precollege students. In addition to serving as the college's President, Dr. Monette is also the Principle Investigator for the National Science Foundation's Tribal College Rural Systemic Initiative. This project provides technical assistance to several tribal communities that are striving to promote systemic change in science, mathematics, engineering, and technology on reservations that are located in the states of North Dakota, South Dakota, Montana, Nebraska, Wyoming, and Minnesota.

Dr. Monette has served on many tribal, state, and national education boards. He recently completed a 30-month term as President of the American Indian Higher Education Consortium. He recently served on the National Agricultural Research, Extension, Education, and Economics Advisory Board, and on the national advisory group to the Washington D.C. based Institute of Higher Education Policy Center's *New Millennium Project*. Dr. Monette also served on the Commission for the White House Initiative on Tribal Colleges (Executive Order). He is the current President of the North Dakota Association of Tribal Colleges.

Dr. Monette has a doctorate in education administration from the University of North Dakota. He is married to Dr. Loretta DeLong, Superintendent for Education of the Turtle Mountain Agency School System. Together they have seven children and seven grandchildren.

Richard Nichols, Santa Clara Indian Pueblo, is a graduate of Harvard University, Graduate School of Education. He is corporate Vice-President and Senior Research Analyst for Nichols Associates. His responsibilities include project administration, program evaluation design, training, policy research and analysis, program planning, and development. Mr. Nichols' professional career has led him from field researcher to counseling coordinator to Director of Institutional Planning and Evaluation (1970s) with the American Indian Higher Education Consortium. As a scholar researcher, Richard has authored many government evaluations, has worked and trained public school personnel, and has served on many national task groups that focus on developing evaluation systems and designing academic standards. He was most currently the lead evaluator for the W. K. Kellogg Foundation's Native American Higher Education Initiative (NAHEI).

Dr. Michael O'Donnell is Director of Distance Education at Salish Kootenai. Michelle Mitchell is a Gates Millennium Scholar and a graduate student at California State University. Al Anderson is Director of Information Technology at Salish Kootenai, former paramedic, and house painting ladder surfing champion. Lori Lambert is Asynchronous Curriculum Specialist, author of 3 books, and Montana dogsled racer. David Burland is a knowledgeable and forgiving computer technician who owns the largest worm ranch on the Flathead Indian Reservation. Kim Barber is Director of Asynchronous Student Services at Salish Kootenai and mother of Mariah and Madison.

Dr. Anna M. Ortiz is an assistant professor in educational administration at Michigan State University. Her research work focuses on multicultural issues in higher education, specifically studying ethnic identity development in college students and multicultural education strategies in postsecondary education settings. Other research interests include professional issues in student affairs such as the collaboration between academic and student affairs. Dr. Ortiz is an ACPA Emerging Scholar and on the editorial boards of the Journal of College Student Development and the ASHE/ERIC Higher Education Report Series. She also serves as the coordinator of the Master of Arts degree in Student Affairs Administration Program at Michigan State University. She has degrees from the University of California, Davis (BS), The Ohio State University (MA), and The University of California, Los Angeles (PhD).

Dr. D. Michael Pavel, ChiXapKaid–Skokomish, is traditional bearer of Southern Puget Salish traditional culture. His training has been ongoing since the age of 13. He also earned a PhD in higher and adult education for Arizona State University. Dr. Pavel is currently Associate Professor in the Department of Educational Leadership and Counseling Psychology at Washington State University. His primary tasks are to advise students, develop meaningful partnerships throughout the university, with community colleges, and local K–12 schools serving American Indian and Alaska Native students. During the 2001—2002 academic year, Dr. Pavel, was the codirector of the Native Teacher Preparation Program, OKSALE, and Northwest Indian College. He is prolific scholar publishing in professional and academic journals, authoring reports and numerous book chapters, and co-authoring books. He was co-author of the book *American Indian and Alaska Natives in Postsecondary Education*.

Timothy A. Sanchez (Jemez/San Felipe Pueblos) is a doctoral student in the Higher Education Administration Program at Teachers College, Columbia University. He received his Bachelors Degree in history from the University of California, Los Angeles and his Masters Degree in higher education administration from Stanford University. He currently is a scholar with the Gates Millennium Scholars Program. His research interest focuses on the effects of the accreditation system on tribal colleges.

Dr. James Shanley is currently the President of Fort Peck Community College and the President of the American Indian Higher Education Consortium, a position he has held many times. He has also served as the President of Sitting Bull College. A strong believer in the power of the tribal colleges, Dr. Stanley has been committed to this movement for more than 30 years.

John W. Tippeconnic, III, is Professor of Education, Education Policy Studies at The Pennsylvania State University, University Park, Pennsylvania. He is a member of the Comanche Indian tribe of Oklahoma. Dr. Tippeconnic is the director of the national American Indian Leadership

Program, which prepares American Indians and Alaskan Natives to assume leadership roles in education at the local, state, tribal, and national levels. He has more than 30 years of experience in education. He served as Vice President of the Navajo Community College (now Diné College) and as a professor at Arizona State University. While at ASU he was the director of the Center for Indian Education. He has also served in national leadership positions as the director of the Office of Indian Education at the U.S. Department of Education and as the Director of Education for the Federal Bureau of Indian Affairs. He has served twice as the president of the National Indian Education Association. In these positions he has worked with well over 180 elementary and secondary schools and with colleges and universities, including Tribal Colleges and Universities. He recently co-edited the book *Next Steps: Research and Practice to Advance Indian Education.*

Matthew J. VanAlstine is a member of the Grand Traverse Bay band of Ottawa and Chippewa Indians of northern Michigan. He received his Bachelors Degree in psychology from Michigan State University and recently received his Masters degree in higher education administration from the same institution. His professional interest is in recruitment and retention of Native American Youth.

Author Index

Subject Index